LIVING
WITH THE
EVIDENCE
2

LIVING WITH THE EVIDENCE 2

THOMAS Q. KING

Rev. date: 06/29/2019

To order additional copies of this book, contact:
Xlibris
1-888-795-4274
www.Xlibris.com
Orders@Xlibris.com
795552

Table of Contents

Chapter 1

Silent Cry - 1/31/17

As I travel around this area, I see many people in my walk along the way. I see hundreds of people and hundreds of differences in them. This makes the world a better place for all, as each person is going through life interacting with the others.

But something is rising out of this, that I am seeing more and more of. It's that cooperation between people is getting more difficult. Many people judge others first, before facts are known by the 'self appointed judge'. They are so eager to stand their ground to protect what is their's, even when the value they are trying to keep to themselves is less than a dollar. They ask no questions before giving their judgement. Their greed sets their mind and they seek a reason to say why I am not like them and I get no consideration for anything.

I see this unfairness several times in a few days. In the other circumstance, I offer a trade so I can blend in with another group of people. I get something, I give something. They do this for another, but I am left out in the cold. Somehow they think that they are better in the eyes of others, they are only fooling themselves.

I have seen this in my past over and over, I thought is would end as people should be wiser as the ages march forward. But, they become like the 'Warden' of my past. Then like today, Nobody listen's to me. It's like I have a Silent Cry. I am willing to give what I can, I really want to blend in, but nobody listens at all.

Chapter 2

Cast Off - 2/21/17

As time goes by, I see many more things that try to divide the lines between the people to form classes of individuals. It's like the have and the have not's. The haves don't want to add others into their events because it could mean less for them. But in reality, they will not have anything less except future friends. I see places only wanting to care for their own. People that don't qualify to be one of them are considered to get in their way, and they become a cast off.

I see this over and over, have not's can't become a have, and accept this fact. Why do they always have to be treated as an outsider. I see that many times I am considered excess baggage to some. It happened when I was younger, I still see it today.

This reminds me of a rich kid. He does not care about the price of anything, because he has enough resources to get anything he wants and still have change left over. I see issues outside of things that have a price. I can be a castaway in a group of people because I can't fit into their mold. They just refuse to 'bend the rules a bit'. It would not change their balance sheet a bit, but any perceived effort, or cost on their part is just too high.

This type of action can harm the innocent, as some of these are in this position in life, by no fault of their own. So this is why, I travel along the path in my life, I keep going forward, but I see a lonely road ahead. I see a strong connection of being a cast off forever.

Chapter 3

Different Drum - 2/22/17

I am hearing a beat of a different drum, it is playing on and on. It isn't in my real world, It's in the folds of my mind. It repeats the beat over and over.

Just what is it saying. My mind remembers back a year or two, I recall the place where my wife was living. She was becoming more and more isolated. I see the start of it happening again. Why is it that places that elderly live, want to make it that the residents are in a sealed vault. Any normal activity that they had in the past gets crushed. The residents begin to see their value as a human reduced. It's like they all have to live like the others.

Whenever they want to enjoy the pleasures that they have had for more that 30 years, roadblock after roadblock gets put in their way. The places want all elderly to be all the same and keep them from enjoying the things that they did in the past. They want all residents to line up to be the same statue and take away their individual identity and march to the beat of the drum. Boom, boom, do this, Boom, do that, Don't rock the boat. If everyone does not do what you are doing, you must be wrong.

The drum beats on.. The longer you are at a place of the elderly, the more the staff wants you to be the same. Outsiders, including spouses, are not going to be considered as having any rights. Giving rights to others is not profitable. Getting the residents to be all of the same, is a way of controlling them so we can cut our costs. The love of money

3

and profit leads residents to be made to give up hope of having things they enjoy, with those people that they love the most.

At times, these elderly living places become like a prison with no locks on the doors, but they can't leave and go home as they wish. Their hope of happiness disappears each day as these places make another road block that keeps their loved ones away from them, more and more each day.

They like to play musical chairs. Pulling a chair out after each drum solo. Little by little, the guests begin to feel like an unwanted child. They can also feel like Jesus, He had no place at the Inn to be with his loved ones. He had to settle on being in a manger, because there was a no vacancy sign visible.

I see a No Vacancy sign coming to a place where my spouse is. And the sign will blink to the beat of the drum. I see more and more things that are shouting at me every week.

I am over half deaf, But I hear the drum beat louder. . . We have no vacancy for you . Stay away, you keep getting in the way and upsetting the apple cart. Stay away, don't upset our world. We want to get and keep our residents in a private club. We want them to be the same. We built our place that says, There is no place for guests at any of our tables, and this means you.

If you don't like it, I hear that the manger isn't being used and has a vacancy, because there is no place for guests at our Inn. I hear that there is free music there, and job opportunities too. They are seeking 3 wise men, But we have nobody at our private club that can fill the position.

Pardon, It's time for you to go, as I restart the drum solo and we want to get all of our residents lined up like little boxes all lined up in a row. Since you are leaving, it's time to remove another one of those chairs. Boom, boom, boom, Boom boom boom, the beat goes on.

Chapter 4

Shadowless Journey - 2/24/17

I am on my journey through life. I see no shadow following me down the path. I am on my own and I have to live that way now. I see my life not returning to the way it was 5 years ago. My life's partner is not on the path with me. She is living at a place where she needs daily assistance and services that I can't provide. I have been on this trail for years and years. While I was growing up at home, I was on my own as this stage in life passed. I was not interested in a life that my other siblings had. I was a trailblazer in life and not a follower. I am a trailblazer today, I have to go it alone on my final stages of life.

Things are beginning to be more difficult as the pages of the calendar flip like a Rolodex. Things take 2 or 3 times longer to complete than they did 10 years ago. Back then, I had others to pick up part of the load, I do not see that now. When I am faced with a task to do, I have to break it up in parts and tackle it one stage at a time. My footprints on the path are a fleeting moment as there is no one near and can't keep the trail in e. The Trail is starting to be overgrown and is going back to nature. Soon my path will be a memory, just like the shadow that followed me along my way for over 35 years.

My path is getting harder to find and soon nobody will follow it because they can't find it. I have seen many trails of broken dreams and promises. I never have found my own, yellow brick road, and it looks now as I will never find one at all. I can't stop moving forward, I will find my way no matter the challenge.

I will be on my way until I find the light at the end of the tunnel. I can't stop now, I am over half way there. Even as the sights and sounds of the past are fading away, the light at the end of the tunnel will be brighter and brighter. And one day, I will find it and it will show me what my future will be, as I will be on the trail alone.

Chapter 5

Fading Past - 2/26/17

I am moving along the time line of live. I think back to how far my roots can go back to, that I have a connection. Today's date for me can go back 121 years to the source of my history that I can connect to. My Paternal Grandfather was born 121 years ago. I can remember him like it was yesterday. Seeing him drive around in his 1950's Buicks and with no Grandmother in sight. She passed away a decade before, and before I was born. So my Grandfather was the key. As generation after generation has not passes away, My generation takes the lead, followed by my children. I never thought I would ever be facing a world where my fellow classmates talk about getting Social Security and reminiscing about the Beatle song, When I'm 64. I can only enjoy their banter about collecting Social Security. I can't join them, I don't qualify. I have seen many things through my life and I knew this time was coming, I made no reservation to be here today. Many decades ago, it seemed like an impossibility for me to partake of the things of today. Little by little, I see the things in my live erode away.

I go back in my mind to see a world as it was over 50 years ago. I see buildings and placed have now changed so much, anything that was there at an earlier time has been removed one by one. A stranger is now in its place. Some call it progress, I see it as a world that I never wanted to see being changed, but it now has changed in front of me. I stand in the center of the highway, I spin around in a circle. I am trying to see if I can find one thing that has stayed the same, over 50 years. I see

Nothing. Even looking down at my reflection in the water puddle, on the pavement, shows that I have also changed.

I block out the sounds of my past, they were to hard to live through them the first time, so I don't want to do it again. The busy highway that was back in my days, has tripled in width. I remember the 55 semi trucks per hour, rumble down the 2 lanes. The terrible accidents that were there. And the souls of those who have left this world before me. Even if I went back into the past, I could not change this, I could only relive the events. I don't wish this on anyone, I have seen enough events in my life that would keep several historians busy.

If I ever was given a miracle to go back in time the 50 years, I would have to refuse. Living the way that I did back then, has to stay a memory and packed in a box high on the shelves of my mind. I remember the tears and pain that has followed me through time. The past has became a thing to look at now and then, But I can never consider doing it all over again. I paid too high of a price the first time. If I had to do it all over again, I might not be here today. I only have to keep walking on my path of life, this is what keeps me going forward and still seeking the light at the end of the Tunnel.

Chapter 6

Granny Wanna Be - 2/27/17

The older I get the more things in this life that I will not get or have. This is not about wealth or money. It's about expectations in life that most people have and most get, but I again am left outside and looking in. I saw this issue with my In-laws.

My mother-in-law wanted her children to grow up and have families of their own. Her oldest child was now 30 and another was 26, and the youngest was soon to be 18. She thought that at least one of these would give her a grandchild, but the clock had years to go forward before this happened.

Months later, Her oldest set the wedding date. Was this going to be the time when she gets a grandchild. Many questions arose as the first faces the alter in marriage. Many felt this was a shotgun wedding and asked questions but thinking that it was. This was not what they thought and no grandchild was on the way.

After the youngest daughter turned 18, she did not take too much time to get married and again the question arose again as why she married in a hurry. No child again, the newly married couple moved to another state because the Husband got a job offer in his field. The waiting game continues for the Mother-in-law.

Years passed and her only son announces that he was finally getting married, he was also over age 30 at this time. My mother-in-law now has all 3 married and she felt like her son would have a child first as he waited the longest, and the child would carry on with the name. But it was not going to end this way for her. News came that her youngest daughter's husband had cancer and this greatly reduced the couples chance of having kids. So, the waiting game continues, as the oldest daughter has now been married over 4 years.

Granny to be, was now over age 60 and 'Gramps' was over 65. She was still coming up with the same question over and over, when? Nature had its own road map and mother nature was to lead the way. 'Granny' was beginning to think that she would never be a grandma, because her time was running out to stay healthy and be able to live on her own. So Time moves along on it's own pace.

Chapter 7

Family - 3/5/17

Everyone is born into a family. A few get scattered from their roots at a very early age. Others, Like me, grew up with members that were not known until later. These unknown members become half brothers or sisters. Sometimes new members are left on a doorstep, these could take years to never to find their families. You are guaranteed to have a family when you are born, but not everyone born will find theirs.

I recall that when I grew up, I thought that everyone that was living in the same house that I did, was my entire family. I was wrong, over the years, unchecked chatter around the house led me and others to knowledge that a part of our family was not here. It took years to understand that a part of the family was far, far, away. The member was across the ocean in a different part of the world.

Hints came up when I and others listed to our parents argue about a woman that we only knew as a stranger with a name. This led us later to discover that a half sibling existed, and that's all we knew. It took me decades to get the story, the names, dates, and events of the siblings past.

Many years ago, This sibling came to America to see his natural father. Many, including myself, found out too late. The sibling was to stay a week, but left early after meeting his biological Father. Seems like our father treated him the same as we were. The sibling felt he was not going to connect to anyone and felt like he also was an unwanted child. The sibling did not know that his visit was kept a secret, and his

Step Mother did not want anything to do with him. This reminds me of the way that I, and the others brothers were treated. When you get 18, get out and don't come back. This sibling did not believe this was possible, until he felt rejected by his own Father.

Chapter 8

Blink of an Eye - 3/11/17

I am sitting here going through my messages on my page. I am using my reading glasses as I comment on the messages. I suddenly feel a strange sensation along the right side of my neck and round my right ear. I feel a chill in this area and a slight numbness.

Then I go back to working at my computer. I then realize that I can't clearly see the print on the page, my vision is blurred to a degree that print can't be read. I check my heart rate and see if its faster than normal, it is not. Part of my face is numb a little bit.

I am expecting to see flashing lights in my eye, but see none. My left ear has ringing in it. It is louder than normal. A hearing loss in left ear is perceived to have increased.

My vision in my eye is improving and getting better, but my left ear is still without its normal hearing ability. I remove my hearing aid from my left ear and I realize that both ears at this moment are experiencing the same level of hearing loss. How or why did my left ear in less than a second now become like my right.

This makes my mind speed back into time to 1983. This was the time where my sight faded away and i thought I would never see again. 1983 was before I had any children, today the children are all adults and are living their own lives. This becomes another close call and then my mind asks, now what.

I don't know what is next or when. I have not had this effect ever. In 1983 the problem was only with my sight. Today, its main assault was against my left ear hearing ability. My sight issue was another with the numbness along the left side of my neck. Even after 30 minutes, My left side of my neck and head still have a area that is slightly numb. This feeling lasted many more hours.

Could this be the time that the events from July 28 finally catch up and play the final card ?, I don't know. I am visiting my wife at this time. She is in the bathroom at the time with one of the patient assistants. The door is open, I hear them talking, but they don't notice what is happening to me. How many times did I hide events before ? Many, and this looks like another one.

I think back to my 1969 poem, I must fight to the end. This is another thing that comes up over and over. So I never know what happens next. I can't expect it because I get no warning signs. I have to take what comes along in life. I am on my path through life and I want to keep going, I need to keep the pace and not let the circumstances win the day.

I may never know when, or if, this happens again. But I can't let this stumbling block win the day. So I will spend the rest of my time walking on the path of life, having another 'Guest' along for the ride. I can't let this one win, as I now carry it along with the others, on my walk along the path of life.

Death made another knock on the door. With my high hearing loss at the time, I felt the knocking. I did not let it in, this time. Within a blink of my eye is all it could take next time. I always have to be on guard, and be prepared. Like today, I never know when its the next time.

I remember that old '78, Will the angels play their harp for me ?,as each step forward is another step closer to see the end of my path. This time, I made an adjustment in my route and kept my time clock running.

Well, I am off walking on my path again, I have things that I can still do and people to see. Today was not the day that I meet up with my Son, or the Son of God.

Chapter 9

Unwanted Bond - 3/19/17

What God has joined together, no man should put asunder. I this of that but around me are situations around me that are doing just that.

Wherever my wife is, there are people and forces that keep trying to go beyond the limits and interfere in the lives of others. Some have no consideration for handicapped guests. This is proven to me again and again. Every thing that they do is causing more problems and they never ask of seek opinions. They just do what they want and does not consider the individuals involved.

I go to visit my wife at meal time and the want to put her closer to the noisy kitchen. This makes communication between a couple difficult, I am over half deaf and background noise prevents me from hearing voices.

Why did they move her closer to the noise, Their clue is the volume of the TV in her room. Whenever I am there, its much louder.

My wife's new location is next to a blind woman. When I went to supper with my wife, I am now next to the blind. Trouble is this is a very bad spot for me, You see, I am more than half blind. My blind side is next to her, this is disaster waiting to happen. Management really screwed this up. Its like the blind asking to guide the blind.

Then Directors wants to limit my using the computer, I cant use cell phone for various reasons. I should be on the other side of the room. But they are as blind as I am, but they have 2 eyes, I don't.

They put wheelchairs in the narrowest part of hall, another absurd idea. This causes me trouble. The even place things in the entry way that narrows that path too. Where is their common sense.

I am a handicapped individual and too many people cause more troubles instead of trying to solve them.

Workers should not re-arrange residents rooms without asking questions.

They need to walk in my shoes and when they fall, I can say, welcome to my world.

Chapter 10

Enter at your own Risk - 3/20/17

As I go and visit my wife at an assisted living location, Its enter at your own risk.

It was not like this weeks and months ago, but it is now. Chairs are left in the hallway, Wheelchairs are placed in the narrow part of the halls. Finding a safe and friendly place to sit with my wife at meal time is becoming impossible.

They moved my wife closer to the kitchen and this is a major problem for me. The noise from the fan gets twice as bad, the closer I get. I have hearing aids and the added background noise prevents me from hearing my wife.

Then when I want to sit next to her, the other side if me is a woman that has the same kind of problem as I do. I have a visual issues and so does she. This is the worst location for me. A blind person cannot be leading the blind. The management must be blind to this too.

They don't want me to have my computer where I need it. I can't use a cell phone, messages on my laptop are mo only link. There isn't even enough chairs to use in the lunchroom. I went to get one and tried to get past a wheelchair in the narrow hall, and found myself running into the side of the hall.

I need to know why ?, I, a multiple handicapped individual has to be treated in this way. I get no respect or consideration to have a enjoyable time, visiting with my Wife. No wonder many people avoid these places. It seems to me, these places try to break up what God has joined together.

Chapter 11

Judy's Reply - 4/10/17

This is a response to her question that she asked. He question was what kind of issues that My Wife and I faced, while she was at facilities that provided care.

I have seen very poor care at the first place my wife was at. The treated Patients and visitors alike, very badly. My Wife's room mate at the Nursing home was not watched, and was left in the bathroom for an extended time. Later on, an employee wanted to offer residents his sexual services. They did not follow her restricted food list, over and over. Some on certain medications, can't have certain foods. They had the daily meal slips with every tray, and failed to follow what was written on the page.

I have seen too many things that were not right and some even crossed over the laws, in the time she was there. I finally got her moved to a different living location. Now we will see what I found there.

This assisted living location does a great job for her daily care, that was listed on her doctor's ordersBut this place gave less consideration to the Guests. They try to control visits, Make it difficult to be with her at a meal time. They create hazard conditions to handicapped guests. It is like they don't want the guests there. They want to control the residents, and the guests too much.

They leave things in the hall, Narrow the entrance with items that do not need to be there. They Only have a lunch room with enough seating for the exact number of their residents. Its like they designed it only for their paying tenants, and everyone else needs to get out around meals. This was an extremely poor case of a lunchroom floor plan.

Why only make the lunchroom only sit the number of residents ? When some resident has a 100th, or 90th birthday party, The guests really have no place to sit and enjoy the event. The room becomes a rat trap of walkers, wheel chairs etc. At times when Employees that get a meal there, I have seen them sit on the floor in the hallway. It just Is not right at all.

They also moved my Wife to the noisiest part of the lunchroom. With my hearing difficulty, I can't hear Her over the noisy fan.. It's seems they did this without thinking that the noise can cause the guests trouble, and residents too.

My problems are the way that others treat Handicapped individuals, Like myself and others. I also have trouble with Nursing homes and assisted living locations. They treat married people, within the place, like a single and the spouse is treated wrong.

Also the place isn't safe as it should be to the Handicapped. If You are not a resident, they really don't care to be thoughtful, some of these things are in my book, but my problems exist today. They do not have any extra places at any tables, that I can sit like everyone else, including my wife. They treat me like I am not even wanted. Some things that are a danger to me. They leave wheelchairs in the narrow part of halls. They leave many chairs in the hall after exercise period.

They place items in entryway, that narrows the way for me to enter. I don't have any depth perception. These dumb ideas caused me to run into a wall. Hallways at times, feel too narrow with items left there. I feel like an uninvited guest.

My Wife feels like we should be treated as a couple, and not as two parts of the group. At times does cry because of this. Like my book says, I started out in life walking my narrow path alone. With them making me feel like I am an unwelcome guest. I am now walking my path into the future alone. These facilities don't honor the bond, By God or by Man, between a Husband and a Wife.

One item about sharing a meal with my Wife, They want $4 a meal. I don't complain about the price, But I do not have an extra $100 a month to afford it. Right now, my Wife and I are spending about 70% of our incomes on rents property taxes, and my utilities (electric, gas, and a land line phone). I can't afford cable. I have to pay part of her monthly fee (rent) for the place where she is living, out of her money. I also have my rent to pay Some of these issues are in my book. I may have to consider making another one. I already have a dozen new writings after the first book was published. Chapter 72, (1970 Poem), was the start of my writing. It is a short poem as what I had to deal with at the time, around 1970. It tells about being a friendless friend. It has been a long time since then.

Some readers are amazed that I can remember things from 60 years ago. There must have been a reason that I can recall them. My book covers my memoirs and my biography. It really covers a lot of ground and truly paints the life that I had over the years.

Chapter 12

They Took That Away - 4/15/17

For decades, the bond between a man and wife are set. But I see where others think they are in control. I see this happening again.

My Wife is in an assisted living location, and our bond between us is being torn apart by those that do not consider a marriage bond has any value, when one partner is confined to a nursing or assisted living location.

They don't consider the needs of the spouse is of any importance. They placed my Wife in a different location at meal time. The new location is in the absolute worst place for me, I have several disabilities. She is in front of the kitchen doorway. The vent fan is extremely noisy. When sitting next to her, I can't hear her voice because the fan overrides anybody speaking, including my wife. This is wrong

This noise overrides my hearing aids, every other noise isn't possible to hear clearly, including my Wife's voice. This is cruel punishment to any hearing disadvantaged person.

It is like, they don't want me there. Maybe this is why many residents see a reduction in visitors. Sometimes the guests are treated like an undesirable.

My wife and I always had suppertime together for over 30 years, to talk and share time together, this was our family time. But now, someone has taken that away from us. Another thing that can harm residents.

I thought these places were to make the resident feel at home. But they are not doing that for us, they are also making her suffer. These places remind me of my past, where I grew up in another house of hades. I know, I am Living with the Evidence.

Chapter 13

The Checkout Counter - 4/20/17

Over the last year, I have been avoiding doing some things. One of these is shopping in large stores that have a multitude of services. But today, I went to a place that I have not been too in over 6 months. I am in need of general items and could not afford them over the winter, as my utility costs were the highest for me. Today I have a few extra dollars to get the basic items that I put off.

I go through the store and my needed items are against the far back wall. Searching through the items, I find a few that I can afford and I do have a need of the items. So now its off to the checkout counter.

I select the counter that has the short line of customers waiting to be served. It should not take a minute or two, how wrong I was.

I remember in the past when one of my relatives worked at a check out counter. All items were stamped with a price and the price was on every item. The customer would push up with their cart. Then place items on moving belt that brought the item to within reach of the Checkout Clerk. She would quickly position the item, with her left hand. Read the price and enter it in a mechanical cash register with her right hand. Then as her left hand placed the item to be bagged up. The customer had the next item ready. Clickety clack over and over until the order was complete. Then the customer handed her cash to pay the bill. The Clerk gave back any change. Then the Clerk/or Helper bagged items and placed it in the cart. the Customer leaves with their goods, or the cart was sent to grocery drive up to be there when the Customer drives up.

From beginning to end this was like clockwork. This is the way it was and should be today. Today it should be faster and better due to advances in the bar code reader and the option of using a credit card or bankcard. All of these things are to save time and be more accurate of an operation. No more buttons to push down thousands of times a day. Today this task should be easy as pie, But it is not, in many ways it is longer today waiting in line that it was 50 years ago.

Today I spent about 10 minutes to get the few things that I needed. Then it was my turn to go off to the checkout counter and complete my purchase. I had cash to pay, so it would be an easy and quick to complete my purchase and leave the store. Oh, how wrong this would be. I look and see one line that has 3 waiting and the other line has 2 customers in line. I pick the line with the 2 ahead of me.

I approach the counter, only 2 customers were ahead of me. One man had already placed his items to purchase on the counter, but placed the items in 2 parts. He declares to the clerk that he wants to make 2 separate purchases. He proceeds with the first part. He wants to pay part with a gift card and then make up the difference in cash. This is not a quick event as he uses 2 partial gift cards and then cash. After this, the second half of purchase is tallied up. He wants to use another gift card on this purchase, then to make up the difference, He takes out a credit card to complete the transaction. Now the wait for the card approval. Now its time to bag the items in 2 separate bags, instead of one. What would be a simple one step operation for me, has taken him 6 different steps. What could have taken me a minute, has taken him several. Now for the other customer ahead of me.

She places her items in one cluster on the counter. The clerk quickly tallies the amount using the bar code reader, in the counter top. Now this customer stalls and says that she wants to buy 2 gift cards and of different amounts. This takes much more of the clerk's time, as she has to load the cards with the requested amounts and have amounts entered into the computer. Then the amounts have to be recorded into the new cards. After this, the customer announces that she wants to pay by credit card. But places card in scanner backwards. the computer rejects the card, this one has a chip installed and it can only go in one way to be read. The customer need instruction as how to place card in reader.

The clerk has to do it for her to get the card accepted. Then the clerk waits for the approval from the customers Bank. This adds more time. After computer clears purchase, then the clerk bags up the purchase. Another multi step event through the checkout.

Now I look at the line that had 3, All of those three already are out of the building and that clerk is waiting on the fourth customer. Now its my turn to buy my items.

The clerk scans the items, requests payment. I pay her in cash, she gives out the change and quickly bags my items, She tells me that my coins as change are at the coin dispenser at end of counter. I get change and leave the store. With all the new innovations to get customers through quickly, I found 2 people that turn the checkout into a formal visit with the clerk. I thought that with all the money spent on streamlining the checkouts, This would save time. 2 people showed me that this was not possible. It makes me wonder, maybe the old way was better. No distractions and issues as how many ways can be used to pay. In the past it was cash on the barrel head. Then checks were added into the mix. Cash, the evaporating commodity, soon to be only a memory to some. Today's methods may not be any better than the past. People find many ways to waste the time, that the new way was to have saved them waiting in line.

One last opinion of mine. I could not hear the change being dispensed at the end of the counter, like I did years before. Why isn't there a light on the unit that lights up when the change is being given out. Does not need to be too large or bright. But something that would help out the hard of hearing.

Chapter 14

The Sounds of Silence - 4/20/17

As I listen to the songs that play on my computer, I have to have my mind fill in the sounds that are no longer there. The songs have lost their top frequencies. The bass has more than doubled. Some instruments that I know are in the song are no longer heard as the song progresses.

The voices all are lowered, I can't hear the highs as they were in past. Frankie Valley no longer sounds like four seasons of sound. His voice is lower than I ever heard.

The depth of the sounds of Spirit in the Sky sounds like a hallway instead of a concert hall. As i approach the sounds of silence over time, I remember how somethings were to me over the past. I had sounds evaporate from my ears in the past, things became a challenge on a daily basis.

I recall walking down the side walk scuffing my shoes along the concrete ribbon. By I can not hear it. It sounds like I was walking on marshmallows. Not a whimper of sound.

Another song starts on the computer, The singer has a raspy voice like an antique crystal microphone, I just can't ride the Locomotion with Little Eva. The steam locomotive must be wearing a face mask to muffle the sound, or it finally stopped smoking.

The lion sleeps tonight, and they will have a real good nap, as the mighty jungle goes silent for me, The quiet jungle will provide pillow time for the lions, but I will not notice the change. It will be silent as I rustle through the brush and tall grasses.

Lesley says it's my party, but I see her in the corner crying. But can't hear her, she is as silent as her tears. Judy and Johnny just walked through the door, like a King and a Queen. She walks in and is wearing his ring, but I don't hear any sound from the thing.

I just checked my computer to see if I could increase the volume, no such luck, it is maxed out. As time passes along with the songs, the sounds slowly drift further away, Like a man holding a boombox playing the songs, walking down the street. The songs begin to go more silent with every step.

The Rag Doll just isn't what she used to be. The band must be really down the valley. I can't hear the story of the Rag Doll, no matter what the season. As the sun rises over the valley, I may discover that silence isn't golden. as the sun becomes like a red rubber ball.

Silence may be golden if my eyes still see. I don't know the future, as it comes at me. It's like a railroad locomotive, chugging down the steel rail. Chugging like a dragon, with a hundred part tail. Days will go by as a train goes clickity clack down the track. I see my future coming, I can't go back.

Will the future be a brighter world for me, I will not know until I get there. Will I take along my partner, or will I be alone. When I get there, will the green pasture surround me. Will there be silent songbirds ?, or will the music of their tunes fill the sky.

My mind could be the only place that plays sounds for me. I would like my mind to record the new visions that will come my way. Then enjoy watching them over and over again, but will my eyes still see.

Oh, I will hurt deep inside. As it will be painful for thee. Because someone I know will be hurting and cry, as the sounds of silence wrap around me.

Chapter 15

I Do, Until Death Do Us Part - 5/14/17

From the moment a person says I do, The 2 people become one as God has joined them together. These 2, a Male and a Female walk away from the alter to sign the legal documents and then it becomes legal to the state. Then the two go off and live a life as a couple and a family.

Many things in life are never easy and many have large setbacks in life. Maybe it is a death of a child, a bad accident, storm, fire, or a tornado. Some parts of the country have hurricanes, earthquakes and floods.

But through many things like this, I have been able to keep the family unit running along, even through the many tests and challenges of life. I have seen many adversities in my life. I expected these to be less and easier as time passes along, but I have met a new nemesis. It is not talked about much as many people try to avoid the issue.

The actual day that something comes up that half of the married couple enters a hospital, nursing home, or an assisted living location. This can happen in an instant, if one of the couple has a stroke, heart attack, or other debilitating injury or accident. This action can break up a couple as one can't relate to the other as they have done, ever since they said I do.

Until Death Do Us Part, or until one enters a nursing home or some kind of assisted living location. This should never be, a married couple should always have consideration as a couple and staff of these places should not be treating one or both as a single person, but sadly, most do.

Chapter 16

Lost Soul - 5/16/17

My time in this world seems like a path that I must be on and make my way through life. I can't escape this walk of life. Along this path, I am confronted by many challenges and trials. I never know what twists and turns are ahead. I have to continue to go forward and do the best that I can. My life seems like it is a very long hallway with many doors. Many Doors with many challenges that I have to encounter, and I will have to encounter them all, no matter if they are big or small.

I am walking my path of life decade after decade. The path narrows over time. I look ahead and see the path is nearing a long hallway, with 10 doors. I slowly approach and come to the hall. I see the long desolate place, with only numbers on the doors. some have locks and others do not.

I see the first door and come up to it and then turn the handle, it easily opens and I peer inside. I see a small house with 6 inside. The smallest is in severe danger, I see the shadow of death over the scene, it hovers overhead like a little storm cloud ready to strike. The house rumbles and the cloud flashed down with fear. Am I going to see an empty crib ahead ? time will tell. I have seen enough and want to close this door. But just before it latches, a demon of the 6 escapes into the hallway.

I go to open the second door and see what is inside. I see the same 6, with the house wrapped in barbed wire and guard towers. There is no escape from this place at this time. I see a second demon rise out of the six, this one has many secrets behind the closed bedroom door. This is the time when the Warden arises and shows herself. This begins her career of greed, pain, and suffering upon the innocent. There is nothing here that I want to take with me, but I can't get the views of this to evaporate out of my mind. It's time for another door.

Door Number 3, I open it and I hear the school bells. I also see those knee scrapers, those high pitched, pint sized opposites that are not found around the house where I live. I also see the meddler has followed me and my brothers, making life not as enjoyable as it should be. I also see some Doctors and others, trying to figure out just what and who I was. And what was different about me. They tried to help, by the family Warden saw to, that they only know what she wanted them too. Time for another door.

This Door was 4 discovery and to see what was on the other side of the fence, for years the Warden had a heavy hand and we were severely penalized for crossing it. But, a few of us crossed the line and started to break away. This room smells of beer and signs from many taverns dot the walls. The Warden begins to take her nightly escapes and the King Of Beers, begins to awake like a slumbering Volcano. Whenever she is away, he begins to develop into a demon of his own and the house shakes as this pickled one raises the level of demon to new heights. He finds out that the basement is the perfect place to create a dungeon. But he has also given his 4 liabilities another reason to plan an escape. There is no relief here, as now there is two demons to roam

Door 5, This one has a small glimmer of hope, as a few of the unwanted began to escape the stalag and some flew the coop. The grip on the remaining tribe begin to get tighter as the restriction began to get tighter and the grip feels like a boa constrictor wrapping around your hopes and dreams. the lighting in this place dims and it's time to move on.

Stranded, as the man's number is 6, the lead Warden's number is becoming 666. This door has a wall painted like a mirial, showing the deeds of the parents as they revel in their great accomplishments, Satan stands by in glee, with a smile a thousand miles wide. He could not be more proud in this pair of recruits. The 3 glisten in a bright red glow.. all 3 start to sing, "There is more to come". It is too hot to handle, as the furnace begins to be stoked and Daniel is forced to enlist.

Door 7 is opened and I see many diplomas adorn the walls inside. The Warden is gnashing her teeth as none of these has her name. But, She rejoiced as she knows of another that turned out just like her. So this is now her time of handing out put downs and slams against those who tried to rise above the ashes. But in her mind, They were just not good enough. This begins, You are worthless, never amount to anything, and when you arrive a 18, get the Hell out and don't come back. Seems like there will be no next generation 'New Warden' from this den. Time for Some Inmates Never to go to sleep.

Number Ate, It seems that way at times. Others have eaten away at the hopes and dreams of the survivors. Some enjoy making life miserable for others, and take pride in doing it. But The downtrodden still carry that flicker of hope, put into them by a stranger or two. But, will it be enough to save the lost soul. Or will the soul of the oppressed sink faster that the Titanic. Satan enjoyed the free tickets on this one. He enjoys turning people into walking stone cold heartless followers. But I, and others have be able to keep the pilot light on, hoping for a better day to arise and warm the heart of your soul. I am still walking on my path, even as I wear out my soles of my shoes. I can't let others step out my kindling flame. I have been nursing it to stay lit for decades. Someday I hope I can bring it to it's full glory and lite the sky for all those to see and follow the light home. My shining star will be so bright and large, that no ocean can put it out. My dreams have been that way for over 60 years. I have not let anything or anyone put a stop to it. It must continue, like the glory of the universe.

Number 9, Number 9, This door opens a stage that show the many wannabe wardens that pop up over my lifetime. These rising stars want to control my life and do it no matter what or who they will hurt. these are power hungry demons that will chew on anything that gets in their way. The enjoy being runner up at the Miss Demon USA contest, and take pride in their accomplishments. They all gather around and sing. They sound like a thousand screeching vultures that are dressed out in red. They swarm overhead watching with their beady little eyes, waiting to strike whenever hope and goodwill arise in the minds of the inmates. They enjoy crushing their promising dreams of the future. Like the moon, falling from the heavens and crushing an ant, as it scampers across the picnic table. Keeping it away from one sniff of the succulent BBQ slathered ribs. Time to see what is behind door number 10.

The last door, as I open this door it becomes very hard to open. inside there is nothing except fear waiting inside the hall. Fear is dressed put in red, and is partially transparent. Looking through, I notice a dim light way down at the end of this room. As I make my way through this dry, arid place, My life flashes before me. Fear turns into a copy of 'The Warden', she has been lurking about for over 60 years.

The trials and tribulations in my life become exposed, as I am getting near the light. Then another light flashes on and I see the writing on the wall. The sign says to stand on the floormat and wait for one of two doors to open. One says Heaven and the other says Hell. I have to wait because there is nowhere else to go. I feel fear approaching and the 'Warden' close behind. As I fidget around waiting for a door to open, my foot steps on something under the matt. I reach down and pull back the edge. I have found a key, what it is from, I do not know.

I stand there as Fear closes in. I feel my body transform into a spirit of some kind. I realize that my soul has been uncovered. I then notice a mirror on a side wall. I look into it and see nothing. I am still grasping the key. Then the key starts to glow, as I notice that the doors also have locks that are also glowing. The key starts to heat up, I can feel it in my hand. Its begging for me to use it or lose it. I dangle the hot key near the door of hell. I feel that I am not worthy of trying the other door first. The Warden finally joins up with Fear, as they both want to usher me through the door. The hot burning key finally enters the lock.

The Warden tells me to get out of the way, She will turn the key so all three of us can enter together. Fear pushes me aside as it jostles for position next to the Warden. I hear the door unlock, as the Warden and fear both squeeze through, as both want to be first. The door suddenly flings open. Hot fiery breath comes out the door. It sounds like a choir of the damned. Then I feel the air shift directions as, whatever is there, seems to inhale. My soul feels like it is being pulled toward the door.

The Warden and Fear are both now stuck in the door opening. The hallway is creaking as the place is becoming a vacuum chamber. I am starting to enlarge as the Warden and Fear turn beet read. The hall begins to vibrate and violently shake. Then, both of them are sucked through the doorway. I begin to accelerate toward the doorway, colors around me are all turning red. I see the Warden still grasping onto the hallway railing inside of the door of hell.

I pick up more speed, I see the Warden lose her grip and grab onto fear. Before my eye, I see both of them vanish into the glowing core of hell. I am almost near the door, the suction effect is growing more intense. Then, the vibrating door suddenly snaps shut, I feel myself bounce off of the door and ricochet back away from the two doors. I hear the key become dislodged and it bounces on the floor. The color changes from red to green, as it cools off enough for me to pick it up. Then I notice that the other door now has a green glow coming from its lock. I approach the door and enter the key. I slightly shake as I turn the key, it clicks. The door opens to a hallway, with the brightest light that I have ever seen. As I enter, my soul is embraced by a silent but secure feeling. I see a green pasture ahead with peace and tranquility. My journey has ended, as I have finally reached my destination.

Chapter 17

Death Wish - 5/18/17

Why do people seem to have a death wish life attitude. I have been fighting to stay alive for over 6 decades and at times it isn't very easy. Many adversities have come my way. I did not create them, at times, I was the victim of others cruelty. So I am not the one that constantly increases my chances to meet my maker. Many others around me have done this over and over.

Along my daily life, I have many things to overcome as my body has many shortcomings. I do the best that I can with what I have. I see others around me that seem not to care about anyone else, they do risky things. They put their lives and safety on a back shelf, because they do stupid things within seconds of each other. Any slip up means that they get to have their name in the paper and a shiny new stone pillow to rest their head. These even come personalized, Their name and even their birthday is proudly displayed for centuries. The problem is, they will not be alive to see it.

I am busy doing my daily tasks that need to be done. I have finished picking up a few things that I need. I am driving back to McQ's to meet with a friend or two. I am on a 4 lane divided highway with turning lanes. I am slowing down, I have my signal on, I enter my turning lane to go east. The rest of the cars in the 2 southbound lanes are stopped, waiting for the green light. I am approaching the red arrow signal for my lane.

I am halfway down the left turning lane. A cycle rider is waiting in line with other cars, then He decides to pass a car on the left side by using my turning lane and my right of way. It darts in front, I hit the brake, The cycle accelerates and go in front of the next car waiting in line. He just missed his opportunity to be part of the pavement, and his blood would mark the spot. And, what a spot it would be. It would last a few weeks, But he would gain that stone etching with his name on it.

After he positions himself further ahead in the line, the light turns green, he then speeds up and cuts to the right lane without signaling and without proper clearance to do so. His cycle could have been clipped by the closest car to him, But again, He quickly speeds above the posted limit and gets away. He missed his chance to be a highway 8 ink blot. He would be, a one of a kind highway marker. His relative then could set up a cross near this spot and proudly display his name, until the snowplows in the fall. The cross would be buried under 6 feet of snow, while he would be six feet under as well.

These careless individuals don't seem to care what the do with the ones that almost became part of their death wish. I do not volunteer myself to be part of their project. I have enough issues on my plate and I don't need more.

In one afternoon, I walked past over 1,000 headstones, east of Pine Valley. I took 525 photos to understand the history of those who have lived before me. I saw many vacant plots waiting for the relatives to show up and await for judgement day. I wonder why, some people want to rush this. I wondered years ago, as a child, in 1960. Why there are fences around cemeteries ?, I was told, "Because people are dying just to get in".

Chapter 18

Knight in Shining Armour - 5/18/17

I am not the only one that has to help care for a family member. I do the things that I can and others provide the services that I can not.

The family member in need, does not like the fact that that they have to rely on others. Most of the time, they have to seek help from others, they just can't do what they did in the past. This makes them feel helpless at times and call out for needed assistance.

I, like others, are always ready to do the best that we can. I listen to every request and if I can't provide the service, I seek others that can. I want to remain part of my family member's life, this includes my wife, Rayne.

While visiting Rayne, she has a difficulty as one of her mobility devices has failed. Now she has to have 2 assistants to help her instead of one. This makes her feel more dependent on others, than she wants to be. I see the problem and understand what needs to be done. I explain what caused the failure and what I will do to fix it. and this makes her feel better as she does not have to rely on another outsider to solve her problem.

I like to fix things that she needs, that have broken down. I have a degree in this field, and to me this repair is a 'Piece of Cake'. So before I leave for the day, I explain to her that when I return, I will bring the tools needed to fix this problem.

I enjoy fixing electrical things and I feel at times like a Knight in Shining Armour. It isn't a pride thing, its a chance for me to feel good about myself and help others. It makes me feel needed, even if, I can't do everything for her that she needs.

The next time I come back to visit Rayne, I have the tools and I am ready to complete my task. Rayne informs me that someone else stepped in and started making the decisions to solve her problem about the broken electrical item. I told her that I did not ask, or need anyone else to help at this time, because I could do it myself, and this is what a spouse does to show concern and love for their married partner.

Then she shows me the bill for the services provided by those who were not asked to help and where I saw that outside help was not actually needed. I told Karen that my cost was pennies and I want to do it myself to show I care for her. Rayne says that the one that did the repair told her, that I have enough leftover money to cover the bill. That I could use what she had left after paying the monthly cost of her living at the facility.

My comments was that this worker should have stated her issue over the problem to Me, But nobody did. Every month I have to pay the pharmacy money because of uninsured over the counter expenses. Some months the costs can take over half of the remaining money of hers, after I pay the monthly rent for her room. I feel that she should have given me a chance to correct this myself. I say it was not needed, I fixed this same item many times before and still could do it again.

This decision of another that should have never entered the equation. I should have been asked how I was to solve the problem. Then come to a joint resolution. The resident and spouse should not have control taken away . The Management moves in and wants to control everything, If I need additional help, I have always asked.

This type of over control, prevents me to be what I enjoy becoming from time to time, A Knight in Shining Armour. This is a way that I enjoy showing Rayne that I care for her, But others have now taken that away from me. Why ? I don't know, as a Spouse, I am now again treated like a 'Second Class Citizen'

Now the Director here is setting up something that will even control my wife's money after I pay rent.

Amy never asked me about this, This new control over my wife need to be stopped. I always bring in Paper products, Pay pharmacy, provide Rayne with Clothes, Shampoo etc.

I do not agree that they should have their hands in Rayne's finances any more that they do now.

Amy must be concerned over the $30 spent on the Chair replacement controller, But is going too far and taking more control over my wife.

She will get her $30 at the start of the month. Amy did not talk to me about this Before or after She dealt with the Chair issue.

I see this is wrong. I can't share an event during the day with my wife, I see this is wrong as well.

Any time an item comes up, they should talk to me first and not march in and make my decisions for me. I do have my Wife's P.O.A. I feel that they maybe stepping on my rights.

She never talked to me, I would have told her that she would get the $30 by the 1st of month.

She never talked to me, but contacted someone else about controlling my Wife's remaining Money.

I say, they should leave me alone in handling my wife's money and affairs. This is what Her Married partner wants to do, And to remain her "Knight in Shining Armour"

Chapter 19

Lost in a Crowd - 5/20/17

I have been in this place many times before and I am there again. I am in a place filled with people and I feel that I am the last man of earth and have no more connections to anyone. Many of these connections have be taken away from me by others that just don't care.

I am being led astray by others that set up roadblock after roadblock. This individuals of the present and the past, just don't care, as long as they keep the power that they think that they have. Some of these betrayers even do it for money and glory from anyone, even if it is the man in the red suit, Satan.

I have been set adrift in a sea of living life forms that are from my hometown, adrift to get lost and ignored by the masses. I am on my own again, walking a narrow hostile path that I search for a place to survive. I am seeing a dog eat dog existence, I am forced to walk in front of the parade. I have been set adrift, alone.

The world is colder to me as over half of the sounds around me have disappeared forever. Some people just take this for granted. I only have part of this sensor system and this causes my isolation in the crowd to be amplified. I look around and see half of the ones around me to be unseen. I have been this way for over a half century, so I have adapted the best that I can. But this does make my situation worse. I am in crowd that I can't tell what it's truly is.

I can only dream as what the sounds should be and where. I can never remember what it would be, if I could only see like the rest of the homo sapiens around me. I can dream this, because I never remembered a time that I could see like the others. I am cast in a world that I am now Lost. Lost to sound, sight, touch of a caring human being. My senses are stranded and there is no place for them to go.

I need to post a notice on the nearest telephone pole. Man Lost, Can't find a connection to the world, or even to his family. If Found, You can't return to sender, the sender had rejected this Man many times over the decades. No Reward is offered, only giving finder a chance to be a good Samaritan. Finding this Man is difficult, as he is hiding in plain sight, surrounded by a crowd, a crowd that treats him like good old Charlie. The man that never returns. He has no nickle to get off of the train. He's a man who never returned.

The Crowd goes home, But I am still in the area, but not found. The Poster fades over time. I am not discovered, as my memory fades from the minds of the countless crowds that follow, and my hopes and dreams fade away from within my heart. I truly have become, lost in a Crowd.

Chapter 20

New Warden - 5/20/17

I never thought that I would encounter another person in my life that needs the name of 'Warden', But I think I have. This individual is keeping me from Her prisoner, that person is my wife. She is alone more and more each day, as the new warden tightens her grip.

I can't be with her in the lunchroom as the place they placed my wife is the worst place for me. She is at the table nearest the kitchen, The fan in the kitchen is very loud, and when it runs, I cant hear my wife that is next to me, talk at all. I am over half deaf and need hearing aids. The sound of the fan over rides and other sound in the room. I am isolated from my wife that is about 2 feet away from me.

I have asked the Director to move my wife to a new spot in the lunchroom, but my request is never honored at all. I have had the request made many times, Is this being cruel to the handicapped. The facility did many things in the last year to make the facility a jungle to the disabled, like me.

They leave chairs in the hallway, this is wrong as it is also a fire escape route. They placed items at the entrance to the building inside the roof supports. This narrows the way to get into the building. This is a problem for me because I am also partly blind. I do not have even 50 percent of the eyes that I was born with.

Is this is another form of who and the heck cares about the handicapped, unless they are a resident and a paying customer.

The Director seems like that she does not care at all about what effects this causes on a resident. I guess it comes on down to the bottom line. As long as money is coming from the resident, this is all that we care about.

Judgement day is coming, I think I have found my Mother's match. The 2 can work through eternity stoking the coals.

Chapter 21

My Wishes - 5/23/17

I am restricted by my income and lifestyle, that includes many limits that my body has. I only see a future of a world of unrestricted dreams. These do not cost a dime, and they take my time, so I do not end up like others. These others wander around town daily as if they are lost and wandering in circles. These repeat their lives, day after day. Never seeming to get something new into their lives. They can at times, look as if they are a wasted collection of humans that stall in the bright sunlight of life.

You would think that my dreams would show a glamorous life that awaits my nightly slumber, But it isn't always so. Also any glittery high lifestyle dreams I have, have one thing in common, I am alone.

My treatment from the facility where my wife is, Could be better. The Director makes a purchase for a repairable item in my wife's room. I have fixed the item about a half dozen times before. My wife keeps mishandling it and breaks it by not using it correctly. The Director then goes out and buys a new part and I get the bill. I know nothing about this at all, Until I am set to repair a broken wire. One broken wire. I have a soldering unit to correct the break, but the controller isn't there. The Director removed the item and purchased a new costly replacement. Why does this seem like she overstepped her authority. I never was told what she was doing or given a chance to fix it, or to even buy one. Her comment was , I have some money that my wife gets in a month and I can afford it. The Director thinks that I have nothing to do with the $25 a week that she gets. She is wrong, my Wife's over the counter pharmacy expenses can consume a good portion of this small amount of money.

I still can't sit with my wife at a mealtime. they will not move my wife to another location, or fix that noisy fan. It could be a work place violation as the noise could be too loud. Since I have to wear hearing ads, It is too loud for me now.

When ever I visit my wife, I end up in her room with the door closed. The bird that the have outside her room will not shut up at times and this causes me hearing issues. Why do they think a place for the elderly is a good place to have noisy items around.

I am beginning to feel like a prisoner in an assisted living location. I am as trapped as the resident who is totally blind, or can't get around without a wheel chair. They want me off in a corner and not to be seen or heard. This Director reminds me of my mother, I wish things were not this way.

So my dreams are being evaporated from my mind. I want to improve the lifestyle of my wife, but they are trying to crush mine.

My wife and I have enjoyed the last mealtime of the day together for over the last 37 years. But they are talking it away from me and one of their residents. This isn't right. My wife cries at times as she faces another thing that has been taken away from her life. Soon they will be nothing left to enjoy. She will be a living vegetable in a way. This control over us is very wrong, I wish for better things for Her.

I want to dream of a retirement life that my Wife and I grow old together, but this place my dream is vanishing away from my mind, as well as my hope and her freedom. Soon they will have a living puppet, that at one time was a wife. Some at this place do not see this. Elderly are becoming a bottom line on a balance sheet, and are turning into a empty shell of themselves. They are forced to give up relationships with their loved ones.

All I have are my dreams, Because I don't have my life partner as a day to day connection, as it was for 37 years. I wish that others do not have to go through something like this.

Chapter 22

Blind Eye - 6/2/17

As I walk along my life I find many things that I thought never would cross my path. One thing is the way people care or don't care about others, especially the handicapped and elderly. As I look into the mirror, I still try to stay 39 forever, but I seemed to have passed this milestone some years ago.

As time marches on, some of us end up in nursing homes or assisted living locations. When this does happen, chances you will enter a place like this alone. And the daily walk of life becomes more and more of a struggle.

The best place to meet and communicate with other Residents is in the lunchroom, at meals. I have found that this isn't to be for me and the other blind Residents.

If I was to sit in the lunchroom, I would sit were another resident was to sit, she is totally blind, I am half blind, But the Director has a blind eye to our predicament, We need to rely on our hearing more that anyone else. So, why does management stick the blind people in the noisiest place in the lunchroom. Don't we suffer enough by not correctly seeing.

To me, This is cruel and malicious treatment to those that have this handicap. Management does not even notice, just how they cause some to withdraw away from others. They can't use their ears here to communicate in the noisy environment around them.

Some say that management just does not care, they turn a blind eye to this type of treatment and just walk away. I guess I am a bit lucky and can walk away, as another resident can't do this. She is totally blind.

Chapter 23

Few Concerns - 6/20/17

A few things have arised out of having Rayne being at an place where she lives away from home.

Two more issues have come up that I feel that this Facility should not be getting their hands into, and these 2 items should not be forced upon Rayne or Me.

1. They now have Rayne sitting out of the lunchroom when I am there to share time with her. It is in another room in the facility. They have a Bird in this room, so at times I have an issue with the noise. So I sit while only using one of my hearing aids. Using it in the ear away from where the bird is. This reduces some of the interference the bird can cause. So I sit at one of the Tables, I want Rayne at my left Side, It has to be this way. But I find that the workers want Rayne to sit across the table from me. This is a dumb for 2 reasons. I can't hear her as good as I could, if she is places across the table from Me. I need her on my left side, this is my better ear to hear with, without using a second hearing aid.

Why can't they stop meddling in issues that cause me difficulties ? Another reason is, my left Vision is better that my right. Rayne belongs on my left side, They seem to think that they know better about everything. But this is one thing where they should leave the seating arrangement alone. They screwed up our time together in the lunchroom by placing Rayne in the noisiest place in the Lunchroom, it is the table next to the kitchen doorway.

The second Issue that recently came up, Rayne tells me that some workers are suggesting that she has her hair colored. I don't think this is right and should not be done. I married Rayne and accept her as she is, I feel that they don't belong in this decision either. They know that Rayne and I are going to an event in July and some workers want her to dress to the nines, This is not a formal event and Rayne would not feel as she was being herself.

Another example of others interfering where they were not asked or needed. I accept Rayne as what she is and who she is, others should not set the standard between a married couple. This happened at the last nursing home that Rayne was at. Too many involved with things that are really not their business to be inKaren is at this place to aid her in issues that she can't do herself, due to her medical issues.

Employees are there daily to assist in helping her needs. This is what is being done, why do some feel a need in going beyond this ? This is a very good question. They can be there to help, if we ask for assistance in any matter that arises. But I feel that others are meddling between a Husband and a Wife if they get involved in things, that We did not ask help from them to be involved.

Rayne and I have limitations, I set things up at meal time to address these things, They are not living with my handicaps or limitations and should Ask first before thinking that they have an answer for everything.

Chapter 24

Nowhere to Go - 7/01/17

It amazes me as how people see the world around them but what they see isn't the real world. I see many vain things that others want to do or become involved with. As we grow older, we expect an easier life ahead and more time to reflect on the past. But, I see too many wanting to push the hands of time backwards and this leads to appointments and failure.

I see many older individuals living out their lives in Nursing Homes and places like this. I also see the eager beaver workers that think that they have a solution for everything. But they do not. These youngsters need to step back and see life for what it is to others.

Many times these workers think that they have the ideal answer for a problem that they perceive that my Wife has. They think that if see looks like she did in the past, life would be better for her. But they are wrong. Sometimes the past must remain in the past.

Some worker that cares for my Wife, got it in their head that my Wife would do better if they had her hair dyed. I see this is asking for trouble. It goes back to the children's story, The Old Grey Mare ain't what she used to be. This is true in peoples lives and some things should be left alone.

They may have extra funds or see this hair treatment as a necessary item in there lives, but it isn't this way in others lives. What you have in the end is, a person looking more like they are in their 30's but still hobbling around like they are 70.

Then there is the person decision between a Husband and a Wife, Many Caretakers think that their way is best, and interfere between a couple that God has joined together. They do this by trying to convince 1/2 of the married couple to go along with what they think is best. But, they did not live our lives and are very wrong.

Remember that some people still follow God's way. The word says do not Mark or pierce your bodies. I and others avoid Tats and coloring the body in any way. These workers should back off before asking the married couple what they want.

I see many things that are forced upon the half of the married couple, the half that is the resident, and seek no input before they start making changes to the resident or the room that they live in.

I have seen this a few times, some worker re-arranges the residents room and makes it a living hell for the married partner. These people just don't know the circumstances and should have asked questions before changing things.

When people enter Nursing homes and Assisted living locations, They don't come into the facility to become a prisoner and have to accept everything that the Staff thinks is best. Guess what ?, the Staff and caretakers don't need to become dictators. Many elderly can think for them selves and don't need to be dragged into deciding things, the way the workers want.

When you don't know what a resident wants, Ask. Don't become a Warden and control the residents like cattle. Don't exclude a married partner from decisions that effect the Resident. A spouse has more rights that the worker. many workers think otherwise, they should change places with the residents and see just how 'the shoe fits'.

Let elderly be themselves, when they need assistance, you are there for that and that's what you should be first on your minds. Stop overpowering the rights of the Residents and their Spouse, if there is one.

Chapter 25

Dead Body in a Car - 7/10/17

I am going through my messages on my computer, I go back to the main page and I see a story from the local TV news announcement. A body was found inside of a car in a parking lot, on the side of a main highway that runs through Pine Valley. I see the photo on my news feed. It's a red car. There is a red car driven by a family member. I begin to wonder if it's the same car. I sense the rumbling of the past beginning to be exposed before me.

A child of mine has stated a few times over the last year that life was unfair and maybe everything would be better if He was dead. Then all of the unfairness would go away, and there would be no more problems that they have to face.

You try so hard to get family members to understand that death is final and there can be no change of mind, after the fact. There is no redo option for them.

They were given a miracle to live, but they don't see it. They are given a chance for eternal life, but some miss that too. They don't see the sacrifice and effort that others gave them. They forget what parents did for them, as they were growing up.

Yes, they can run into a so called brick wall. They should accept help when offered. But they think that nobody else understands their problem. But, the real reason is, they never gave anyone a chance.

Some think that they know everything that there is to know. Because something in their lives are not like others, They feel that they are a failure. There have plenty of options, but some want to take only one choice. They think that a world without them is the way it should be.

Many then make a list of their failures and assume that there is nothing that they can do to make life better than themselves. When offered professional help, they refuse. They think that the final solution to there problem is ending their life.

Suicide, is the silent killer that sneaks up inside of a person and snatches their life away. Everything ends for them, they threw their chances away to be saved, but never consider the suffering of those that they have left behind, whenever their friends or relatives read their name etched in stone.

Chapter 26

Wrong Solution - 07/17/17

Assisted Living and Nursing Homes seem to have answers for everything, But I see flaws and at times they are not that hard to find. When you live at one of these places, you never know what is needed from day to day. Medical support items are provided like clockwork, as a few are responsible and have been trained to do what they do. So items needed for medical care are there for the Resident, on a timely basis.

What I see as problem has to do with personal care items. Some at these facilities have everything taken care for them. The Facility has legal and financial control over their income and assets. This works for some, but not for all.

I faced a situation where the Director was planning to take the financial control of my Wife's remaining income, after the bulk of her income went toward paying the room fee. I have a document that says that the Director is taking steps to control the remaining amount of Her income. But the Director's plans hit a roadblock, as I have the Power of Atty and it put the brakes on her plan, to control any remaining funds.

So, the next thing that the Director came up with, was a plan that I would deposit some money each month in an account for my wife. This would be used for personal items that residents run out of, and at times, a social event or a shopping trip to a local store.

During the first few days of the new month, $15 was applied to her fund. Within a day, a product that She was using ran out and another one was needed. This sets the stage for a problem to arise.

A worker asks is there is more of this item in the room. My Wife indicates that she has none. So the worker tells the Director that an item needs to be obtained as a replacement. The Director then decides that she is going to get the item and use some of the money, that my wife has on account.

Days pass by, my Wife does not have what she needs. It has been about 2 weeks and the product has not been replaced. I am told after 2 weeks that the Product has not been obtained by the Director.

So in the end of this experiment, having the Director handle this part of my Wife's care, is not working out. I gave it a try, and my Wife did not get her needed items in a timely manner. Having the Director control her resources was the wrong solution.

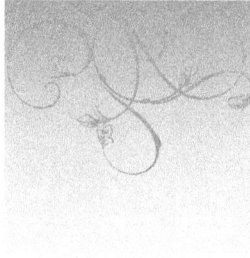

Chapter 27

Whispering Headstones - 9/1/17

I walk around many places in my everyday travels, in my part of the world. I walk the streets to see the history and the lessons of the past. I drive through the counties and nearby states where I live. I have flown across the country to see the power of the ocean. I have seen the wear marks in the ground, that others have made before me, at the places around me. I have seen a lot of different things. I also walked through the rows of written history, that I find in the dozens and dozens of cemeteries, that I visited over the years. These places also have a hidden history, and tell of events that most people cannot relate to. But, I have encountered many as I walk along, and pass over a thousand or more headstones in an afternoon. I walk along and see the history of the past and encounter events that are present. These are the lessons of the whispering headstones. Some echo a past that was long before me.

The past is not laid out in order, you have to see every stone and the history of the past unfolds before your footsteps. The stones can't hear you coming or see your shadow as you pass by. But something is here that is hidden from most of the people that visit them. I see the tragedy of the past as I see the names of four children that lost their lives in a fire. I see a pair of brothers that took a risky chance and lost. They were buried, side by side, their school photos were on the stone. I see the man that had to have one more drink, for the road. It turned out to be his last.

There are headstones with names and dates displayed in stone, but the place is empty. The person who's name is here, never found there way back to this place while they await the final appointment on judgement day. They ended up elsewhere, as they became an Unknown John Doe. I went to a place and found a headstone with my name on it. I had my Son next to this stone and took a video. It was unusual to have three people in one place with the same first and last name. While at this location, I came across a woman who had become a victim, in a crime that was committed near my home town. Many were never told where she was, as the crime remains unsolved. I happened to see it and remembered Her. Her photo was on the stone, I would like to see this solved and the Family can find eternal peace,

Another day, I was over 30 miles from home, I went through a church cemetery and saw a few familiar names that I knew. I researched this later and found that both families had Grandparents in this area. Later the children branched out and ended up in Pine valley. One relative happens to be a classmate of mine, and another was from my Grandmother's neighborhood. I know both of them.

Over time, I also would find classmates of mine that passed away years ago. Many lost their lives in accidents and nothing could have prevented it. The hardest things that I see, are headstones that say Unknown, John doe, or Jane Doe. Other graves have no names at all. I know a few of these. These individuals led a different life, and when the passed away, nobody knew where they came from or where their family was. They lived as strangers among us.

I saw several Lost Cemeteries. These were made on private property, and after the farm was sold to a new family. These places had become forgotten in time. I know a few of these. Another was an Indian Burial ground that was made over 200 years ago, and is hidden in my home town of Pine Valley. Even the people who live near it, do not know that it even exists. An archaeologist found it over 100 years ago. He kept the facts written down and did not talk about it. We want the place to remain undisturbed, as it is a important Indian place. There are homes built all around it. So it is well hidden, even if it is in plain sight.

Other places with missing headstones are the places that have names of the disease, that took their lives. The Small Pox Cemetery, and the one for Diphtheria, are prime examples. I walked into the Diphtheria Cemetery and see a row of about a half dozen graves. The first 3 have the

Headstones for children, the next one has a simple marker for a teenager, the last two have no headstone or marker. The last two were the parents, and there was no money left for even a simple marker. Entire families were lost to this disease

I found the cemeteries of the poor. Some worked at the county poor farm. These people tended the fields and the cattle, for only room and board. When they passed, they went to the same place, out in the middle of nowhere and forgotten by the masses. Some that died, had names that they made up for themselves. They were at the poor farm as they had no marketable skills to earn money for themselves. The County usually ran these places, hoping that some would improve their skills and then get hired in the community.

My biggest reason to walk along the etched stone hedge of our modern times, was doing family research. I was involving myself on finding out where my father-in-Law came from. I had a few clues and went south of Pine Valley by a county or two. I began to go to cemeteries that I have never been to before, and found answers. Some places had 3 stones with a version of my Wife's last name. The more places I went, the more I found. 3 places gave up the secrets about his past. The name had 5 versions, and found siblings in a half dozen places. I contacted another relative that was also working on finding answers. The two of use fine tuned a booklet that covered the history of two brothers. One was my Wife's Father and the other was his Brother.

I then looked into My family past and filled in the missing parts. I can go back through the generations of people, that became my family tree. I can take my Paternal Grandfather's side back to the year 150 BC. On my Mother's side, I can get back to the year 500.

Some places I walked past more than a thousand headstones. I took a photo of every one with a date of 1900, or before. I took 525 photos that day. In the cemetery, that had 3 relatives, I took pictures of all 1,200 headstones. This way I can see what names that the family could be related to.

There was also great works of art hiding in the cemetery. Like an etched aircraft carrier, A woman harvesting from a rice paddy. Some have the picture of the deceased etched upon the stone. Others have their farms and tools used in their work. Semi trucks, Tractors, airplanes, and their antique cars are displayed. Many have symbols of sports teams, their Religion, their schools, and some have actual tools of their trade. hundreds of versions are all around.

Every stone can tell a story. Even the date can reveal things. Many have poetry, others have scripture verses, and there are those that tell a story about the person. Few of them have a statement, and some have a joke. I told you I was sick, was on one of them. Many have the symbol of the branch of the military that they were in, along with their rank, and division that they served in.

Other stones have Police badges, Club emblems, or what religion that they partake in. I saw candelabras, the Star of David, and others had their political party mascot. I saw school names and sports team logos.

I saw damage done by others, as the people that do this, could not respect anyone, not even the dead. They damage the property of those that did nothing to them. They should know that in the future, others can do the same thing to them. This type of thing needs to stop.

The ones that have gone before us, should be left in peace. Let them rest in peace, as they await those in their family to join them, and be together forever.

Headstones also tell of Love, and history between a Husband and a Wife. The marriage date and the names of the children are also there. Some even have there favorite Pet etched on their stone. I have seen thousands of different themes. Each stone has a story.

Maybe you should all see the things that I have seen in any Pine Valley Cemetery, or anywhere else. Next time you visit a Relative that is there, Look around and see the things that I did. Places like this should be a peaceful time for all. It can calm your soul and give you a break from the your daily routine.

It is time to give peace a chance. Some have even provided you with a bench to share time with them. Visit the ones that came before you. Without them, the world would be without You.

Chapter 28

Rough Roger - 9/24/17

Roger Achenman walked a beat every day. He had a job, and was a very hard worker. He could have lived off of the government. I the early years he worked on a potato farm. He had many challenges in many areas, and was a hard worker and honest man. I have seen people with less issues then Roger, whine to get SSI, or welfare. Roger set out to get a job and did. He worked for Highroad Distributors, and took pride in his work. Many remember him riding on the delivery trucks, and having big hands.

I saw him time to time going to his favorite hangouts on Riverside Street. He was 5'6" of muscle and liked to wear apparel of the 1950's. He liked to enjoy his beers and this was his entertainment. He relied on other person to provide him with a few of his barley pops.

Roger was grandfathered in to keep his job when the business was sold. Roger did not let down the new owner as he worked as hard as ever to prove that he was worth his salt.

After work and weekends, Roger was a very nice person who liked to drink. He could pick up a half barrel and hand it to you like it was a sack of potatoes. He was a fixture, for sure. Once assigned a nickname, he played the role. Roger also liked to talk to the many girls that came into the establishments, He became a legend around UWPV. All the Girls at that time, knew his name and recognized his face.

He honestly thought the people he met in the bars were his 'friends'. Unfortunately a lot of them made fun of him or took advantage of him, & many of them "borrowed" money from him.

Roger liked to call the girls "Mother." Other times the Girls would say that he was always bugging them to get into a conversation and to be at the bar near them.

Area kids got mad when some people would pick on him or make fun of him. Others said that it was infuriating knowing how someone like that was treated.

Roger was a fixture on Riverside street for many years. On his 47th birthday, students applauded him when he entered a bar while shouting 'Author! Author!' He didn't understand what was going on, but did enjoy the interest that others gave him. He liked to drink, that was what he did for fun. When he wanted a beer he would say "I'm as dry as a fish." Other times he used to love to get in your face & would call some girls "Honey", He called other girls "Sissy".

He was impressed as what others could do. This may have given him ideas to set goals and move forward, but the tasks became complicated at times so he did the best he could with what his abilities were.

Others who knew Roger, got mad at times when people would pick on him or make fun of him. Roger did not quit understand that there was students out there that did stick up for him. Many did not know the story behind the legend, they knew his name and recognized the face. Yet I'm sure only a very few knew where he came from and what ever happened to him ? Others did not know him well. What I do remember, I kid you not, he was a very sharp person.

Roger proclaimed at times that he was strong as a bull, He could pick up a half barrel and hand it to you like it was a sack of potatoes. But He was still a sweet guy, that was misunderstood.

Roger had a life of a set routine, when he was hungry he went to the nearby fast food restaurant, he had his favorite worker to order from. He was harmless man that had a simple life and he was a very sharp person.

So what was Roger, A man that became a fixture around Riverside, lived an honest and life as a hard worker. Some thought he was a bit creepy, others knew he was a man that acted like a shadow at times. I have not found anyone who said he broke any law or actually harmed anyone, some had their opinions, but that is all that they had.

Roger was a hard worker and honest, even if his knowledge and skills were not up to par with the others. He lived a peaceful and simple life, he worked for a living and gave much more that he received from others. He wanted to be accepted by the people that he met at the local bars, especially the girls. Some said that he would stare at the girls too much. Even if he did, He intended no harm.

Rough Roger may have been that way to some people, to others he had a heart of gold. Even if his social skills were not the best, he did not intend to harm anyone. He may have not done the best things around others, but some got to know him and realized he was only doing these things to be accepted as a person, and to be a part of the world around him. All He may have wanted was to be like the others, even if he knew in his heart that he would never be.

Chapter 29

Where has She Gone - 11/27/17

Nearly every day of the week, I do the same thing. I run errands, get to have a meal and catch up on daily tasks. Around 4:30 I head to visit where my Wife is living at a facility. I arrive at my location and enter the building.

I enter with my things and go to be with my Wife, But I can't find he in the place where she should be. I go and search the room, She isn't there as well as her wheelchair. I go to the main lunchroom and she isn't there. I go back to her room and find no notes or messages as where she is.

Why is this happening again. Just like the last place she was living at. As a spouse, I am given no consideration as to be informed as where my wife is. Is she in the hospital ?, this happened twice before. Is she in the office ?, I look in window, but room is dark. Why do places who care for the elderly, not give a tinker's damn as to informing relatives to their events ?.

I have to think of the possibilities as where she is. I remember seeing the transport van when I arrived. If she was aboard, Why wasn't I told. But places like this have an attitude at times. If you are not a resident, you have little importance.

Then I remember about a yearly event. This place takes the transport van and takes some residents on a trip to see the Christmas lights at a Local Park and Zoo. This must be where she could be. But, Why was

I not told ?. I arrived before the transport van ever left the facility. So my hunt was on.

I then took my camera and headed off to see if the Park with Zoo, is where she went. I run the camera as I enter the downtown area of the next city to the north, of where my wife lives. After recording a drive through downtown, I restart the camera to record my drive through the 'Christmas Village' lights in the park. Halfway through my first drive through the park, I see the van parked just south of the animal cages. Now I finally know where she is, but she did not see me drive by, as she was sitting on the side away from the traffic flow. I then completed my video drive and took some photos of the lights.

I arrive back at the facility and find out that my Wife arrived back about 20 minutes before, and she did go to the park and saw other city house displays. Now the $64,000 question, Why was I not informed at all, about the facts of this trip ?.

One time before, she was not in the facility that she lived and did end up in the hospital. Her fever has high and was a serious risk to her health. Don't they see this ?, A Spouse should never be left guessing as to what happens to the other. It has happened in the past, and has happened again. The question is still the same, Why ?

Chapter 30

Yes, Virginia, There is a Grinch - 12/3/2017

The Ghost of Christmas past has caught up to the Ghost of the present. I am beginning to see the same things after 50 years, in a new shape and form. I'ts beginning to look a lot like Christmas, in the many places I go.

I can recall the shadow of the Grinch that was always around the house, sitting on the self made sofa indentations, and bellowing the same commands for over 10,000 times. This Grinch was always huddled around a pillar of smoke and his hand around a Bottle.

Many others tried to get in the festive mood and set the stage for a promise of brighter things to come. I saw this, but the Grinch always got his 2 cents in, over and over. When he gave his 2 cents, he took back a nickle. Always a spoiler in the scheme of things.

As the years tumble by, I again see the shadow of the Grinch. This one has an unknown face to me, and is hiding out in the shadows of their bright Christmas decorations. They are saying," don't look or take pictures, I made these for Me, Me, Me". They wear other colored clothing, to hide their skin of green. They end up just like the ones I knew, with their own cup full of mean.

I have seen the prophecy written in a book, that talks about the baby in the manger scene. They must have missed the message that they are to spread the joyful event, and never end up like the Grinch.

This Grinch has brightly lit their lights and wants to cover them up with a basket. They are suspicious when anyone else wants to enjoy them, then proclaims to others when they do. Why would they put out the bright lights and react negatively when others want to look at them ?. It cost then nothing to share.

They seem to have inherited the Grinch from the ones I knew before. This new Grinch needs to quickly change their ways, Or the Ghost of the Future will present them with a not so pretty picture.

There will be a chair in the corner, of a large fire pit. Next to a cane, on the back of it, will be their name.

They could not see the value of their own holiday lights, and have became another version of that old green man, Mr. Grinch.

Chapter 31

Trapped in a Box - 12/30/17

Trapped in a box, called Home. Some who enter Nursing/assisted living locations, can end up feeling like the person is living in a box called home. Everything can start being the same, day after day.

To Rayne, it felt like she was in a place that was surrounded on all sides. She was raised in a rural farm setting, and you could be outside and feel no restrictions from nature or man. There was farm land in every direction and only see the trees that made the windbreaks and the trees around the homestead. This is not what she encountered in her life during the last few years.

Rayne felt like being in a box, she wanted to see all around her, and not behind a wall of trees. She wanted to see open spaces, but none could be found. As time went by, she could do less and less things. This caused even more stress as she could not do the things that she could do, just a few years ago. Live began to resemble hotel living, and your car was not working, so you could not even leave the place.

This caused fear in her at times, as she began to think about her future. What if some type of medical issue caused her to be confined to a bed and never use a wheelchair again. This would confine her to a single room and never allow her to mingle with the other residents of the facility.

This struggle lasted for years, and as time passed She began to lose her expanded world around her. First it was the freedom of going places with others. Then it was the places where she went to in the past, at the facility. Now time that she spent outside of her room became limited.

Time was not on her side. What if ?, She fell and caused her to be bedridden for life. The thought was on her mind over and over. She started to see less and less visitors that came to her room. The trees bringing on their spring color of green leaves, blocked what she could see off in the distance.

Rayne repeated over and over as what she wanted. She wanted to go home, but this would almost impossible with her medical outlook.

So She had to make the best out of what she had, even if Her life where she was, felt like she was trapped in a box.

Rayne is not alone with having this feeling, I am living in a box, dictated by costs and others restricting my choices, as the way I live my life. We are both living our lives differently of each other. In the end, We feel that our lives are like the both of us, are living in a box.

Chapter 32

Miracle from Above - 3/14/18

As I walk along my path of life, I have experienced many things that others have not, I have experienced many things that would never confront them. I have mostly done the best that I could. There was times that I should have taken another route, but I did try to solve issues instead of running from them.

Today, I think back to 1991, Our 2nd born Son should have celebrated his 27 birthday yesterday. But, He never got a chance, there was no miracle from above for him. I always wonder why this event happened. There must have been a reason, but I never found out what it was. One thing did come out of this, we had another child. This was not a replacement for him, as the child born was a girl.

Later this year, Rayne and I will be married for 37 years. I also can't understand why We have now been married longer than any brother that I grew up with. This seems as a miracle to me. Also raising the two children to adulthood was a struggle, but we did it. Many things that we encountered must have had helping hands from above. When things were down to a slim chance, there always was something that pulled us through.

I hope that things in the future will be in our favor. I want to have a chance at things that my brothers had. Having a chance to give my Daughter away to the man of her future. We want to have a grandchild or two. I know a few brothers have more, this is not a race to have the most. We want to have our own 'Slice of the Pie', We don't need the whole thing.

We want to enjoy our golden years together, life needs to slow down and We need a chance to enjoy the fruit of our labors. We will not have anything fancy, but it will be what we have spent a lifetime to get. The amount of these things isn't the reason as why we have them. These items will help make life easier for us for five or 10, or 20 more years down the road.

We may need another miracle or two, as we grow old together. I always want to look for a brighter tomorrow. I want some more time to walk as a team down my path. Walking the path daily with a life partner is better than walking it alone. This has been difficult over the last 3 years, as she lives in an assisted living location. All I can do here is take her places for a few hours in the afternoon. This is what life is like at this time.

She keeps saying that she wants to go home, but her ability to move around in the world around her is limited. I don't see this changing as time goes forward. I am left with the vision of Me pushing her down the path in a wheelchair. This is better than nothing, as I see no change in allowing her to go back home. This is what she wanted the most. But moving down the path is still taking steps in the right direction.

Also along the walk down the path is my guardian angel, I feel the presents of this angel, as all 3 of us are on the path. I know it has been following for my lifetime. Most of the time, I am not aware as where it is. I just keep going and at times the presents of this Angel is known to me. I need to keep the 3 of us together as a team. I see many road blocks ahead as I travel forward into tomorrow.

My greatest Miracle from above is the fact that I am still alive and doing many things that I was told that I would never do. As time passes, I don't know when my life will be changed into something less than it is now. I can't speculate on this, I just have to keep us together as a team and move forward. For better or worse, We are in this together. I want this to remain for years to come. I don't want to see a detour sign, as why we can't be on this path.

Any miracles that I was given, was given freely. As I could not ask him for the first one, because at this time, I could not talk or walk, or even know that I needed his help at the time. I see this power as a friend, and more. Others see him as the Creator of all things. I at times, I can't let go of Him. I see him as the best Father figure that anyone could ever have.

Chapter 33

Just a Minute - 3/19/18

I'm off to go to My Pharmacy, where it has been for decades in Pine Valley. I have been going to the same place for years, I rarely had any issues. Now I see too many issues that come up. My normal response from the Employees is, just a minute.

But on this day, I inquire about a medication that I have been using for over 40 years. I am told that my prescription had ran out and I need to have a new prescription, so they can refill it. I am also told that there is a filled prescription, but it's at another location. This place has same name and it's on the same named street. What?, I have never gone to the other location for any pills. How can that be ? I am told that Dr's Office may have sent it to the other location in error. I am asked if I want it transferred, So I can get it where I always did. I said yes, transfer it and I will be back to this location to get it.

Two days later I return, expecting 2 filled prescriptions. I find None. Doctor's office where I was days earlier had still not called in refill order, and the transfer of my other prescription was not done.

Seems with all their new computer systems. A solution can't be found. Computer results are this ... Human Error

Medications are needed by people everyday. Missing one dose of a medication can have an effect on a person's quality of life.

I found out that asking for my medication and expecting a response back like just a minute, is becoming a thing of the past.

In the past, every pharmacy in town had a personalized name, no two places were named the same. There was a Westside, Johnson's, and Rex's Pharmacy. No confusion about the location.

It's time to end Pharmacy chains to have more than one location, in the same town. If they do, the named should not match. Make it so it's not confusing to the masses.

When I get an order filled, Having 2 non-matching names of the place, I can always know where the correct location is to go pick up my prescription. Now I can have it in my hands, in just a minute.

Don't get me started on medications having more than one name. This issue should have been addressed years ago. I have 2 bottles of the same medication, but the name isn't the same. The pills are not even the same shape or color, but actually the same item.

Stop confusing customers. A medication should always be a match, so the patient does not get confused and take the wrong pill. Safety first, it's the best way to design things. Taking a pill that may be the wrong one, may be your last mistake that you will ever make.

Chapter 34

The Braggers - 10/01/18

Along my daily path in life, I find many things that are out in society. I like most things and deal with the rest of them. One of the things that I am coming across more lately are the Jabber Jaws in society. A person like this is not easy to deal with, But I come across 2 of the same. Their talk in life is jabber and use their spring loaded jaws like an electric stapler.

They enjoy talking about themselves constantly, only stalling to breath & not listen to the others, hearing their latest story of glory, from the past. Both center the conversation about themselves, or their Me, Myself, and I. Some days they would starve as there is no chance of food getting past the flapping tongue. Their's are flapping more than 100 flags in a hurricane.

At times, they start conversations with complete strangers, so they can share their story about their lives of the past and present. But rarely let the stranger change the subject. When they have time sitting around with out someone to listen, they walk up to strangers and give them part of their life's story. They do this a few times a day with different people. It's like they have a script that is memorized.

They enjoy involving others in their sermon about themselves, other times they give a lecture about care of car batteries. They act like they have bi-polar disorder on steroids. They change the story in mid paragraph. When they change the subject, they do this to attract another listener for their spin on things, but rarely listen to the stranger.

This leads to stories about their opinion as why someone else failed in their lives, and how they are so tough.

Their stories get larger and larger over time, They have many examples. As a farmer, they could grow anything and enough to feed Paul Bunyan's crew, and a thousand Blue Oxen. They can remember when their mother talked to them while they were still in the womb. They talk about their medical cures, and how Madam Curie stole her ideas from them. Then they state how they survive in life, even say that they do not follow doctors orders, but you should. Then they talk as if they did every medical procedure known to man, then start giving the details, step by step .

They bring strange or old things to show, they do this to bait others to be nearby them. Then tell the merits of every restaurant in town, or stories from the pages of their Religion, but they want to quote every scripture story, and their version of it too. They are eager to attract your attention, in a twinkling of an eye. They should walk with their tongues, if they did, they would win the Boston Marathon.

Some sit and make strange vocal noises to attract attention. Other times they could account for every penny of the National Debt, then state how much money that is in their bank accounts. Then they whine about the cost of everything that keeps them from piling up their money, a $500 cost for a bottle of eye drops. Their Doctor is so greedy that he even considered a fee to park out front of his office.

Braggers even say that their children were told that they could not live in sin. They strongly re-enforced the rules, but I want to tell you about a few of my one night stands, one was in a gravel pit. Another time was in a house, down by the beach. Then there was that final one riding downtown, in that old Chevy. Then again, the time in the hayloft was something else. When they 'take the stage' it's them, them, them, they go so far as bragging about their sinful past. After this sermon, they want to known if you want to go, with them, to church.

They talk about medical cures and then state how they survive in each day of life, even say that they do not follow doctors orders, but you should. Then talk that they did every medical procedure known to man. They start giving their details, of being lead surgeon in a 6 hour operation to save a few lives. Then jump to their military tour of duty and say that they had 500 soldiers lost in an average day.

Some talk for an hour going through the stages of an operation, and that this is not for a public forum, but I am going to tell you about it, as a favor. Then comes the horror of the highway accidents, and how they saved 9 peoples lives, that were in a 65' Volkswagen rollover. Medical procedures abound out of their mouth, telling every detail, until they have to stop to pickup the phone call, maybe it's from President Lincoln. Then describe how every relative died over the past 100 years, because they were there.

They complain about the bad weather, yet brag that they came anyway, even if every bridge was in pearl, along their path. Then say, It was really tough growing up. I had to walk 5 miles uphill to school, both ways. My sister even learned a craft from Betsy Ross, who was a relative. Where are the shovels when I need them, they could teach entire FFA chapters to raise polka dotted Cows.

Then there are times when 2 'Jabber Jaws' get together, it's like Noah and the flood. Nothing stops the two. Then one jabber jaws, tells the other to stop talking so they can stay on center stage. The other does not hear him because his jaw is just warming up, waiting to take off in the wild blue yonder. A pair of these tongue flappers could start their own hurricane, in different oceans. I wonder when they let out so much hot air, and then yawn, could their lungs explode.

Others at times, greet them with a Hi, How are you, but keep walking fast past them. This prevents the 'Jabber Jaws' from getting to 1st base. But Mr Jabbers follows them around like tailgating cars, their eyes twinkling like directional tail lights. When the both of them arrive at your table, their head swells with enough air, that could make the Hindenburg blush. Then they stand next to your table like a statue, and take most of an hour to empty the contents from their brain into your ears.

No wonder, this world is becoming more of a me world. These tongue tweeters even say things about the stupid things they do, and feel proud of this. They should stick knitting needles in their tongues, and the could manufacture enough sweaters to put China out of business.

I sometimes hear so much info from a few of these that I could write a set of books. Other times, I get a break from their fire breathing sermon because I hear something else in my ear. Battery, battery, then click, my hearing aid tucks itself in and turns off. Silence is golden, but they don't know that my hearing device cancelled the rest of their sermon from the mandibles. I can still see them rant and rave, getting steamed up so much, that the thermostat in the room, could be turned down.

They sit and talk at places for hours, and would starve until they get others to be slaves, and get things for them. Some of these eat like their proclaimed Uncle, Paul Bunyan. How do they get the spoon fed items past their tongue is amazing.

These lip vibrators never will learn that there are better ways to get an audience. It's because they never listen to others or even themselves. This may not dawn on them, until they are older and alone. So alone, that they will hear the pin falling through the air as it is dropping to the floor. Once the pin hits the floor, it will be like a pair of cymbals. I hope that these jawbreakers learn to slow down, and share time with others when they communicate, or in the future they will be alone. They will have all the time in the world, by themselves.

Chapter 35

Museum Memories - 10/10/2018

As I set out to research more history and the names that link to the my family's past. I came across a name that links me to an old house in my home town. So for an upcoming weekend I see there is an open house that lasts 2 hours. I decide that I need to go there because the last name of the 1871 owners, can be found in my family tree. I decide that I want to take photos, never know what I would find there.

I arrive at the historical house down town with my camera ready. I want as many photos as I can. I take photos of the outside and the entrances. I enter the museum and the clicking from the camera begins I am taking another photo about every 7 seconds. I do this for 2 hours. When I was end of the 2 hour open house, I had taken 842 photos and videos.

I visited every room and nook and cranny that I could find. I looked at my watch and two hours had passed. I began leave and went down the steps from upstairs. I walked through the parlor and sitting room, on my way to leave the house, the 2 hours had gone by too quickly.

But, things begin to change at the end of my photo shoot. when I stepped into the last of the 2 Rooms and stood in the middle of the room, my body feels like I am up against an iceberg. My back is cold and my legs chill rapidly, then they would have a tingling sensation. My feet begin to feel like they are warming up, seem to be sending a clue, a clue for what?

I look around the room and see many old items, but nothing stands out to me. Everything is an antique, that set in the time frame of the house. I look down and my body reacts again, the sensations in my feet are increasing. My first thought was this, what did I hit with my foot or did I step on something. But, the answer soon revealed itself.

As I look down and see that nothing happened to my feet. I finally realize that I see something I have not seen in over 50 years. This house may have been built in 1871, but it now sends my mind back to memories before 1971, 100 years after this house was built. As I stare down, I slowly focus in on what I am seeing. It's the antique rug. The last time I saw this style of rug was over a half century ago. It looks like the rug from the house I grew up in. The rug from the house of hell.

My mind flashes back thinking, could this be the actual rug?. only way to know, is to inspect 2 of the corners for cigarette burns. My Father was a chain smoker, going through several packs a night, He occasionally would drop a lit cigarette on the floor, and at times on the carpet. So I inspected the 2 possible corner locations, I was relieved. This carpet was exactly the same size, design, and colors, but no burn marks were from a cigarette. But the carpet was an exact match.

Seems like I can never forget what kind of life I had growing up. It follows me around like a shadow. It lays silently asleep for years, then when I least expect it, a reminder appears under my feet. Who knew what things are kept in a museum for decades, like a rug that sneaked under my feet, causing a reaction that sent me back over 50 years.

An old rug that blended into the background for decades, only to be stepped on by countless visitors. This time around, when I stepped on it, My mind raced back through time and visions of the past danced around on the rug, and from within my mind. The memories of the past came back into my mind like a rumbling railroad steam locomotive, pulling a thousand rail cars loaded with pine logs.

I took home more than 800 photos from this place. not knowing that the last photos of the day would be the most valuable. They were from a dormant decorative rug, that was overlooked and stepped on by thousands of strangers over the years. To me, it was something else. It showed me that my past was remembered, but it is still in the past.

I walked over the unforgettable rug, not letting it, or the memories from it, stop me. As I walk along my path in life, I am still living with the evidence, that is within me.

Chapter 36

Cookie Cutters - 10/19/18

Growing up was like being in an assembly line. Stamp,stamp, stamp, make them all the same. Everyone in the family birth order was set up to be and do the same thing. Since our parents knew very little outside of the box that they were living. All 4 of us had to be the assembly line stamped as what direction we were being led down. But I was at the end of the line, stamp, stamp, stamp, crack ... After me they broke the mold, and changed their expected results.

I picked another path in my life, but over and over, I was redirected to the chosen path. One by one we were in a line and expected to follow the leaded. There was many examples of this, the biggest was Cars. My Father expected all of us to be grease monkeys. Well, it worked for the first 3. But, I wanted to be what I could imagine myself being.

I wanted to understand what made Mickey Mouse look like it was alive, when I knew it was an character thought up in the mind of a man. I wanted to break the dilution of the television. This box of hot glowing cherry hot chambers, wrapped in glass, was going to be revealed by me. I set out to solve the puzzle.

I set out to work on the mystery, but the Wardens of the house acted as if we were prisoners. We had to conform to the laws. We could not leave the yard, playing with the neighbor's kids with a wire fence was between us. The Pine Valley Berlin wall was as real as the one in Europe. We then had to be involved in the production line of painting cars. Just because it was their way to make money, and left nothing to jingle in out pockets. It was like being on a chain gang. Each of was given a task and every car that came to the house was the same thing for us. Over and over, year after year, these 2 ton skin shredders marched into the garage and out again. No consideration was done by the Wardens for safety. It was do it so we can afford to take care of the worthless crew, that will never amount to anything. The paint dust, lacquer thinner and never ending orders from the Mr. Warden, while he was polishing his elbows and keeping his cool by switching his empty beer cans for new ones. He would bellow out, get me a beer. This lasted for two many years.

Stock cars were also involved. The Wardens had a Studebaker and raced it at two local tracks. We became, at times, a kind of a pit crew. This lasted until 1960, when another co-worker of the Master Warden dies in a track related accident in September. This was just months after one of my grandfathers died, while on a trip. This ended the stock car fantasy, but did not end boot camp living.

Over time the camp operated year after year. One year, as I started a new school year, the last 3 on the chain gang looked identical in our clothes. We had matching shoes, pants, shirt. This was from our Mother, who also wanted to be leader of the chain gang. I could only imagine as what the others kids at school though about this.

When the oldest graduated Lincoln High School, We thought that things would get better. It was not this way at all. They had one less kid to control, so the pressure on the others increased, and it was like a Spitfire airplane was chasing us, at full speed. This made the next in line hit a brick wall, His solution was to run. Run away he did, and this started a career that would involve reform school, foster homes, and eventually finding another kind of warden to watch over him. This Warden was federal, and his new form of prison had steel bars and one room to share with another. So convenient, the bathroom was included in the room. Food came to you and every one got the same. Just like the order at home, 4 of us at the table, all fed like a soup kitchen, we had a separate color of dishware for each one of use. The Oldest had gone to a Camp called Camp Phillips, operated be the Boy Scouts. Now this one got to see a camp called Leavenworth.

This is the time where I found a way to escape being cut in the same pattern as the rest of them. In school, I picked something other than the field of cars. I remembered the warning on the back of Mickey Mouse's magic box, Danger High Voltage, 17 kilo volts. I found something that the home Wardens knew nothing about. This became my way to escape, in more ways that one.

The 3rd brother had problems with school, and after he left, He joined the Army, but never gave up being a grease monkey. The oldest spent 4 years in the Navy and left, he joined with the Marines and found his way back to the grease monkey ways. I kept my goal on the traveling electrons, as I dissected many things with the internal organs of copper and carbon, and a brain made of Transistors. These things lived on a bloodstream of moving electrons.

I had advanced ahead of the den of wardens. I was in a world that they did not understand. I finally broke through the chains by finishing Lincoln High and then completed Technical College. I walked along my path to the beat of my drummer.

I was not under their thumb and I bent the shape of their cookie cutter. The first thing that they did after I graduated for the 3rd time, was to kick me out of their unauthorized prison. I was on my own and out of bondage. I was expelled from their prison camp and had to start a life on my own.

This is where my path walked back in time and lived the life as some did 100 years before me. It was a hard time over the next few years, but I accomplished many things that the home brewed wardens said that I would never do. I broke out of their assembly line of having all 4 become the same. They said that all of us would never amount to anything and were worthless, except as being cookie cutter home grown crew of slaves.

My path is still not an easy task, But it has not stopped me yet. I took my Mickey Mouse early question all the way. I wanted to know how Mickey got on TV. It took me to a place where I ended up on TV, and I was in Color, unlike Mickey. All he got was red pants with white buttons. As Mickey turned 90 this year, and I uncovered his way of life. I think back to the simple idea that got me on a different path, so I never ended up in life as a grease monkey.

I found a way and this started me to my next stop. The narrow path took me to my little house on the prairie days, for starting a new chapter in my life.

Chapter 37

Link in the Chain - 10/24/2018

Along my path in life, I keep coming up with the same things over and over. It should not be this way. Man has evolved enough to find a way to cut down or errors and misunderstanding in an event.

I am contacted about an appointment that my Wife needs to be at. She has been told the basic information about the appointment. When I ask her for this information, she can't remember everything, as she feels that she was told 2 different stories about the upcoming appointment.

Too many workers, at places that care for others, assume that the patient understands things that they are told. This is a wrong assumption.

I go to meet with my Wife around 2 in the afternoon, expecting that she is getting ready for her appointment. I arrive and see that she is prepared for this.

She tells me the time she was told by a worker is 3:15 pm, so there is plenty of time to get a ride from a service provider to see the doctor.

It is now 2:20 pm and she is worried that she will be late to the appointment. She summons a worker and asks the question, "When is my ride going to show up ?". The worker says that she will check at the office. The worker returns and says that her ride will be here at 3:15, her appointment is set for 4:15 pm. My Wife is confused as she was told that it was 3:15. The worker said that 3:15 was when the transportation would be provided. But, her appointment was at 4:15.

My Wife isn't happy that she has to sit and wait for another hour. I ask "Why?", She says she heard different stories from her care providers.

Write all information down, is all that I am asking. Write down the time for the ride to show up that takes the patient to any appointments. Sometimes patients can forget things in 5 minutes, or the don't understand what is being said.

Have the actual appointment time written down, as well as the Doctor or event, with the address and phone number.

Caregivers are overworked in providing services, and all they want it a smoothly ran operation. That's all that we ask.

Chapter 38

Not Listening - 10/26/2018

As people pass by me everyday, I hear the same things. Complaints about their lives and how they suffer because of disease and afflictions of their everyday lives. They whine and complain about the same things over and over.

The warning signs have been exhibited for decades, but they avoid it year after year. Some, actually are proud of their accomplishments that cause them to suffer today.

They have more pride, than a group of lions, about the large meals that they eat and then describe every tasty morsel. These also are the ones today that run to the Doctor, wanting a cure in a pill. After they get assistance in losing a few pounds and feeling a bit better, they rush out to celebrate their victory. They then sit down ad eat a meal for three, Me, myself, and I style. Soon they are at the revolving door to the Doctor's office, seeking another pill to solve their problem. They don't care about the cost, as they are not paying it, Uncle Sam is. Uncle Sam then passes the cost to you, in taxes, fees, and higher Doctor's bills.

These never listen or see the importance, because they never earn enough to cover their costs, not even enough to rub two pennies together. So they just pass it along, and along, to you.

These are like the welfare Cadillac families, that live in rundown housing and live like they are at so low, that they sunk below the basement of the poverty line. Yet, they have a shiny new Cadillac hiding next to their shack.

Some even live on handouts and social services, some are drifters on the street. Then while they are waiting in line for another freely given handout, eagerly grab their over $500 phone with the high monthly fees. They answer the call to find out when their free ride is coming to get them.

Meanwhile, their bodies and society are screaming out giving them a push to see the errors in their lives. Some cough and cough, just before lighting another Cigarette. Others can't pick up the quarter from the floor, that they missed getting into the candy machine. Others reach for another beer, but they fall off the bar stool while reaching for the barley brew, that is as cold as the waters that were along the route of the Titanic.

The problem is that they will not listen, they again rush off for a quick cure. Pounding on the door to get the, Me first treatment. Their heart rate ends up being as unstable as the New York Stock Market. Once the door is opened, they scream out and cuss like a sailor. Why did it take so long, I have been waiting longer as the last ice age.

I recall something from my past, It came from an unlikely place. It was this, your sins will find you out. Your errors of your youth shall follow you around like a thousand starving Hyenas, each waiting to nip your heels. Your transgressions also have a cost to pay. Pay now, or later, the cost will be as high as the Federal debt. Your cost is your very own life. The wages of your transgressions is death, Your death. You will not see the final bill, your kin will. One item that will be factual, Your charge account of your transgression will end and you cant hurt yourself anymore. But, there will be others in your life that still will be paying a price for your recklessness, for decades.

Your line of Grandchildren will still be paying money to Uncle Sam, for your me first attitude, They will pay in hidden fees and the hidden suffering that you caused decades before. Your little 'One Night's Stand', will be written into your judgment day Personal file. It's too late for you to repent now. It's too late, you missed ride on the forgiven express. All because you wanted more and more of that piece of green apple pie, But, a piece was not big enough. You wanted the entire pie, as large as the playing field at Lambeau Stadium.

You were eagerly waiting for your next phone call, before answering the warning calls coming from your Creator. He has been calling very,very, long distance. You have been putting him on hold, you had no consideration to priority. You wanted to get in a few last transgressions in, before you were willing to pick up his call.

You wanted your next nicotine taste, your last Beer for the road, your last addition to your harem. You felt that your creature comforts and pride of them, were worth more that the long distant call, that was kept God on hold for decades. He sent a family member as an ambassador for you, You kept putting him off. You felt that he could wait, He came to visit, and has been calling to whoever answers, and has was waiting for you for over 2000 years, But you only answer the $500 cell phone in a 'twinkling of an eye'.

People, get out and smell the roses, don't be controlled by man made devises and temptations of sin. You don't need extra servings of Devil's Food Cake, or a spare spouse on the side. You don't need to 'test the limits of your bathroom scale', or the limits in the world around you. You error's could leave you as a pillar of salt, as tall as Paul Bunyan.

Your Creator could not wait any longer, You had your chance, the call was free. Your last dime entered in the slot of the game of life expired. The cab came to pick you up, in a twinkling of an eye. It came to you, no matter what your address is. He knows, and does not need the GPS to find you. This time, You became his Top priority. God paid nothing to make this call, Your cost was everything, because you failed to answer the warning calls for decades.

Chapter 39

Judgement Day - 10/27/2018

I have been in line for an unknown amount of time. I am the next one up, in front of the Judge. The man before me is as nervous as a Clowder of Cats, in a room full of rocking chairs. The Bailiff says, "Step up to the bench". He staggers up toward the bench. The individual as now standing upfront and awaits the decision of the court, and is asked what he thinks the decision should be, He says that he wants to be rewarded for his efforts and be allowed to enter. The answer comes from the Judge, "You shall not enter my house". You have done many things, including abuse of my Son.

The Man then cries out, "I have worked and worked all of my life to end up in the house with you. I have paid plenty to keep the doors on your Son's shelter open for years. I celebrated his birthday every year and have given all of the spare money that was in my pockets.", I mentioned your Son in front of my friends."

The answer comes from over the bench, "You did mention my Son, But when your favorite team lost a game. When you were angry with your kids, You even mentioned My name over and over, what this had to do with regulating water on my rivers, you never explained this. You even enjoyed my creation of 'Eve' so much so, that you have thousands of them on your walls, in your computer files & in your mind. They are dressed the same way as a new born baby. I have sent many others to tell you to change your way, but You refused and rebuked them.

I sent others before you, and they asked you for help feeding the hungry. You said that they don't deserve anything because you never took a handout, and they should follow your footsteps, and pull themselves up by their bootstraps. You whined the homeless were making bad personal choices, and you were hoping that they would just go away. One a cold day, you were taking your extra slightly used coats to be sent to the dump. You could not be bothered with the needy, because if you give them one thing, they will whine for more. You said, Poor are to be sent far away and have nothing said about them again.

I saw you sitting inside of your gleaming castle on the hill, sitting in your easy chair, stuffing your face with every tasty treat. Then You let out a roar, load enough to wake the dead. Then you wanted your Wife to do a task, and said, Hey You, get me a beer, and while you are at it, I want a bacon burger and fries. I saw you when your team lost the game, you called out to me again in anger. I got blamed that you were going to loose a bit of money to your co-workers. Then you mentioned my Son, but wanted nothing from him. I rarely see you put your hands together, except to prevent others from taking things away from you. You keep saying that others have better things that you, but when I give you one of these things, you still are not happy. You stand up and bellow loudly at me, cussing me out because you can't have it your way.

I see you blame others, that your children are not turning out like you want. You turn into a raging firestorm because the children missed a step in your army. The voices of them are silent some nights, I can hear their whimpering as they are trying to fall asleep. You don't care, because you are trying to have it your way. You don't care about the cost, and long as it does not affect your wallet.

I have given you many chances, All I wanted for you is to have a personal involvement with my only begotten Son, and to share his ideas. You refused, but sent your Wife and Kids to see me. I have prepared a place for them, but you now are going to hear my final Judgement.

My final decree is that you are too late, the Roll call was made and you were warned many times. You were worried more about why the chicken crossed the road, and once she got there, can you eat it. You never paid attention to the Rooster, as he crowed the 3rd time.

I rechecked my book of life again, I just had to be sure about you, I can not find your name. Sir, Please step down .., and down ., and down. Next one in line, please step forward.

It was my turn next and as I walked slowly up to the front, I faced the Judge and was ready to plea my case. The Judge says, "My door is open for you, You knew my Son and he has paid for your admission to my house, Please step this way, my banquet awaits you."

Chapter 40

Second Chances - 10/29/18

There was a Woman that had a dream, it was something that she dreamed of, over and over. A business of her very own to operate and communicated with the people in the area. A simple dream that worked for awhile, until the noise arouse out of the chatter and the Iceberg arose before her very own eyes.

She was a hard worker and invested in her future. When it came to open her dream, she hired others to share her dream. She had good times in the first few years. She replaced employees as needed and kept the ship afloat. When others asked for a new start in their lives, she opened her heart and gave them employment.

It was not easy for them, but the workers all formed into a team and provided the customers with the best. This worked fine for a while, but the storm clouds were coming from afar and from within. She was happy with her business and even offered others a second chance, for them to grow in their own lives.

This worker repented of the things that they did in the past, and then humbled himself and asked for a job. He never hid his past and laid it on the line. The Owner decided that she was willing to accept the challenge. The worker was given a 2nd chance in their life to start anew. But, some patrons resisted this effort and refused to use her services again, and soon the business could not survive. They saw a splinter in another's eye, but not the log in your own. They concluded that this person must be judged because of their past. It did not matter to them that the worker did outstanding work on the job, and paid the price to society that was demanded.

More and more patrons jabbered like a thousand flags fluttering in the wind, and began to avoid the business that the owner put her heart and soul into. They expected perfect people that were employed here. One patron bragged about what they do for their church and complain when others did things that they don't like, and this employee should not have been given a second Chance.

Some chatter too much and involve themselves in correction others, when they should be looking in their own mirror. Moses committed a murder, But he was given a 2nd chance, So what was wrong with giving another person a 2nd chance? Plenty proclaimed the users of the booths. Some said that could not risk their safety, others said that it was something that they wanted nothing to do with a man like this.

After a while, this robust place turned into the Sahara Desert. Without the support of customers coming for a hot meal and friendly conversation, and sharing their events of the day, The till became as bare as old Mother Hubbard's Cupboard. and the decision was made to close. The employees suffered as well as the Owner. They put their heart and soul into making it work. But the gossip condemning another's past, sank the ship.

It did not have to happen this way. The owner tried to make the restaurant work, in every possible way. But a few stubborn customers came up with a common goal, crucify him. They even judged the remaining workers for putting up with a sinner being in the place.

In the end, the whining customers got their way and the business closed, putting this worker out of a job. Some of these past customers rejoiced in winning for their cause. Or, did they ?. One day it will be their turn to be judged and they will not be listening, as there minds are on all of the great things that they did to make the world a perfect place. They will not get the facts correct, is that they are not perfect, and shall never be. It may come to them right after the Judge pulls the lever and sending them Down to meet their fate.

They are now back with their buddies from years before, back in a familiar booth awaiting their food orders. This time, there is a new owner and staff. Ding, ding, goes the bell, as their treats are ready. The waiter comes over and hands then their snacks, and says "I hope you enjoy these red deviled eggs, and your complementary order of devil's food cake"

Chapter 41

Personal Master - 11/01/18

They bow down their heads daily in front of their master, it is their iPad or tablet. Some even are using earphones, while they salute their tablets and watch for hours. They see their tablet as being very valuable, as the set that was carried by Moses. Their thumbs are their contact to the world of the master. They trained their thumbs decades ago with a man named Mario. Some even have a device that their voice can control.

They watch the screen without moving their body. They could easily blend in with the wall design of King Tut's tomb. They could fall victim to a pick pocket scheme and never know it. They stare down like a statue of Paul Bunyan. Some even hold their tablet pen so tightly, as they would the Holy Grail. Some live like squatters in public places and business locations, to use the airwaves to communicate with their master.

Hour after hour, their eye's have seen more letters, that what goes through the New York's post office. They watch videos and think of themselves as a reincarnation of Elvis. Then, others spend money as fast as it is printed. They want everything available to them. The bleed their bank accounts until it no longer has a pulse. Some make so many posts, that they could fence in all of the land out west, including cricket ranches and worm farms.

They are under machine control that they allowed themselves to be controlled by. They are not even paying attention to other things, even if the cost to them is free. They avoid others that are not in their screen worship activities. Life is passing them by as fast as a meteorite on a drag strip. Most of the time they are on the Internet airways. WiFi ?, Why not read a book ?.

Finally, they are tired, after more than 12 hours saluting the screen. The screen that provided entertainment, knowledge, and contact with unknown others. The screen even provided a way to have someone else assemble, bake, and deliver their pizza of the day. But, a bird just came along with another twitter, so they grab the tablet once more, just to see what the current message was that could shake up the world, like Atlantis is rising out of the sea. But end up with a Go Fund Me message that wants to raise money, to buy shoes for homeless dogs.

It's time for a snooze for themselves and the tablet time to recharge its battery. They finally fall asleep with there cell phone near their hand, their i-pod cooling off in the table, and their tablet used as a pillow. They never know what they missed in life, as they are no longer living it. They are on standby, having a great relationship with their electronics, even taking one to bed with them. It waits along side them with the window open, for the next flock of birds to fly in with an ocean full of twitters.

But tomorrow is a new day. Another day to do it all over again. The new sunrise soon appears in the morning horizon. This offers them a new chance to get out and explore the world around them, and be part of it. But, will they take advantage of the opportunity?

Chapter 42

Stolen Dreams - 11/06/2018

I have walked on my path for decades thinking that I would never see a close call of death that I had went through in life. I was only 30 days old and I was abused by the 2 people that were there to keep me safe. But in seconds my life was altered forever. I went through a severe head trauma that the Warden herself started the event, and her other half finished. I was in pain and had a head trauma that showed. It took 3 days before I received medical attention and a conclusion from the Doctor, I had less than 6 hours to live. Somehow, a higher power decided that it was not my time. I live with what my parents did to me, and I never could get back the things that I had lost in a matter of seconds. I wished this on nobody else, but an event like this has happened. Not identical occurrence, but one that made me relive and recall the events in my life, by the evidence that I still live with.

I was following a news story where several Girl Scouts died because of a driver trying to get a high. He was huffing a chemical that altered his ability to drive. He drove into a ditch, causing several deaths at the scene. He then drove off and went home, He committed a hit and run. Then, the next story that came up. This happened a few days before, around the same city.

A 10 year old girl killed a Baby boy, that was around 6 months old. She was holding the infant and dropped the child, hitting his head on a piece of wood furniture. The child wailing out in pain. Instead of seeking help for the child, she stomps on his head, and soon his life was over, caused by the deliberate recklessness of another. This is what happened to me, recklessness of 2 others, it was the married couple that lived in the house with me. I was in the hospital for months and lived with their sin for decades after decades.

This event awoke parts of my memory that was sealed as tight as Mr. Scrooge's Coin purse. My suffering over the years had stolen many dreams away from me. I could never get them back, even for all of the gold hidden in the Valley of the Kings.

Now I see another that never had a second chance. 6 months will be etched on his headstone forever. The Child who did this will never find a way to correct this travesty. What was done to stop the child's cries, shall reverberate in her mind through eternity. I live with altered dreams, this baby had every one stolen by another.

This event echos in my mind, as an echo travels through a space, as large as the grand canyon. Causing me to recall what happened to Me as well as to another. My mind then shifts as fast as a comet going to infinity and beyond.

I find my thoughts going back over 20 years, pacing along a stone hedge of headstones. I suddenly come to an abrupt stop, then I see what I knew existed. As I scanned the silent landscape, as still as the surface of the moon, I then glance down and there it was. I saw a cemetery stone that had my name on it. This now sends chills down my back, as if I were bonded to an ice burg that was as large as the Titanic.

Why did I get a chance to live, and this young baby did not. I will never know. Many things are the same, but I was allowed to live and this baby boy was allowed to die. Both of us would have had a better life, if only, someone stepped up to the plate and defended our right to live, but in both cases, nobody was the only person that answered.

I did the best I could do to survive, without having a full deck of options in life. But, this baby was dealt an out. What are his innocent parents to do ?, I don't have an answer, as my parents were guilty of the crime and hid the complete facts from me, for more than 60 years.

Oh my God, what have I done..., screams at me from the written page. This was on a hand written note that came from my mother, over a half century before. I know what they did to me, my body tells me so, as I am Living with the Evidence.

The Baby boy's body also included evidence, that told the Doctors his own story, as how his life was ended so soon.

Chapter 43

Pages In My Mind - 11/13/2018

Life is moving along at a faster pace, it's like flipping the pages in a book that you have read a dozen times or more. The years in life are beginning to act that way as well.

I keep saying to others that I am 39 for another year. I have been doing it for decades. Time really does keep slipping into the future. But my mind can flip the pages of time, and the years that have gone by. I still can remember the unusual stories behind the few photos that I have found, that show my past in many stages.

But one keeps coming back, this one is over 60 years. 60 years and change, I am sitting on the backdoor steps. these were poorly constructed and I could sit backwards on them as if I were sitting at a school desk. Life was bad enough already, but the future looked bleak. I see no way of escaping the circumstances around me. Living where I am, is like something that I don't know actually what it is, a concentration camp. My Father keeps bringing this up, and someone that has the name of Rosie. This name keeps coming up again and again, all I know it's someone that he knew a few years ago and does not live around here. I thought she was a close friend of the family, but my mother wants nothing to do with her. My father has only one close friend that he wants to hold on a daily basis, something that he calls a Fifth.

The house echoes from the sins of the past and present. My brothers and I, are like an inventory of slaves. My father had big ideas for himself and we were along for the ride in his schemes. The planting of 5,000

Norway pine trees to sell years later as Christmas trees, These did have a small payback, but I saw none of the rewards. After a few years, and no attempt at pruning these to look like a Xmas trees, sales of them, were no where to be found. The thousands of trees we planted because of a man's dream, ended up under a bulldozer. This wasn't the only thing that he started out to do to advance his glory and his pocketbook. But the others attempts ended up the same way, like a flash in the pan. Racing, Ski Jumping, and Bowling made the list. Only night he waited to have a relationship with his 5th, was on a bowling night.

Selling onions that were grown by others, was another flop that started out with him crossing the finish line before the race even started. He would buy 10 and 50 pound bags of Spanish onions and resell them for profit. But, as usual, This relied on him not doing much of the daily effort that it took to run a home business. After some time, even this began to fall apart as a way to keep his bar tab paid. One brother got fed up with this charlie brown operation, and took some of the money that was earned and ran away from home for a week, ending up past the Dakota's. He was back in a week, but all the money was gone. He took the money out of the 'Queen Bee's Cookie Jar'. He came back to a world that the he left, but now the Sofa King had another reason to say that we were no damn good and to this wayward son, He had one more reason as why he would never amount to anything. This was the turning point. After this event, the Queen Bee began to use his ill gotten gains to her advantage. A few of the items that he stole, ended up in the Queen Bee's hands. She later proclaimed that the items were hers and kept them for decades. She even raided a woman's apartment before she had her last breath. I have seen so much in very little time.

As I remember resting my head on the top step, I recall that in a half dozen more years, I would endure another night of going down the hallway and behind the closed door. The place were the Sofa King lived, after he had his 5th and a 6 pack. I wanted help from his other half, the Queen Bee, or what she began to act like, a warden over fenced in prisoners. But, I got no help, She let it happen and knew something was going on and did nothing. Night after night, she would go off with her Mother to have coffee and left us with the Souse in the House. This put in question about what happened to me just 10 years before. I later found out that She started the events back then and He finished it. This may help explain her final decree/judgement, I could not attend his or wanted at her funeral. I was more unwanted than the family felon. At least, He was wanted by the Queen Bee, she even copied his work. Today, He and I are the only family members alive, that lived in the house of hell. The paint on the walls of this house tell a story of many things, they are like that house has a set of fingerprints, each pattern tells of an event from the past. The house had a checkered past, and rooms of green, blue, yellow, red, and white.

My mind recalls chilling sounds from the past, like kittens screaming out sounds from hell, as the Sofa King cuts off a part of their tails. The Dog howls out as scalding hot liquid seeps into the hairs on her back. The sound of a rumbling thunder coming from the garage, as the air compressor sucks in enough air to fill a blimp. Then the rattling of wood arms, sounding like bones, that are on the water pump. This is pulling up and letting down a rod that went deep into the ground. This noise existed for the life of the house. This was 25 years, and then the noise ended. The house met it's fate by being destroyed and ran over by a bulldozer.

Before it became a memory, it was allowed to show its battle scars from over a quarter of a century. The house was a landmark to many travelers, but when I grew up, it was a bunkhouse to a wire fenced Stalag.

I recall the night when I was 4, The Sofa King and Queen Bee went off to a Ski Club meeting, This Club was something my Grandfather cherished, but my father used to his advantage. On this day, we were kicked out of the house all day and received no crumbs from the table, I knew what a church mouse must have lived like. All 4 of us kids were outside looking for food from nature, this is all that we were going to get. There were plums, choke cherry trees, and acres of wild sauerkraut in the fields. Inside the house, the so called baby sitter, had her boyfriend and 2 other couples that she invited. They ate anything that they desired and when they desired more, they went for it and this included anything. Every bedroom in the house was used for any of their lustful desires. My oldest brother was the only one tall enough to see into Sodom and Gomorrah. When our parents returned, were were all outside, cold and hungry, like a pack of wandering hobo's. This babysitter never appeared at the house again. We thought that this event might make our parents care for use more, but we were wrong. They thought of more ways to hide events and use us for what they wanted.

I saw more scams and cons from these two, than what you could find in the entire series of the Dukes of Hazzard. My mother wanted to be like a man in a man's world, and instead of being Boss Hogg, she ended acting like him and became Boss King. The number of scams and schemes could fill a filing cabinet at the Pine Valley Court House.

I dozed off a few times that afternoon, on the backdoor steps, hoping and dreaming of a better world. But it would take decades more to have a life without the Warden using her control. So this banning me from family functions, may have been another way for the Queen Bee to exert her power. Her Will delivered another way to show her power from the grave, I was given no crumbs to nibble. While another brother lived like a Hogg, But, in 6 short months, His bloated lifestyle came to a abrupt end. He ended up along the side of the Queen Bee, awaiting judgement day.

I can still place myself back on the steps, hearing things that I would know nothing about for the next 10 years. Some have asked me if I had a chance to live my life over, would I ?. I tell them No. I might not survive going through it a second time. My mind is like a Jukebox, I can select one of many platters, each with a horror story or one of dreams of the future. Problem is, I never know what one could come up as a selection. As my mind wanders down the grooves of the platter, I relive the events that were pressed into my mind. I can replay the event over and over, and never skip across it's history. I recall that in my lifetime, I had over 11,000 records that I played on my phonograph. I don't know how many platters are recorded in my mind, 11,000 does not seem if that number is large enough.

Time to turn off the music & put the records away. They just don't sound like they did in the past. My abilities are not the same as in the past. I can only remember what songs should sound like. But I can't make life what it should have been. I only can continue forward on my path, my shoes show the wear of treading down the beaten path. The evidence of the past, follows me like my shadow, as I await for the sun to reveal it's face from behind the clouds. At times, its rays help evaporate the tears from the past. The creation of the sun became an inspiration to man, to go forward and build a better tomorrow. This shadow follows me around every day.

I can never forget sitting on the back steps, as I have done it several thousand times. Each time, giving me a chance to dream of a better life.

Being 4 years old, did have it's limitations. I was limited, but the King and Queen of the house never could take that away from me. I am that last surviving member of the family, that is free. The only other living member is in a new stalag of man's, built with concrete and steel bars. He is caged inside of a place known as the big house. He forfeited his dreams and freedom, for his crimes became larger and larger. The two of us, that fell under control from a family ran stalag, ended up on 2 different paths. I dreamed of a better life as I sat on the back steps. I knew that life had to be better, and I was given a 2nd chance to see part of it come true.

Never give up, The hare had everything going for it, But it did loose the race. The steady tortoise had a mission to walk along the path, not knowing that he would win. I went through life, not knowing that I could stay on the path, or see part of a life that never was in my dreams. I have made it this far, and I am still moving forward. I can see the light at the end of the tunnel, and I don't plan on losing my way through the darkness.

Chapter 44

Final Order - 11/17/17

In my life, I wanted to know more about where I came from than were I would end up. I went back to the places where I lived and what happened along the way. Later I wanted to know where the people were before me and my time on earth. This led me to study the family tree. The best place was old documents, newspapers, and looking for the answers myself. How was I going to do this? I had to go where my past relatives are now. Some are among the living and others are among the dead. This fact led me to start searching the ones that have passed before me, so cemetery searching was what I began to do.

Some afternoons, I would walk past over 1,000 headstones in 3 different cemetery locations, this took about 3 hoursHad a camera with me and took photos of the ones that I felt could have a connection to me or my past. In the 3 hours, I took 525 photos of the names and dates, etched in stone. In a few years, I visited over 150 locations that were close to my hometown. I discovered many things that I did not know, and this knowledge was not in any paperwork that I had or read. Several of my past relatives had a last name that did not match today's version. Some names changed a letter or 2, others switched 2 letters around in the name.

Traveling to the many places on a weekly schedule, filled in the missing pieces that gave me a stepping stone to discover the location of more family information. This led to finding more paperwork and documents that filled in the missing pieces. But, by seeing tens of thousands of these etched book marks in stone, I also discovered a world that I only came across by asking questions, over 35 years ago. A personal tragedy led to the questions that I had to know.

Decades before, after I became married, We decided to start a family. But, life did not go as planned. Our 2nd child died in less that 3 hours after he was born, and this led to questions that needed answers. The nursery was ready, but the child was never going to be there. His first stop that had a place for him was the funeral home. This was never on my mind when you start having a family. The first signal was the Black Rose that appeared outside of the hospital room, that my Wife was in. Then the other questions came at us like a tidal wave.

We heard too many of this kind, what did you do to cause this ?. Then we got many like this one, you should have done things the way that I did them.

But, in the end, I had to handle it myself. I saw no other way to keep peace within myself. I had to do it my way. When all things were considered, I did the best for me and my family, and I am at peace with the choices I made. I did the best that I could

Chapter 45

Twas the Night in the House - 11/23/2018

Twas the night before wrestling open the boxes to be,
the ones beneath the tree that we hoped we would see.
The flying delivery man was yet to be there,
even if his sky riding deer were fast as the Hare.
We had all gone to bed, hung out our pajamas to the back of a chair.
We were waiting for a jolly fat man to bring some gifts to be placed
there.
We knew the man of the house had a beer puffy belly,
All stuffed with beer and stinky cheese from a cheap old deli.

Stuffed and pickled, was time for the old man to hit the hay,
Trips over a pair of old fuzzy cats he met along his way.
He rolls down the blankets and jumps into bed,
Visions of a Keg party still in his head.

We were soon awoken by a crash above our Heads,
This large noisy impact knocked us out of our beds.
We jumped to our feet and we raced out of the house,
The glowing red object we saw was not a mouse.

But a strange red battery less object, was all that was there,
He was pulling behind him Paul Bunyan's giant blue Ox wheelchair.
Sitting on the Handles was a fat man in white trim lace,
with a long curly smoking pipe stuck far into his face.

Looking for our house that was as Red as a Beet,
He finally arrived with a hole in his seat.
Growing up in the red brick house where and when I did,
There never was a question about Santa, from any kid.

The many clues spoke for themselves and one by one,
My brothers and I came to the same conclusion.
If Santa entered the house, he would be smoked like a sausage link,
because the chain smoker stained the walls, and the double kitchen sink.

It was impossible for cookie stuffed Santa to be,
He would never get into the house, he has no key.
He began to huff and puff, as he tried to squeeze with all his might,
A 44x belly down the furnace's brick lined exhaust pipe.

He would then keep from being trapped in the chimney with his butt,
Otherwise he would end up being roasted like a chestnut.
But that did not stop Santa, He sucked in his belly and came through
the damper,
straining and squeezing so much, that he might be needing a new large
blue pamper.

Arriving on the floor of the basement, he was lucky to have his boots,
He would have a new pretty name, "Flower". But not the kind that has
any roots.
He would have a long white stripe down his back,
That would make him very easy to track.

He rubbed the side of his nose and the itch would stop,
He then puffed up like he was a king sized Jiffy Pop.
Stumbling around, He entered the room of the water pump,
He almost got his white beard knitted into a lump.

Bouncing off the shiny metal, cold water tank,
he felt the concrete floor vibrate and then it sank.
He came up the stairs with a heavy load on his back,
Dumped off all that he could find from within his big sack.

His work was done and Santa felt proud, like he did years ago as a hippy,
After scarfing down 6 large Jars of Smuckers, and a gallon of Skippy.
His time was up and he ran from the red brick house,
Tripping over the couch sleeper, the old grey souse.

The Liquor Lover would have put enough holes in Rudolph, and the
other reindeer,
That you could sew them up and make the Jolly Green Giant, a 6 pack
holder for beer.
On Smasher, On Slasher, On Mindy and Candy,
On Cuspid, On Polar, On Grumpy and Handy.

Time to leave, hurry it up and get out of here,
This place was smokey and had the smell of cheap beer.
As Santa leaves with his 8 pork belly reindeer,
Rudolph went missing, it's like he was never here.

As I see Santa fly away, it was never too soon,
He went to hide until next year, by living on the Moon.

Chapter 46

Where's Santa - 12/11/18

The night was a bit colder than usual, with the ground covered in a fresh blanket of snow, that tucked in the plants, and to keep the hibernating animals warm. The place where the family personal Santa had lived, was all decked out in lights and soft music could be heard.

A family was gathering for going on a Christmas present safari search, in a dozen scattered stores around the area. They began to come across a few Santas decked out in red, with a big belly and a ding a ling bell in their hand. They did this work for free, to help others in this time of need.

The family members began to discuss their past and their personal Santa. Over the next few hours, they all had a memory of what their Santa did for them and the many gifts over the years, that he had given to them.

The youngest member in the group spoke up with a very unusual question for a child of his age. I want to see Santa, There is one in the Mall, but where is ours ?. This got the chatter among the older members going like a avalanche.

He was good to all of us over the years. Maybe we should go see him, after all, its been about 10 years. Another spoke up and said it was more that that, I recall it has been more than a baker's dozen of years.

They then decided that they would take the children home and wrap the presents later. After this was done and they assembled the group and took one car on the trip to the place where their Santa lived.

As the entrance request button was pushed, a light on the inside panel glowed like Rudolph's red nose. Within a minute a worker appeared at the door to let the strangers enter. They came to see their Santa, the one that filled this role as they were growing up

The several guests that came, quickly entered the building, and went to find room 8, That was Santa's favorite number. He would joke about counting the legs of his reindeer and divide by four, this gave him the number of 8. But, time has passed by in years, and the reindeer moved to Florida to keep themselves warm.

Along the way they picked up a few elves, and found a place to retire at. Their Grand Reindeer had the job now of pulling their jolly old fat man around the hall ways. This allowed another to do the job, that the Family Santa had, as he found his own place to live, half way between the equator and the North Pole Toy factory. The Family Santa made enough toys to make the largest Toy Soldier army that the world has ever seen.

Tiny Tim also was where the Family Santa lived, He retired after making items that made life easier for the handicapped children of the world. Tim never wanted to be a scrooge, so he worked long hours to give children a gift that money could not buy, a smile on their faces that reminded others of the curve of the runners on the sleigh.

The guests entered room 8, and said that they did not remember their Santa's room looking like this. An old man was sitting in a big stuffed chair, looked at them and raised his cane, striped like a barber pole. Then he said, I don't know you, what are you doing here.

One of the guests said that they were looking for our Santa, He was in this room for over a decade.

The man in the chair said to them. That Santa you are looking for left about 3 years ago and took his last sleigh ride, Rudolph was too old to pull him, so 6 of his trainers took your Santa to a place where he would forever be.

One guest blurted out, Why did no one tell us that he died ? The Old Man in his chair proclaimed, Why were you never here and know what was going on with your relative. Without the pictures that I saw, I would never have know that he had any family at all. I only knew his nickname was Santa, but never knew from where he came.

The oldest guest said, "We were too busy, and we had a life to live. It was not that we forgot about him, We had to work long hours to get what we wanted and see, We have a gift for him ".

"See my name is Chester, it's on the Door Tag. That gift will have no use now, He could have used it 3 years ago. before he got a change of address, to Lakeside section 9, This is where some of his friends are. You should have been here years ago. I do have something that is not mine. Somebody said it was to be a gift to those seeking him out, to give him a gift. So this unopened box must be yours."

One of the guests opened the box and many photos fell out and filled the floor of the room. Then she fell to her knees and saw a photo of herself, being held by Santa. She felt like she always had time to make things better and always could put it off until tomorrow. At that moment, the clock in the hall, tolled 3 times on this hour.

As She sat silently staring at the photo, the others began to realize that the remaining pictures told of a man that always remembered them, But when they stared at the pictures, they began to see the strange look of their faces reflect off the photos. They finally realized that they were beginning to look like their Family Santa.

They picked up the pictures, and saw hundreds of memories that were on the photos. Each one could never be again, they waited too long. After they refilled the box, it was time to go. They thanked Chester for saving the pictures. Chester said "It was the last gift that your Santa had on the sleigh. This was a gift that he could not deliver himself, and now his final delivery is done".

The guests left and it would take a few days before they finally realized just what they have lost. They knew now that they themselves, were at fault. They were chasing their dreams, instead of living their lives in a world with their personal Santa.

All of them went back home. A home that had everything that they had worked for. The front yard was all filled with every item that shows the neighbors that they have the Christmas spirit. Everything was there that they wanted. Rudolph was out in the yard, his nose was ready for takeoff. The elves were all decked out waiting for Santa to arrive on Christmas Eve. But Their Santa would never arrive, as they have no memories of him in resent years. They let things slide along and now it's too late. Even the memories in their minds are as scattered tumbleweeds, marching across the desert.

From this day forward, they could never forget that their Santa would never come to enjoy the fabulous store bought Cookies, and the glass of Swiss Hot Chocolate. They always said that had everything at

Christmas. But, now they knew now that they lied. They had forgotten the most important thing of their past, their own "Personal Santa". His knowledge and memories went with him, and this was more valuable that anything that money could buy.

Chapter 47

Phonograph Flipping - 12/13/18

Back in 1974, I was like Gilligan, He was making a 3 hour tour, and was stranded on an island. I was packed up and shipped out of the home where I grew up. I was facing a 3 year tour.

I was stranded out of town in a house, with no phone, no heat, and no motorcar, and very few items of luxury I had the TV and the refrigerator. and not much else. Some days the house was chilly, and other days is was cold.

I had to do things that kept my body moving so it would generate heat. So music was the way that I could beat the cold indoors.

The level of the Audio was no concern, I was in a house and was all alone. It was not a problem even if the glass windows vibrated in sync. I could feel the beat of the drums with my body. The sound waves were invisible, but I could sense them anyway.

To sort out the songs in my collection, I could swap 180 records in an hour, on My phonograph. Nothing to worry about, I had thousands of these black platters, I was getting 10 used 45's for less than a dollar. Also got some out of local Bar jukebox.

I moved to the music and my temperature started to rise, I needed it as the room was in the mid 50's. I could not turn up the heat as I had no heat source. I had to warm up the body by motion.

The Faster I changed the 45's, the faster the songs would play in my mind. My Cobra turntable had an adjustable speed, it could go as high as 90. This made a 45 ready for takeoff, heading for it's own zenith.

My mind would go back and forth in time, remembering the past to the present. This would clock along like a railroad train clicking along the rails, running at over 300 miles an hour. The drums in the songs would be like main cylinders on the side of a Big Boy Locomotive.

The calorie burn began to be cranked up. I could even imagine being in the band, of the song that was playing. If wanted to increase my motion more. I did not need to play air guitar. With an electric guitar in the corner, I had a chance to work on this skill. This allowed me to play along and try to keep up with the rhythm of the song.

Other days, I would leave the house and ride my bicycle for hours. Some days. I spent 16 hours on the road. So I had 2 things that burned energy and warmed me up from the inside out.

The days like this can never be repeated, as I can't hear all the parts of the songs now. They are only a memory to Me, But this memory of my past, will remain with me for a lifetime.

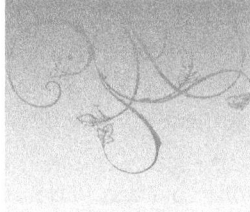

Chapter 48

Game Changer - 1/1/2019

The day starts out different as today is a holiday. Not everything is open and business locations are closed. I start out my day and go out to get a meal at the usual location. I spend time chatting with a high school classmate and another friend of mine.

I spend a few hours being online and updating information and adding things to my websites. It is around 4:20 in the afternoon and it's time to go visit with my wife, she is at an assisted living location. I pack my computer up and it's time to go to her location.

I arrive and enter the building. It is strange that the lunchroom is half empty and the usual chatter from the residents is missing. I pass it off due to today being the start of a new year. I continue my walk down to my wife's room. I find the door to the room closed. This is not normal for her, The door isn't closed until I arrive there.

I open the door and the lights are off. I turn on the light and step further into the room. I see that she is not in her chair, and the room has been re-arranged. The two small tables have been moved and the one I use is folded up. I then turn around to see where she is in the bathroom, but she isn't there. The wheelchair is empty and pushed back into the corner by the sink. I seem to remember that in the past, if she had a Doctor appointment the wheelchair should have been taken with her. Where could she be ?

I remember being with her after 11:30 last night. I set the TV for her to watch the new year fireworks. I left a few minutes after that and got home around 11 minutes before midnight. Where is she now ? I begin to search the room and see many things out of place. and I am moving around the room, a worker from the assisted living location enters the room and begins to tell me that my wife is in the hospital.

This worker came in around 7 am, and could not awake her in the normal way. It was time for my wife to take her meds and get ready for breakfast. But my wife is a bit groggy. The worker thinks that my wife has another infection and seeks help from others. Soon it is realized that they can't quite pin down what the problem is and a call is made for an ambulance to move her quickly to the Hospital. So the gurney is brought to her room and the over 4 mile trip to the Hospital has to done.

The assisted living personal fill me in with what they know, and I am on the way to the hospital to see how things are. I need an update on her condition, and what may or may not be needed. All that was brought up was that she could have another internal infection or it could be a stroke. This conclusion was brought up because she had some weakness on one side of her body. An infection could cause this or having a stroke could do it too.

I arrive at the hospital and enter the Emergency entrance. I talk with the women that are behind the desk. I of them take my information and find my wife's assigned room. She walks with me to the elevator and to the waiting room, nearest my wife's room. The Worker leaves the room to find the Nurse that is in care of my wife. It takes a few minutes and the Nurse comes into the waiting room and starts to inform me of my wife's condition.

After being told that she does not have an infection, the real truth comes out. My wife had a stroke overnight, between midnight and 7 am. Because it happened over 2 hours before she arrived at the hospital, they can't use a blood clot removing medicine as a treatment, that some do have. They also know that my wife had a heart valve replaced and this complicates the options. They want her in surgery as soon as possible.

It is around 6:30 in the evening and they all ready have her on a gurney.and once I sign the consent form, she is off to the races to get the procedure started. I was told it could take 1 to 3 hours. Nobody knows until they actually finish, as how long it will be.

For me it's a waiting game. I have to find things to make the time go by. So I am writing this to keep me occupied and prevent my thoughts from time warping into the past and having it act like a prewound double tornado.

My mind begins to have its first flashback. Its about the actual tornado that struck in the early 1950's. This tornado passed within yards of the exact location of the Hospital that I am in now. It damaged the ski jump that was built before the Hospital was, and then it went across highway 3 and went between the house where I grew up and the nearest house that was 200 feet to the west. It damaged the roof on our red brick house and heavily damaged the attached garage on the house to the west. Then the tornado started to lift back up into the sky as it passed over the Pine Valley city dump. My mind is full of the events of the past that I could fill a museum.

But it does not get any easier, the next flashback places me back almost 3 decades. I am inside my house and the smoke is increasing, the house is on fire and I have to get my pregnant Wife and son out of the burning house. I manage to get both out and I am the only one inside. I feel the floor shift and the bedroom doors are starting to close by themselves. I have to get out, the countdown to flash over fire has began. Stresses of today bring back the stresses felt from the past, I can't escape this. I can't replace the past memories with good times, as good time events are very rare. I can related bad times of past with current events because there are too many to choose from.

It's been an hour that my wife has been is surgery, I still do not know how long it will take. My mind is acting like a roulette wheel, I never know just what past memory that it will land on. I try to think what I could have done to prevent this stroke from happening, but I can't find none. I was getting her the best living arrangement that I could for her. She had 24 hour around the clock care, and was getting the treatments she needed, determined by her Doctor. There is nothing else that I can do, I have to leave the fate in God's hands, as mine are not big enough to be a replacement.

I now wonder what path I am being led on. I don't know, I can only imagine as what lays ahead of life for myself and my Wife. Do I see images of a cemetery or do I see a medical victory. I am only 1 person among 7.6 billion. I have to let the one God do his job. There is no way in knowing just what the answer will be. I cant sent him where I want, He is going to take me where he wants.

An Hour and 10 minutes have passed since she went into surgery, a Medical staff technician comes to where I am and informs me that they can't remove the blood clot. This is not the information I wanted. So my mind is adrift as the best scenario has just passed from my fingertips. It now becomes a waiting game. I was informed as why the clot removal procedure did not work. This cause was also was out of my hands. As people get older you never know what you your body will be like and what medical issues you will have. Having known that I could do nothing to prevent this and I could do nothing to insure that her blood clot could be removed, has me feeling like the captain of Noah's Ark. As Captain, I had no rudder to steer the giant vessel, and all I can do is watch as it meanders around the oceans waiting for a place to settle. As usual, I do not know where this address will be. My mind is afloat as the Ark was, on the open sea.

It now is a waiting game. It could take days, weeks, months of time, or never. She will be alive for now, but what type of person will she be. Will she even know my name or her own. The future is very cloudy, as I have spent the last few years like I was a widower, I see no change in this until the unthinkable happens. She has her last breath and ends up in the hands of the creator. This feels like the day the earth stood still.

It's now 7:57 pm and the next round begins. I see her wheeled past the waiting room. I still have to wait while they get her in her room and connect all of the needed equipment. It's just one thing after another, and another. I see no end in sight. The roulette wheel has stopped spinning, but I can't see where the ball has landed, or even if there was a ball at all.

As time sneaks around to 9, I finally arrive at her ICU room. This one is in a different part of the hospital that she was in a couple of years ago. The more it looks different, the more it looks the same. It feels to me that I have been here before and before. The Nurse and I discuss her abilities and come to same conclusion, she needs help and I am not trained in this field. All I see are the clues, as she twitches her legs and grabs the bed railing with her right arm. I see no movement at all with her left. Her tomorrow will be filled with many strangers that will only be known by their medical title. I will be a busy and confusing day.

As midnight gets closer, I need to go home and get refueled for another day. I had a chance to sleep over in the hospital, but this is not the best for me. I saw the list where visitors can go out to eat, but even this is out of my price range. Everything is now calculated to the minute and the penny. No time for error in anything that I do. Communication to me is the keyboard on my computer, or nothing at all. A mouse can get into the house before a phone call would go through. It's just the way it is. I can't stop the world to get off. It spins just like the roulette wheel.

In the background as I write this in her room, I hear the constant churning of the machines that have become a part of my wife's life. Occasionally an alarm triggers and the crew comes running to see what needs to be done. I feel helpless at times as I can not do anything to lesson her discomfort. I have become the invisible man who is a witness to the things that affect her daily life.

What do I do, and when do I tell the children and her side of the family, or do I ? What do I do if things happen, that cause her to join our Son. He has been at the Lakeside Cemetery for the past 28 years. Then what do I do ? A million Dollars can not solve this problem. The path before me is beginning to narrow and I have to pick up the pace the best that I can. I never can seem to avoid the rocky path that I have to enter again and again. I want what is best for her, but what if things don't turn out this way. Who will have to tell her that she now has things that she will never be able to do again. This event also ends her biggest dream that she has, of being able to return home again.

How can I be the Rock of Gibraltar again and again, and not show the stresses that could tumble down the great pyramids of Egypt. My guardian angel must be working overtime, as I have no emotions to show at all. It seems like they are encased in concrete. I can't turn them on, even if I find the switch. They are locked up inside and nobody knows the combination. What event will cause my walls of Jericho to come tumbling down ? I do not know.

Chapter 49

Stroke of Midnight - 1/7/2019

New Years Eve countdown has started, anticipation of the local events at midnight heighten the time elapsing second by second. Time is down to 19 minutes before ringing in the New Year, of 2019. I am on my way home to watch the local event on the Television. It will be an eight minute event down town where the 2 rivers combine into one. Pine Valley river and the Indian river combine their power together and this was the reason to the creation of the city of Pine Valley. The saw mills gave birth to the town.

I left my wife at the assisted living location that is near my house. She is awake and waiting for the light display, as I can't take her there to see it in person. It should be a good show. She was awake and wanted to see the entire fireworks display, as it would fill her room with the various lights and sounds.

Since she needed a wheelchair and walker to get around, going to these events were out of any possibility for her. She only had the memories of the past ones in her mind. I did have a few recorded on videotape that she could watch if she wanted too.

She was in her room and watching the TV event countdown. When I got home, it was almost midnight. I watched the same Downtown Pine Valley fireworks display that she did. I wanted to ask her about it, later in the afternoon. I never got that chance. Her life would change forever after the Stroke of Midnight.

Her life would never be the same again. A worker came into her room about 7 hours after the fireworks were on TV. One worker could not wake her up, as they normally did. She summoned another worker to come and help. The second worker, also saw problems with Rayne, So they had the Director of the Assisted Living location, come in and see the situation. It was then determined that Rayne had a medical issue and the ambulance was called.

The worker said that the TV in the room was turned off. Rayne did watch the entire fireworks event from downtown. What time she fell asleep that night is unknown. So the mystery of when it happened would never be found. There was not going to be an easy solution to her problem. It was time to get her to the Riverside Hospital and see just what the medical issue was.

Her life would never be the same again, as it was determined that she had a stroke sometime after midnight. Since the time it happened was not known, several medical treatments could not be done. The damage was done and she still had a chance to get outpatient treatments and reduce the affect upon her. So even, if she had a major setback, there was hope that she could partually recover from this.

She was transported by ambulance to get the answers and work on Her recovery. Her future was now in the hands of the Medical Staff and her Creator.

Chapter 50

Last Dreams - 1/08/19

Time seems as if it's at a stand still, after a person has a stroke. Life becomes a waiting game, as I and others do not know what comes next.

Will time begin to heal what went wrong, or will the time run out on the patient and their span of living on this planet end. So a waiting game goes on and on.

Multiple tests are done and repeated to get the information to use to take a step forward, or will it show that the person is beginning to accelerate to their final destination ?

In the meantime, what does the person do that is confined to a bed and connected to a gauntlet of instruments, that fill the room in the light glow of green and blue lights.

Without the patient knowing, many are making decisions and setting plans to match what may happen to them. This is a task that needs all questions answered, for every day after day. Each day new questions arise.

The problem is finding out what needs to be done and who will do it. This becomes a task that keeps relatives busy for day after day. The patient can do not of this, others have to do it all. sometimes you have an easier task if the patient has written down what they want, but not everyone does.

The waiting game goes on, but what is the patient doing while the tests and decisions are being done. I look at the patient and I see that they can't do anything physical besides small movements. So for the patient, all they can do is remember their life and their past. They will not be aware what others are doing for them or around them, all they might be able to do is dream.

Dream of the world that they had. Remember the good times and push back the bad times. They will review their life as long as they can, their memories last until they take their last breath, other's will not have access to them because they were taken with them.

There is a lesson here. Share the memories of your relatives and friends now, as you never know when the time runs out, and your chance to do so has expired.

I hope that they had happy memories, soon there is a a big rush as lights go off and alarms start a choir. The population in the room jumps by leaps and bounds, as they try to help the patient.

Then they know, dream time for the patient has ended. They pack up and silence falls within the room. The patient will have a new address, that has no post office.

Chapter 51

No Care for Compassion - 1/11/19

My days are double booked as I try to deal with the Fact that my Wife was taken off life support machines. Nature, with direction of God, are now in Command. I don't know how long she has left. Every day I have to check my Email for any updates.

This day, the first thing I see is from the people that was managing her needs while she was in an assisted living. This message says that I have 2 days to empty her room, or they would donate everything away. I don't know when my wife will die, and they want this short time frame to get what they want done.

They should have asked Me my wife's current condition and how I was getting along. This may help them understand humans under stress and come to a compromise as when I could remove her items.

This is like me being slammed by the door, as I was told to get it out or else. I have found an example that shows No Care for Compassion.

Chapter 52

Silence of the Lambs - 1/13/2019

As I awake to a new day, The last thing that I expected this year has happened. Things around me do not seem real. It's near the middle of January, there should be more than a foot or two blanketing the ground. But it isn't there, the ground looks like old Mother Hubbard's Cupboard. As I scuff along the ground, I pass many people along the way.

My mind still has to register that Rayne has passed away. I don't want a million questions asked of me. I need to find a place that I can collect my thoughts. Some place where I have people that know me, but do not know what the current event in my life is. I need to stay out of my current traffic patterns and how I spent my day. I have to face my life without my life partner. I have to walk along my path, alone.

I pass by hundreds of living specimens of the Human Race, But I know that they do not know what I am going through, I have too many things that have to be done alone. I need to finalize the place, date, and time, for Her funeral. I have to finish contacting relatives. I need to handle the legal paperwork. Decisions, decisions, I have to make them all. Even getting the money to pay for the costs. I walk around trying to make sense of what happened yesterday.

Why was I the only one that knew that She passed away at 4:16 pm. There was 4 others in the room. Maybe I was to be the first one to know, and it ended up this way.

People walk by Me or I walk by them quickly, they stand like statues and some look like i feel, a Zombie. Images in my mind spin faster than a tornado, thousands of photos go past and cover over 60 years of my life. Then the channel switches, I see thousands of pictures of my Wife and family. There will be no more pictures ever again of the 4 of us. There never was a photo of the 5 of us, since out second Son passed away before our Daughter was born. Then Silence fills the spaces of my mind.

Silence is the time where my mind has to reset and snap back into the real world. What tasks that I have to do seem to come over me like, a 67 foot tidal wave. I then realize that in order to solve the problems ahead, I will have to do one thing at a time. I have to continue walking forward on my path, by stepping forward, one step at a time. I will get where I am going, and complete what I must do in stages.

I have tried to walk along my usual daily route today. I try not to reveal what My feelings are, or what is on my mind. It is too early to let my feelings show. So I will use my pen and paper to write down what my mind is going through. When I pass by anyone today and it seems as if they are as Silent as a Lamb. I am not ready yet, it may take days to let down my guard. I have to complete what I have to do first. I am responsible for the decisions that must be made. This is to handle the tasks that are ahead of me, It will take many days before I finally tell others why I changed my routine.

When I do open up, all the decisions have been made and they will be told. Now begins the final steps to complete my responsibilities to my Wife and family. When all is said and done, My writings will reveal what was on my mind, as I walked through one of many tough times in my life. To complete my tasks, I had to have time to be within the Silence of the Lambs.

Chapter 53

Aftermath - 1/14/2019

It's been only a few days after the loss of my life's partner. Questions have arose as why I changed my life schedule. I am not aware of this drastic change and the days seem shorter. I can't plan one day before the other. Stresses of this event strike like lightning bolts. I never know when, how, or where this will happen.

I try to get back on my regular schedule but this isn't possible, It may take days, weeks, months, or years. I will never know until years tumble through the hour glass. The days will be remembered from our past that we had in our lives.

Every thing I touch could cause a flashback to the times we had. I never know when a sad remembrance happens. It is tough to prevent and I can't get them to stop.

My mind flashbacks 39 years, as I remember the time that I first saw the woman that would be my wife. I was not looking for love in any place at all. I walked by her as she worked in a different department than I did. She was just another person that punched the time clock. She worked in the printing shop and made things for local stores, businesses, and local events. I was in an arca that I rebuilt small ovens. Our 2 lives was not expected to ever cross, it was only possible in one of the lunch breaks or when we passed through the halls. She was a faceless female among the many in the crowd.

I had been dating another within the last year and we were still friends. She had 2 that she dated over the previous 2 years. Or destiny seemed never to be. I had a vision issue and being in a printing department was not on my list of things to do. She would never ever understand electricity and the internal workings of appliances. It was like 2 ships running into each other, when the ships were in 2 different oceans.

Then the odds changed. The City Park and Recreation expanded seating and picnic areas in local parks. They needed more garbage cans. The city dropped off over a dozen 55 gallon drums. A crew in the reconditioning department began to work along side of me, cutting off the tops and sanding the barrels and then painted them green. But they had to be made with Pine Valley Parks and Recreation Dept. Nobody in the area could hand paint decent letters on the barrels. They sent a message to find an employee in the building that could do the job. They found one in the sewing department that was a past worker in the printing Department. So this employee was transferred for 2 weeks into my department to hand letter the barrels. They needed white letters on the prepared green barrels.

So destiny was set to be, as my future wife was in my department. I was rebuilding ovens and she was along side doing what she does. In a few days we said a few things to each other. Every day the chat increased. She knew others in my department so she was a chatterbox to many. I heard a few things about her and I got he courage to start asking questions. I knew my mother was still trying to interfere in my life and got nosy many times. I found out that this woman was not born or raised in the Pine Valley area. This intrigued me to know more, because my mother would take years to snoop around to get information on her. I was seeing 2 others on and off during the last months. One woman I dated could never work out, and the other was on and off dating. Nothing was written in stone.

My mother had began to investigate my on and off romance with this woman. She thought that she knew everything. She knew I went to church with her, went out to eat at various places and discovered that she was some kind of nurse, working at Lakeside Hospital. My mother was on the top of the pile of Queen Bees.

As the 2 weeks started to come to the end, it was an off time with the nurse. I had enough courage to enter in to a conversation with the chatterbox. I spent the last 3 or 4 days starting to know her, Her name was Rayne. On the end of the 2 weeks, I knew she would go back to her original department. So before that, I asked her to go out to eat. She said that after work she always went down to the Country Boy place to have coffee and maybe a Country Girl Meal. She told me that she walked down there after work, and later went home. I had a Car and offered her a ride there. She agreed and we had our first dinner date. I had the Country Boy platter, she took the Country Girl. We were there for over and Hour. Then I took her for a ride around town to show her the sites that were not on the bus route. after that, We went back to her apartment, a place where she shared it to a Legally blind woman. She had other roommates in the past as well. Before I left, we set another time to meet Saturday.

The months flipped through the calendar, one by one. My mother knew I was dating, but the nurse was the one she was involved in tracking down. My uncle was dating a coworker of the nurse and his comments led my mother to still stick her nose to the ground and her ear to the rails in town.

We dated for a bit over a year. We decided to be engauged and I gave her a ring. We then went headed east so I could meet her parents and siblings. I spent overnight there in a room off the living room, she shared an upstairs bedroom with her sister.

A week later, We went to go to my parents house. After arriving and entering the front door, My mother was silent and perplexed as this strange woman was in her sight. She expected the nurse to be sutured to my arm. Then she saw the ring and wanted a million questions answered, But she got scraps. I told her only the things that I wanted her to know. I told them what day we set for marriage. I gave them no options at all. I began to see that Queen Bee was not happy as she knew she had lost control of everything in my life. Her grubby hands could not control me. I brought a woman that she never knew existed, Check Mate. Wonder how long she kept looking for the nurse ?

In November, about a year and a half had passed since we first met. The marriage became to love and cherish, until death do us part. My parent were there as well as my wife's family. We went from the church to go to the dinner. My parents gave a lame excuse and did not want to make the hour trip. Only a few on my side of the family went. We had the meal played tunes with the glasses, Had toasts that required no butter. After this, Most of my family members went home, instead of going to the Gift opening event held at the Bride's Family house. All of her family and friends were there. Only the Best Man and his mother were there from Pine Valley. All other skipped out. The Best man was a high school class member.

The gifts opened, the snack items were invisible, and the card games were done. We were not going to a hotel for our wedding night. We set out to go back to her apartment to live. Her roommate left town months before. The apartment was ours to do what we wanted.

We had all our gifts packed up, Rayne still had on her white dress, she had the top of the wedding cake on her lap, and I drove us home. It was night time as we were on our way back. About a third of the was back. I saw something near the road. I hit the brakes, It was too late. A deer jumped in front of my '71 car, Its head smashing out the headlights on the left side of the car. Its head was tangled in the grill, its body whipped around to the drivers side and dented the fender and door. The deer's head was now battered and it broke free of the car. The injured deer darted off into nearest field and vanished. I was surprised that the cake Rayne was holding, was still in one piece.

Our travels continued through the 2nd third of the trip. Then it happened, A police car was on our tail, it showed me that the roof lights and siren on his patrol car worked. We were pulled over. The officer then approached the car. He wanted to know why my headlight on the driver's side did not work. He saw my suit and my wife in her white dress. I explained the accident and he was looking at my bride and wanted to know how many drinks I had. He never expected my answer, I do not drink alcohol and neither does my wife. He then took out a flashlight and inspected the front. He found antler parts stuck in grill of car. He then sniffed to find alcohol use. He could find none. He then congratulated us and told us to use caution and drive safely home.

We arrived home without anything else happening. We brought our gifts into our apartment. Our wedding night was to be the first time that we used the same bedroom. We wanted our lives to start out the way it should be, and it was.

Remembering the past is all that I can do, My wife is a memory that I don't want to have escape my mind. Writing my stories makes living without her easier, but can never remove the pain inside. I don't know if anything ever will. She has become part of me forever, No one can remove her from my heart.

But times get tough, as I now recall the storm of tears that flowed out of my Daughter, as I had to tell her that her mother had just passed away. At times it truly has become a cruel world. But I have the memories that they can't take away from Me. At times, my mind activity reminds me of the old video game, Frogger. You jumped the frog from one car top to another vehicle top, over and over to a semi, truck or car. One slip up and you would miss the next roof and fall to the pavement, and be run over. The screen brightly displayed, Game Over.

Chapter 54

Rayne Obit - 1/15/2019

Rayne Marie King, 67, of Cinder City passed away on January 12, 2019 at Riverside Hosp. and was surrounded by family at time of her passing. she suffered a stroke on New Years Day.

She was born January 23, 1951 in Neilsonville, to Max Jr and Helen (Trusp) Maspohl, of Chili. She grew up on the family farm. She graduated from Devoted High School in 1971. After graduating She moved to Pine Valley in mid 1970's. went on to work at a few jobs, She worked in a printing department and later in Sewing. ending up working at Howard Johnson's, W Clearmont Blvd.

In 1981 Rayne married the love of her life, Thomas Sr. They had 3 children and 37 wonderful years.

Rayne enjoyed knitting, sewing, and reading.

She is survived by her Husband, Thomas Sr; son, Thomas Jr; daughter, Rachel (Fiance Ray N.); Sister, Mae (Marones) of River Rapids, WI, Mother Helen (Trusp) Maspohl of Mayfield, WI, and many Nieces and Nephews. Sister in Laws Jane King, Rhoda King, & Susan King ; Brother-in-law George, Greenville Illinois

She was preceded in death by her father, Max Maspohl Jr; brother, Alan R. Maspohl; Son, Ray G.

Smith's Funeral Home, Pine Valley is assisting the family with arrangements. Online condolences may be shared with the Family

Chapter 55

I Gave Her Back to God - 1/16/2019

My mind many years ago, really saw nothing for me,
I became adrift as a vessel in the Sea.
I waited a long time for one to be given a chance,
I wanted one of those things, you take to the Fournier's dance.
Then it happened while I was at a new place to work,
For once, a filly female did not consider me a jerk.
We had fun together and the time together we did grow,
This would be the girl to marry, this I did know,
We had everything ready and set, for the big Show.
I had her wrapped up like a fine lace present,
I liked the way she came and the way she went.
We knew about everything that we did not need a teacher,
So we rented out a Church and we sent for the Preacher.
We did our vows, and married after every thing that we said,
It had nothing to do with the fact that my hair was bright red.
Our lives had many more downs than ups as we lived each and every day,
We had 3 children, but only got to see 2 grow up all of the way.
Her time on this world was way to short. then got called without a phone,
The call came down from heaven, God was sending her a long way Home.
Was hard to stay on the narrow road built, out of a tight rope wire,
I believe that she was good enough to stay out of Satan's Fire.
She spent her time on this planet like a tourist with everything to see,

God said that it was time he wanted the Girl that he just loaned to me.
I had her name tag on the package, the shipping was free.
God came to get his present, after spending 37 years with me.

FYI - This was written in 37 minutes

Chapter 56

Silent Theft - 1/17/19

I felt as if a thief came in the middle of the night and stole my wife from me. The robber did not break in from the outside, he broke in from the inside and raided the parts from within the control panel of her life. I have to ask why, but the answer will never come anytime soon.

In the end this robber stole everything including her last breath. There is nothing I could do. I tried to do anything I could. I was the only one that saw her almost every day for years. I saw her more Days that the workers that cared for her. I can count the number of visitors she had over the last 3 years on one hand, I am one & the children were 2 more. The Ones in the Homes and assisted living locations can't drag people to come and see them. It was the same with me.

I remember when our son came to see his mother the last time he was there. He walks up to the door and stands there, says nothing, and in a minute he walks away and never sees her again.

He knew she was there and could not visit others. But he never spent a second visiting her. She did not know he was there, she could not see where he was standing, Only I could see him. He became the invisible son to her. If the bets were placed on him coming to the funeral, I don't know who would win.

In his past there was the funeral of his Paternal Grandfather. We arrived at the same funeral home that my Wife is at now. This also was the same place where we had taken our 2nd son that died on the same day he was born. As a family of 4 we entered in the funeral home to visit my father, and I was heading up to sign the visitor book. My mother stormed up like a riled rhino and in her raised voice and terms. Get out or you will be arrested, We had to leave. On the was back to the van, my 9 year old Son asked one Question, Why does Grandma hate me ?

He has lost his chance to ever see his mother again. The Funeral will not have an open casket. Will he even be at the funeral at all, Your guess as as good as mine.

The silent thief has taken my Wife and turned her into a memory. The thief has a chance to break the family apart even more, if my Son fails to show up to give his last respects, I will also have another loss as he becomes more and more distant.

I have walked along my path in life and have seen more than 3 lifetimes of difficulties, and I am partially a blind man.

Many say that I should remember the good times, But I can't change the channel. It could take years.

All I can say is, I was there when the life of my wife was passed into the safe arms of Jesus, but when will I ever see a lifeline for Me. My Guardian Angel has been with me for years. I will continue walking the my path of life, and knowing I have a backup shadow behind me. My Guardian Angle was with me, when I wrote my Wife's Obituary for everyone to see. Time to get back walking forward down the path. Oh, how narrow it seems.

Chapter 57

Band of Gold - 1/18/2019

The Time line of life has many steps along the way. It starts out when I was born in Lake Shore Hospital. I was the 4th born into the family. It went fine in my life until the 30 day mark. Every thing was normal until this fate full day.

I was invited to a sporting event. It was football, In the house style, and I was the ball. The pass was thrown and the receiver dropped the ball, it was 4th down. A kick was attempted and the ball hit an upright. The Game was over and I lost in the game. It took 3 days to get the players to finally do the right thing. The QB in the game ended up posting, My God, What have I done.

This sent me to the hospital after the event and given 6 hours to live. I had a close call. Later I was sent home to face the house of horror. The Warden had sentenced me to 20 years. During this time, I learned to walk, talk and be like others. I had multiple setbacks as I had to learn some things twice. I got a chance to have a personal Sodom and Gomorrah traveling event to preform in the house.

Starting school had difficult times. I had to have glasses faced the next 57 years with them. I had to change schools 4 years years in a row. This disrupted normal advancements in the yearly years. I tried to blend in over and over, I was rejected or not to allowed to enter any competitions. My social calendar was almost as deserted as the surface of the moon. I saw no future as I was restricted to the back yard. I was 1 child that was made to look like my brothers. Having a difference from the others was frowned upon. I did not want to be a grease monkey. This is when other relatives gave me the tools to set myself free, I took the chance and took this vocation to the limit. I was now approaching the end of the 20 year home prison sentence.

Then I heard the words I have heard a thousand times before. Get the Hell out, and don't come back. All my things and I were loaded up and shipped back to an era of 1874, It was Gilligan's Island without the Island. No Phone, No stove, No Car, No heat, No modern conveniences to speak of. I spent 2 winters with a back yard swirling in a snowbank that could not lend a cent, and blocking the path to the outhouse. By some helping hand of others, I found myself in Shaw town. It was a bedroom rental, but I had things that were missing for years. But I became a friendless friend. Several attempts over the years to connect with an Old Babe did not pan out, as I could not overcome the obstacles. I was still adrift on the sea and saw no land for years.

Life was not fun enduring a daily struggle, I thought what the world would be without me. I gazed into the water and saw that this never solves anything. So It was back to the drawing board. I then set out and made a new trail. Through the help on an agency, I was given support from job testing and training. and a part time job. All I saw was the poor meager pay, 60 cents per hour. I saw a dead end job, and a future as dead as the Woolly Mammoth found in the arctic. My life was so far out of normal that I could write a Book, and 37 years later I did. But, I accepted the challenge and went to a work place that I was to meet the girl that I was to marry. About a year and a half, we married. and we both sported a Band of Gold.

The Band of Gold, I remember buying one at Ed Phillips and Sons. This place is now long gone. We both wore these bands as a victory over living a live of Mr Lonely. After 37 years and 3 kids, we encounters many tragic events. A house fire, auto accidents, and the death of our 2nd Son. This was only a taste of things to come, as the rings still shined brightly. After about 30 years, the cracks started to appear. My Wife had her 1st stroke, it was mild and she did recover from this event with little to show. All it did was slow her down a bit and she left work and was getting an easier life. Then it was the time to add in a pacemaker, Her father had one so we did not think things were out of the normal. This helped her over the next few years.

Then on New years Day, she suffered a 2nd stoke that had a large effect on her abilities. It looked like she would need 6 months to a year to recover enough to be active again. We waited 5 days to see if her swelling was down and progression was normal. It was, in the next day and into the night, was the last time she had a chance to recover. Another event brought her chances of recovery down to Zero. The bands of gold were about to lose the reason as why they existed. She dies a few days later, the rings lost there reason and became just another piece of jewelry.

Until death came, the rings had a significant meaning. Now they have no meaning at all. The sparkle had gone from my Wife as she passed away in front of me. Still embraced around her finger was a band of gold. Now the band played no music. It could offer no pleasure because the meaning was gone. It just became the worlds best electrical conductor for the masses. Without the person, the band is just an object.

Chapter 58

Incoming - 1/18/2019

Times are tough when a loved one dies. They can do nothing to help, all the responsibility falls to others. In this case I have to do everything. Some of my choices are coming down because of the dollar. I am doing the best that I can. I did ask my Daughter about her opinion on several matters. It took many days to do it all. I went the next step that most do not do. I wrote my wife's obituary and sent it in, this was something that I had to do. I had to keep on the path and move forward. It seems like every word I added in the Obit, there was a new memory that raced across my mind, as if it were the Indy 500. I could go forward and backwards thru all the 39 years that I knew her. I have to keep steady, The finish line is within sight. I can't stop now.

I can't use the weather report about this incoming storm. If it comes, it will enter into the front door. This has been a possible storm brewing for the last several years. I hate to have the storm front come through this funeral. This may have been brewing for the last 23 years. But in the last 2 years, rumblings from this threat has been increasing. At times I hear the thunder day after day, the floor and walls vibrate around the house and the voice of the storm can travel through the walls. It's a chilling feeling, I feel as cold as deep space, and it haunts me still as what happened 23 years ago.

I have seen this once, not all that were there at the time was a witness. As family members could not escape this fate, as the the wicked witch of the west was there, and there was no house landing scheduled.

I will have to be on guard as this storm could be on it's way. If it does, Hold on and let it blow through. This is all that I can do. Storming people have a mind of their own.

The aftermath of this possible storm, would then continue generation after generation. and it will be as the warden had started it in 2005. This event scarred the hearts of the innocent.

This is the calm before the storm. The countdown has began. I am a survivor, as I have been tested by living 20 years by living in the house of Hell. At this time, I do not know if I will be facing only an event to send my Wife to Heaven, or facing that, and another round of Hell on this earth.

I have seen so many things, that it would take 2 lifetimes to study it all and take it all in. The Lord is my shepherd; I shall not want. He causes me to lie down in green pastures; He leads me beside still waters. He restores my soul; He leads me along many paths. I can't stop now. My Wife could not do it without me. The power of the word is impressive. Yea, though I walk through the valley of the shadow of death, I will fear no evil: for thou art with me. I have to continue along my path. I brought along my Guardian Angel as my Guide.

Chapter 59

I Am My Grandpa - 1/19/19

Never in my life was a time, where I thought that parts of my life would look like a copy of someone else. But I am seeing it unfold before me. I am becoming a shadow copy of my Grandfather.

My Grandfather and I have many things the same. We both got married while in our 20's, both married before having children. We both married older women, He was 4 years younger than my Grandmother, I was 2 years younger than my Wife.

Both have a person named after them. My Grandfather has a nephew, I have a Son named after me. Both have a red hair person in the family. I have a type of red hair, and so did my Paternal Grandmother.

Both my Grandfather and I have a connection and interest to the Local Ski Club. There is now 3 generations that were involved in the Club, this means that 1 member of each family was involved in the club.

Both my Grandmother and My Wife, passed away before seeing or holding any Grandchild. My Grandmother passed away knowing that 1 grandchild existed (Was 6 months old, living in Germany),and a 2nd one on the way. My Wife had no pending Grandchild.

My Grandmother and my wife have the same middle name initial, the letter M. The two middle names are Margaret and Marie.

I ended up wearing a few dress suits that my Grandfather wore years before. I was the one that ended up with his suits over time. Other relatives were a bit too tall to make use out of his suits.

I started my writing career by using the exact same typewriter that I saw my Grandfather use in his home office. After He passed away, I was given the typewriter as I was writing poems at the time.

My Grandmother & I had same hair color and Both of us married at age 28. My Grandfather was 24, My Wife was 30.

My Grandparents, and my Wife and I, Both lived like it was like in the late 1800's, it was Little House on the Prairie style.

A son of my Grandfather is in the same Cemetery family plot area, as A son of my Wife and I. My Grandfather and Wife are also in the same Cemetery. My Grandfather is next to his Wife, as I will be next to mine.

Another match to my Grandfather, We were both with our wives when the end of their lives came. Also more than one other family member was there as well.

The next thing that matches is that both of us ended up as a Widower, as in both cases, the wife was the first to pass away. It should never have been this way, But it has become a reality. I have copied many things of my paternal Grandfather. This is not what I wanted to have repeat. I looked and saw that we were the only 2, in 3 generations to match this fact.

Now the last matching piece, how our names are etched in stone. My chosen headstone for my Wife and I, will be a match to my Grandfathers.

Chapter 60

Last Time - 1/19/2019

Life can go on and on, and nobody really notices until someone steps off, And this is what happened to me. She was given the road map to take a trip, one last time, on the highway to heaven.

I remember it was decades ago that was the last time that all of the family was complete and in the same place. It was in this same building after we said goodbye to our newborn Son.

I can't remember our last embrace we had, as she was bed ridden toward the end of her time on this earth. The halls and rooms of the Hospital was the last rides she would get. Her bad hip limited her to a van to carry her to appointments before this. It has been over a half of a year that she had a ride with me.

Things were confusing and in a hurry at times, near the end of her life. I try and try, but can not remember when we had our last kiss. She was in ICU more than once.

On the 12th she had her last breath, and ended her constant pain. it was also the last time that she had to be given a pain medication injection or pill. It was also her last time to make use of her heart.

She tried something new today, she was embraced with the angels, But I could not be there to see it. She was set free and it was her Last time that her soul would be called home.

Today will be the last time we will be together in the same place and room together, on the surface of the planet. So when I will be with her again is not know, but I can get things ready when my number is called.

So I am to remain and pick up the pieces and do the best as I can. It is also be the last time that the both of us wear our Bands of Gold. I may shed a tear today, but it will not be the Last Time.

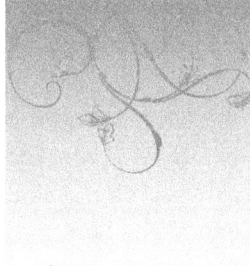

Chapter 61

Death, Round 2 - 1/20/19

After the death of a loved one, others think that the ordeal is over. This is not so. I am facing an onslaught of things that need to be handled.

There is legal issues and getting my wife laid to rest. The funeral is over and a day slipped by, but her final trip to her resting spot is tomorrow. When they place her in her final resting spot, then I have completed the mission of caring for her every need. I and anyone else, could not grant Her," every things that she hoped and wished for ". If this was the case, the world would have too many Chiefs and not enough Indians. I have done what I had set out to do, and then some. Now comes part 2 of dealing with a loss of a loved one.

Clearing out the room where she lived for over 2 years, was the biggest challenge. A room full of things that to be moved to my house with no extra room. This will take time in sorting out each and every box. Each piece has to be looked at, because I had to pack the boxes in a hurry and I was doing this alone.

Then there is the final legal issues. Then giving things of hers to others, to be used to help those who helped her.

Financial matters will take months, but you have to start soon, so things don't fall behind. After this there is the sending of the thank you cards.

All during this time, I have to keep myself healthy and not end up with too much stress. There are many things that can cause this.

Also during this time, others will ask may questions, I will be hearing many "I should have done this for her, I should have visited her at least one time"

I Have to do what is best for her, and best for me. I can not be railroaded by others. I have to keep moving forward on my path of recovery, feelings of grief will last a long time.

I can not do what a friend of the family did way back in 1964. This Woman died of cancer, her husband was in worse shape than I am now. The day of his wife's passing, He came home and closed the door to the bedroom where she was in her final months. He left everything the way as she left it, before making the final trip to the hospital. This was her final journey and a trip that she could never return.

He left his room alone for many years, only having it cleaned and dusted as the years went by. He had turned this room into a shrine. A place for him that time that seemed to be, frozen in place. He done this as a way to handle the loss of his wife. I can't do this, I have no place for a shrine as I am dealing with the loss, in more than one way.

I must make it as if, part of my wife lives on in others. I can not see her memorialized and everything she left, be stored in a room, like a time capsule. My wife would want the things of her life to benefit others, and not be kept inside of a locked vault.

After some time, there will be very little left to show the physical existence of her, Her things would be in the hands of others that would keep her memory alive, for decades to come.

She will still be in the photos, videos, and in the hearts of the ones that knew her. Nobody can take that away from them.

Chapter 62

Secrets of the Father - 1/20/19

I saw the Problems That Rayne had when others asked her about her families past. She could not answer the most simple questions. Her Father Never discussed the past at all. He was hiding it, thinking he was protecting the family.

He also did not have many answers because his real father left for good when he was about 8. There also was questionable relatives, as one ended up behind bars for moonshine running. When Rayne's Father died, his secrets went with him.

Over the Last few years, a wife of a cousin of Rayne's, and I, Did the research. She went to the courthouses in the area to get the census reports, To get her knowledge of her past and more. I searched over 175 cemeteries in the area around Pine Valley county.

I found Rayne's Grandfather's 1st wife's grave. Cora was found in small place called Montana, southwest of Pine Valley. I searched Cadia area, found 3 more, I found more in Glencove, and to the next state to the west.. These are in a line from east to west. I know where the farm was.

I saw why the family broke up, When Rayne's father was put up for adoption, with his brother. I saw where they changed his Last name. Rayne was over 62 before she saw this information. I did not want my children to be left without any information where the families came from, and what life was like for them many decades ago.

I remember taking over 1,200 headstone photos from one cemetery. This way if I find relatives of relatives, the headstones could point the way to find others. The answer I may never find, Where is her grandfather ?. All I know is he left the family when her Father was about 5, He came back to visit when he was around 8, they never saw him again.

Some say he went NE to the New England area, and some said it was farther away in Canada. I may ever find him, But the Story of her father was given to her before she died. The look on her face was priceless. When I ask my daughter's fiance about his father, he answers the question. I tell him I have been there and I know what it can do to a family.

My family story about drinking abuse is in my book. But my memories go back more years and reveal the hidden, dirty family secret. My father thought he could hide his drinking, but his errors caused it to blow up in his face. I have seen the hell and learned from it. My daughter's fiance and I have a connection. I understand where he was coming from, because I was there.

I set out to write my book, in first person style. This gave a look at almost every basic thing about the ancestry of the family. I answered the tough questions. My Daughter had to know and not wait another 40 years.

Now that her Mother has passed. There is a file that has basic family history from her side. She soon will have 2 books and over 300 chapters that have the answers. I could not buy a family history book, I made it myself. I want it to tell the past, the good and the bad.

I remember taking over 1,200 headstone photos from one cemetery. This way if I find relatives of relatives, the headstones could point the way to find others. The answer I may never find, Where is her grandfather ?. All I know is he left the family when her Father was about 5, He came back to visit when he was around 8, they never saw him again. Some say he went NE, and some said it was farther away in Canada.

I may ever find him, But the Story of her father was given to her before she died. The look on her face was priceless. When I ask my future son-in-law about his father, he answers the question. I tell him I have been there and I know what it does to a family. This story is in my book.

My memories go back more years and reveal the hidden, dirty family secret. My father thought he could hide it, but his errors caused it to blow up in his face. I have seen the hell and learned from it. My future Son-in-Law and I have a connection. I understand where he was coming from, because I have been there.

I wrote my first Book about my past, and this gave her the Facts before she asked.

Chapter 63

The Funeral - 1/20/19

It was the Day of the Funeral. There was also a Mini Class Reunion that was scheduled today. That was scheduled weeks ago. But the Funeral was placed on the calendar by the Angels.

God wanted her to end her suffering, and so did I, But this was not my first solution. I prayed to God for the best thing for her. His answer was that time had ran out. Her body was sending her strong painful signals, and in her heart, she was asking for forgiveness to her sins. She was asking to join our son, that was in Heaven. She wanted the angels to care for me, I had to stay to be with our other 2 children.

She said that God's angels advised me, that he had a talk with King David and 70 years was the ideal time that we are to be away from the house of God. My wife almost made 70 years, but her body could no longer keep it ticking like a fine oiled machine. So she passed into the arms of the Angels. I was in the room and felt chilled as she had her last breath. Then her heart stopped and surrendered her soul to the lord. It was his will and not my choice.

When the Doctor said that her days were numbered, I then realized that She was going to pass away before me and was older than me. My mind began scanning through the hundreds of relatives in several levels, and realized that my Paternal Grandfather was the other Widower in the family tree. My mind filled with enough information to make a list of many of them.

The hospital wanted to keep her alive at any cost. But my Wife placed conditions on the final events. She stipulated that she was to surrender her life to God when he made the reservations.

Within minutes, I had many tasks that I had to do. I spent days getting the documents and signing what was required. The biggest thing I faced, was I did not have enough resources to meet her final needs. So I had to do the bet that I could.

With the help of the Funeral Home, Over half of the cost was met by applying for aid. I realized that I had spent money over 25 years earlier and had cemetery lots, So she could await her salvation. Things were worked out that I had a chance to provide for her needs.

A Idea was brought up that the Class Reunion could be moved back a week. I said that the show must go on. This may be the first one that I could miss, but they understood why. So the stage was set for the day of the funeral.

I only had 6 hours sleep and I was restless. I got up and dressed, realizing that I should eat before the long day ahead of me. I was nudged the night before to have my camera charged up. I also thought, why can't I stop by the reunion and have a meal, spend some time with my classmates and then arrive at the Funeral Home for visitation.

So I arrive several minutes after the moved up starting time of the reunion. I have my camera with me. As I walk in, many eyes look my way, as they never expected me at all. One classmate changes there location, so I can get power for laptop. The laptop is my replacement for a phone. One asked. are you sure you want to be here ?

They don't know the real reasons. I tell them what these are. I can do 2 things by coming, getting a few pictures to continue my contribution to the class reunions, and eat something before going to next event. I know my time is short to be here this day. I also have to order meal as soon as I get there. After I put the cook to work,I go around and take my photos.

The other reason is to see how I would react to others when someone brings up the funeral. In the past few days I caught myself shedding a tear or two, so I worked on this to keep it to as small of issue as I could. By going to the Mini Reunion it would be a test as how I could hide the tears from within. This would be a challenge, But if this fails, better it being here, than later.

Then my food is delivered. Time is evaporating away, but I leave in time to get to location of the visitation time. I first talk to the funeral director and the clergy. My Daughter is there, this provides comfort to me. I spend the time meeting with the visitors. I had made a plan if things get out of hand. I remember back 23 years ago, when I came to my father's funeral, and my mother tells me to leave or be arrested. So, I know things can happen, as I have witnessed it. I was on my toes now for any trouble that arises.

I found my wife's side of the family and other friends that were not relatives. While on the lookout for trouble, I was amazed that the first person to sign the guest book, was a Classmate of mine. She was not at the reunion as her schedule was as crowded as mine. We had a talk and she gave me a hug, This helped me to begin to relax. I never expected her to show up, as I know she spends time caring for her husband. This was a surprise that helped me. It gave me hope that other good surprises could be coming my way.

I then saw my wife's old co-workers and my cousin, who was her boss. Then I saw my Daughter's relatives to be, as her wedding day has been set. Soon several class members show up that were at the mini reunion. local friends show up and more that I met over time. I felt that I was beginning to be among friends. Time for the service. The Pastor takes the stage.

The service is held, Things go smoothly, it was not what I expected because of past events. I am content that this is trouble free. The Pastor even uses one of my writings and reads it during the service. I wrote this for my wife as well as her obit. I gave her something that money could not buy. The poem I made and was used in the service spoke to her as well as the guests. It was priceless. I had a feeling that I did something right for all, the living and my departed wife. This helped me go forward through the rest of the time I spent there.

After the service, I had more time to spend with my only daughter. Her Fiance, my sister-in-law, nieces and their friends. We spent time talking about the past involving good times. Time to wrap things up, I had to meet with director and wrap up the business ends, and I was the last to leave. I took the flowers and shared some with my daughter. It will help her to remember her mother. I gathered the visitor book, cards and final documents. It was time to leave. God in a strange way, helped me to a smooth event, unlike past ones.

I have good memories to take with me from here, except one. My Son failed to come. It was his choice. The biggest thing that I got was, Rayne is free from pain and sharing lost time with our 2nd Son. Their souls will be in the Heavens above, and someday I will be joining them, and be Home at Last, Home at Last.

I later found out that a free will offering was taken among the class members, at the reunion. It will help with the expenses of the day. I can't thank them enough. They did something that I never saw while I was growing up. A bunch of friends offering help expecting nothing in return. The Guardian Angels must be working overtime.

Chapter 64

A Visitor - 1/21/2019

Life has picked up the pace and gets me running down Path, instead of walking. Things at times are buzzing around my head like a cluster of Bee Hives, filled to the brim. But I need to get things back to normal as best that I can.

I started getting home at an earlier time. For the past 4 years, I had 2 places to live part of the day. I had a daily visit with my wife, and then went back to the house were we lived for over 30 years.

Activities are a plenty. Sorting out her personal belongings is never going to be easy, as there could be a new surprise in every box. Decisions must be made by me, I have to do this as the final things that She can't do, and She left no directive about this matter. I have to take this task, like all of the others, one step at a time.

Settling down to some kind of routine is best. So I do things that were done year after year. This fills my nights, but the flowers in the room emit there own choir of smells, The Roses want to strike up band. Then I notice that there was only 3, One rose for each child.

There are many matching things about this event. All are trying to be a message from her. These help but it's not like the real thing.

Trying to get back to a normal cycle will take it's own pace. Time to get things done and meander down the hall to fix the fence, as those pesky sheep keep escaping by jumping over the fence. I now become a lumberjack and start sawing logs to earn my Z's.

Morning gets to start a bit later that usual. Nothing wrong with that. I am awake. I wait a bit before I roll out of bed, taking all the Logs that Abe Lincoln would be proud of to put his name on.

While I wait to get out from under the covers, I sense the bed move,. It's like someone was sitting on it and then gets up off of it. I look and see nothing. The bed did respond to something that I could not see. This reminds me of the times where my Wife would get up in the mornings, ahead of Me.

Could it be ?, She came for one last visit before her final resting place. She was not taken to the cemetery after the funeral, it was planned for today. This has a strange feeling that this event was touched by an angel. Was it her guardian Angel that has to get a new assignment, or was it mine.

I will never know. I will have to check back with the Funeral Home to see what schedule that they had for today. If it matches with the time of my visitor, then I will know. Day by day, I have a shadow that watches me, otherwise I would be all alone.

I just have to keep the faith and move forward along my path. I can't take the detour, and I can't turn around. I have set my route decades before by choosing for myself, to be baptized under the waters. This is part of my protection, as I pass very close to temptations that could cause the Satan's fires to rage. The firestorm hoping to vacuum me into them. But, I am still be there, walking on my narrow path, to stay now and into eternity.

Chapter 65

Caged In Animal - 1/21/2019

Not all stories I write about are all about me. I started that way so that I would not reveal any secrets of others. I did not want to go down that path. Even if the stories were greater and more involved others. I wrote my book as a history book for my Daughter to know more about me. It came out this way, I changed the names to protect others, but still had the stories tell my Daughter what the last generation was like. This story is about her Mother. Rayne had one thing that was repeated more that anything else. She stated over and over, I feel like a caged in animal. Just how did her life develop that this was her most used line.

A few things in life bonded us together. We both had a mother that was over controlling. I noticed this from the first time that I met her. She was like my mother, But only to the Girls, My wife and her sister. My Mother-in-law loved her Son more than the others, and I saw that as well as all the others. He lived at home the longest. He could get away with things that the others did not. My Father-in-law did not resist this too much as he favored Daddy's little Girl. Rayne's sister had a medical condition before age 5, and a lot of their money had to be detoured into this issue.

As the children grew up, they also had the 'Hand me Down syndrome', again the money went to pay or dealing with the youngest child. Many things matched my mother the Warden, except this major fact. Rayne's parents were willing to share with others. My mother's goal was Me,Me,Me. My mother married for money, power, control, and things. Kids was one of the tools to get what she wants. Rayne's parents married for love and the combined goal of running a farm. But the condition of the youngest detoured their lives, but did not turn into selfishness, greed, and the me, me, me, attitude.

Then what caused my wife to say, I feel like a caged in animal. It developed over time. I don't know what was the final straw. But her mother ended up like a Drill Sergeant of the K.P. division. Even I saw this issue rise it's head. As time went on, their lack of things did show up. and this caused the Drill Instructor to put the heat on Rayne. This started in the kitchen and it never ended.

Her mother in the kitchen was a slave driver. She offered no 2nd chance. Whenever Rayne did something that wasn't right, Smack went the wooden spoon on her hands. Rayne was too slow or something did not turn out right, Smack went the spoon. Rayne was blamed for anything that went wrong in the kitchen. Her sister was 12 years younger that she was. So she was too small to be in the kitchen. Rayne spent alot of time in the Cagen, I mean Kitchen. She felt like she was in place, where it was like she was caged. Also childcare for her sister became another chore, during winter the house become another cage. At times, weeks went by in the house, Rayne only left the house to go to the outhouse in the back yard. A version of Prison live is what she thought it was.

Rayne saw this year after year. The family did not go to church, or other events away from the house. In the summer, Rayne would sneak over to the neighbors house. She treated the woman next door like a mother. She saw a more normal life there. But over and over as meal time approached, the Drill Instructor had her follow in line or, whack, whack, whack. It was the same year after year. This is the biggest flaw in my mother-in-law, too over controlling to the girls. But later her Son got away with too many things. But Her only Brother had to deal with the same thing I did. His father was like mine in one way. Rayne's father kept telling her brother, You are no good and will not amount to anything. My father's version was, you are no damn good. But as a father to my future wife, they got along.

When it was time for us to get married, He father did not have all the money in the world, but he gave his daughter the dress, reception at the Kitty Kat Inn, on highway 1. Her parents did what was expected, without doing getting too fancy. He walked her down the isle and gave his little girl something she could feel proud of her father for.

So if Rayne lived in another county, how did she get into my daily pattern and end up in my sight, so I could snag her. When it was time to get training and a job for Rayne. There was 2 choices, a county to the east or a county to the west of where there farm was. But Pine Valley County was farther away that the other. Because of the actions of the Drill Instructor Mom, Rayne did not like being treated like a caged in animal. So to break free, it was get away from the D.I as far as possible. So she moved to Pine Valley and started a new life. But she feared for her little sister, she thought that her mother would act like a D.I. to her as well. She was right, D.I. Mom got a younger drafted recruit and the daily grind continued.

My wife stated when she left home, she felt that the cage door swung open and a new life was to begin. About a half dozen years later, I arrived at her work place and was there when they transferred her to do the letters on the Park & Rec barrels. She and I started a life that lasted for 38 and a half years.

We shared this Caged in Animal thing in two ways. Her cage was the Kitchen in the house where I grew up, and my Cage was being locked in the basement. She had an understanding of my basement cage, and I understood what the Cage was for her around her D.I. Mom. We would later find other things that we had in common.

When we married there was nothing forcing it, and we were there to Love, honor, and obey, to death do us part. I look back at this and truly believe, that if had to do it all over again, We would.

Some classmates of mine say that they really did not know my wife. I say, she was a lot like me in many ways. They just don't know it yet. We were both a kind of 'Caged in Animal'. Rayne did come to a few 5 year Class Reunion events. She wanted to come to the Mini reunions, but her health was causing great pain. She enjoyed me telling her about them, and I did.

Chapter 66

Flashback - 01/21/19

Nine days have past since the loss of my Wife. I am getting bombarded by flashbacks as fast as the song of the flight of the bumble bee. I am seeing photos pass in the mind as fast as the U.S. Treasury prints One dollar bills. I recall the only baby picture that I have of myself, then I flash to the one where my wife was 4, I see a rapid flash of the progression of our ages. I see family members come and go.

Then the flashback of holding our 2nd Son, He was already deceased. My wife never saw him alive, But I did. In less than 3 hours, a life came and went. Now I see the tragic things that affected me, Images, one after another falling over the cliff, like a waterfall that reaches the moon. I then see several dozen movie screens playing different things.

Crossing the Wabasha bridge, Locomotive 2719 entering the park in 1960. Then the Warden standing in the place of Satan bellowing out, Get out or you will be arrested. I try to get a glimpse of the casket with my father in it, but the Warden has blocked the view. My mind flashes back to 1960, where I see the maternal Grandfather with a red flower in his lapel, then it flashes to my Aunt in 1984, then it goes back to my 2nd son, He is buried next to her in her grave space.

Meanwhile my body temp feels like I was cast in a block of Ice 3 miles thick. My hands shake and my pulse rate climbs, my fingers are typing like a 30 year seasoned secretary. Then the song switches on You tube, get some flowers in her hair, the song hints. But I don't want to go to San Francisco. Stop changing the Video disk player in my mind. I am doing other things so fast I can't shed a tear.

Then my mind switches to the flowers at the funeral. My mind is spinning in circles. I notice that this is the fastest typing I have ever done. I don't even have to look at some of the keys. My brain marches along as easy as q w e r t y. My mind is acting like the movie of Clockwork Orange. I hear a different language on the computer, the next song starts up. I started a joke that started the whole world crying, I didn't realize that the joke was on me.

I finally saw the image again that my wife was finally dying. I then flashback again as I see the face of my daughter, as I told her that her mother just died. I am starting to shake as I begin to tear up and my breathing rate rises. My fingers are getting to feel the pain of typing on the computer, as fast as morse code.

The Piano starts a familiar tune, Can't you hear my S.O.S.?, nobody can because they are as deaf as I am. My brain screams for oxygen. Then I see the earthly goods that are not my master. I then realize that I have no darling that I can have near me. When you are gone, How can I carry on. I don't know, as Fernando wants to take over the choir. The drums begin to beat a new tune, as this starts up, the photos restart and begin flashing in my mind.

My body feels a cold blast as cold as a grave diggers knee. Then it talks about a friend Fernando, but how can that be. I labeled myself as a friendless friend. I am typing so fast that I can feel the pounding of the keys, with my knees.

Then I see a hundred of our wedding photos flash in my mind, several at a time. Then I realize the statement. Will you honor and obey as long as you both shall live. I never thought that I would hear this line, but I did. Now, since a death has happened, what Next ?.

I face a cold world that I have never walked down a path in it before. The pressures of the past 3 weeks have worn a path across the rug and within my mind. This is what happens when stress has to unwind.

My computer is panting like a cat. No, I was not going to use dog for that lion. Yes, lion is the word that I want to use. Then I get hit with realism, My dancing Queen will be placed in her final resting spot on earth today.

She can't stand and be my dancing Queen, to me being King. It's not easy now, as ideas bounce around in my head like a red rubber ball.

I took it full circle, as I keep coming back to the woman that was my living wife for 37 years.

My breathing rises as rapid as the F-15 Eagle takes off of an aircraft carrier. I am no top Gun, I just wonder what I am.

Writing was never in my system through out 16 years of school. I was as interested in English as I was in the girls. My body was wrong in many places, and this made me make a wall, like a prison. This was to keep them away from my mother, she represented the Warden. She ruled the house of eternal Hell.

I switched women on her, and then I came to them, to announce that I wanted to marry the woman of my choice. She was so dumbfounded that her mouth dropped as low as death valley, Checkmate. This led my life for the next 37 years. I wish I had 13 more years.

None of the siblings lasted as long as I did. Pretty remarkable to a man, that life looked as bleak, as a full moon that's so bashful, that it pulled a little white cloud that cried over it's face and hid for a month. I felt at times that I wanted to join it.

This will take a lot of time to get through this, I can't help it. I am all alone. I see many cats, but they will not help, as every one is stuffed. My computer begins to vibrate, as I shake a bit, trying not to give that little white cloud any more tears. I need to save these, I need them for the next time.

Then I ask the question, Why did my wife have to die at this time. In 3 weeks it was from the beginning to the end.

Today she will be in her final resting place. I remember the flowers, all given as a gift. I now have to await the final cost. I have been walking a rough rocky path for over 65 years, When do I get a break. Or is that coming only when I met up with my wife again.

So many questions still unanswered. Why did my Son fail to come to his mother's funeral ?, At this very moment the song changes again, I get a terrible chill as I know what the Bee Gee song is, Tragedy. This in a one in a million that i would randomly come up at this time. The drum beat is as fast as my heart.

The screen on my computer is filling fast. The Lord is my shepherd, but I am the friendless friend. Then I rub my brow, as the hands on the clock are playing paddy cake, paddy cake.

Then the next song, Staying Alive. What are the odds of this ?. The Bee Gees should go look for their honey, as I don't have mine. The drum beat sounds like the Telltale heart. It beats and beats like it has it's own pacemaker.

Then the Bee Gees are telling that there is too much Heaven. That's ok, I only need a small piece of it, to make reservations, to get back with her again. People told me I don't know what it it's like to lose a loved one. They are very wrong. I have it in writing, Do they have it written down ?. No, they do not.

Hello darkness, My old friend. I hear the Sound of Silence. Can I ride their subway, or their Heaven express train. I need a free ride, as all I will have with me is my soul. The words of the profits are written on the subway walls, giving me directions to the Heaven Express train.

Along the way, and out of this world, I will be California Dreaming. See this is what the human mind can do, as it struggles to make sense out of a death in the family. Each one of these events is never the same.

As I pass the bashful moon along the way to Heavens above, I finally will be at rest with my loved ones. It hurts a lot, that during the last 12 days that my Wife had to live, It made no difference that I was half deaf, She had no voice to speak a word. She could only scream in pain. That was real hard to witness, Just like it was to see a loved one actually die.

It's takes a toll on those left behind, and I did not have to pay the fare. My body heats up as I realize that this event is over. I am typing so fast I think the keys would melt. So many things, in such a short of time.

Now it's off to get back on the path. My path, that I have worn as smooth as the surfaces of my computer keys. And to think, these keys unlock nothing except my memories spilling out of my fingertips. I want to place a call to her, but there is no phone exchange in the Heavens above.

Tonight is an example of an event that happens when my mind takes a slight turn back through time. This has now tired me out, it's off to chase sheep over the fence.

Chapter 67

I live in a Museum - 1/21/2019

When I look around the house I see many things of the Past that travel along in my life. These are big or small items that were a part of my life. I still have my Draft Card that never would be used as I knew I was 4F years before I got it.

I have my High School Bus Pass, Laminated Diplomas, Bus Token, My Class schedule, book of poetry that my poem is in. The Parrot, this was the Junior High publication. As for High School, I can find a few copies of West Wings. I have baptism papers, Confirmation Photo and more.

I seem to have something from every stage of my life, Including my mother's written line that she wrote after I was injured in '53. It is written, My God what have I done. it's the smoking gun.

It seems that I have more that papers and small items. I have my 1st tape recorder that I bought in 1968 for $18 from the Coop. I have my 2nd one. A Realistic 333 recorder, and the next one, a 7 inch Reel to Reel Realistic 909. I need these to play the tapes, some tapes are over 50 years old.

I look and I see a 1970 Color TV, this one is a tube set with a wooden cabinet, with rotory dials. I see my original Video Game system, the Atari 2600.

I even have my 1st computer that I bought, Its a 1977 released computer that I bought on Jan 2, 1980. This is a TRS-80 model 1, it has a B&W TV as its screen and comes with 48k memory. This computer was used for years. Then I upgraded to a Model 2,3,4,4P & the 4D. Later a model 16b & then the first MS-DOS unit that was the TRS80 model 2000. Later I had a color computer. I also had 4 apple versions. All of these used floppy drives as its main storage. I spent hours making my own programs.

Slot cars were another thing. I had Aurora as the main brand. There were Vibrators, T-Jets, Tuff Ones, A/FX, Magna-Traction, Mini Tjets and more. These were designed by me that put real drivers names on them. Some cars are over 55 years old. These required practice and skill. They don't make them like they did years ago.

I have old radios, one had WPV as a Radio Station, One portable Radio requires no battery to run. Old toys too, the Vacu-form, Mold Master, 1960 Etch a Sketch, Kenner sets, Erector sets, 50 in 1 electronics project kit, a 75 in one. The toys of the past were great creative things.

I have a Beta Max & VHS Video Recorder. there is a Beta Cam, and a VHS Camcorder. today these are all outdated electronics. But they are a part of my past. and in the future end up in another museum. I want them to be seen and share the knowledge of the past.

I look around and I see Bingo the Bear, this had a chip inside that it would speak random statements that kids would enjoy, like "Are your knees made of Cheese". Other items are the 78 & 45 rpm records. Audio cassettes and 8 track tapes. Who knew that these would later be replaced by new technology.

There are more things, But my memories get re-enforced due to the reminders that I see from time to time. Kids today stare down at their, Do everything cell phones and forgot how to learn to be creative. They walk on by looking like zombies and risk there lives walking into things as they don't look where they are going.

I will save these items and get a place for some, so others will know just how and what Grandfathers did to learn by playing. I have the number one kid toy of the 40's and 50's, the Electric Train. Some kids have never played with one. I still have a Zero-M Camera, that can change into a Cap gun. But these again are not for the kids of today.

I recall a friend of mine that made the Eiffel tower out of an erector set. Creativity was everywhere. Even when using Silly Putty. Kids look at it today and think it's chewing gum. There creativity switch in their brain must be turned off.

They live with their cell phones 24 hours a day. No wonder I see kids applying for Jobs at local restaurants and they have a hard time blending in with Co-workers. Their number one need for the money. They want to keep their cell phone alive and play games, watch videos, and let everyone else work for them. They can even order a Cheese burger by using their phones. The get lazy, enter in a phone number to call once, the phone remembers. I had to stick my finger in the holes and dial the number every time I placed a call.

When I look into the mirror, I see my Grandpa. But that's another thing. Even if I have a mini Museum, Go see the local museums in your area, See what they had years ago, like chamber pots. Give thanks for the great advancements today, or you could get to town like Great Grandpa did years ago, with a horse and buggy.

I am thankful for the many things that I have, it makes life easier. I am this way because I see what it was like years ago, because I live in a Museum.

Chapter 68

End of the Tunnel - 1/22/2019

Now it's time to turn the page. This has been a rough 3 weeks. I was called upon to complete the care for my wife and do what had to be done, in the days after her passing. I had to do things that I never did before or wanted to do. I was called to do it as the surviving spouse. I remember the paperwork, The meetings to get the questions answered. I was the one that had to make the tough calls and notify the relatives. I left the final choice to God, as he placed the call. I later found out, he was calling her home.

I stayed on my path and did the best that I could do for her. My plans started back in 1993, for what happened this month. I never thought that it would be needed this soon. I now will do as I am asked. Because of this, I carry memories of her and us, In my heart.

I recall many times that when I went into the hospital, I went alone and had no visitors at all. This happened many times that I spent 5 days there. I could not see this happening to my wife and when she was admitted over 3 weeks ago, I was there, I could not see her being without a visitor on any day. I saw what the possible outcome would be on the 2nd day. Nobody expected the setback days later. I knew of this 2nd problem, but did not expect it to affect the final outcome.

I knew the end was coming. The end of my walk with her ended as I reached the end of the tunnel. When the final breath was taken, I was there and had to be the messenger of bad news to my daughter. I knew then, that my wife was looking at something that I would have to wait for later. She saw the light at the end of the tunnel, during her final change of address. I saw in my mind, She was arriving at the Pearly Gates. Angels were there to greet her, and She is now at peace, She is in pain no more. Soon she will enter the Pearly Gates, after getting her pass on Judgement Day.

I will turn the page, with the changes in my life. I have friends now that have helped me through this, and will stand beside me as I go forward. I am a bit shaky at times, but I have not lost my way. In the future, I must now stand fast and continue forward, and not be derailed before its my turn to see the light at the End of the Tunnel.

Chapter 69

Tumbling Tumbleweeds - 1/22/19

The winds are unpredictable, its the same for the Tumbleweeds, as they travel around the isolation of the desert. The roam around at the suggestion from the winds. Different sizes of them and no two are the same. They seem to be lost with no place to go. These nature powered puff balls leave there prints behind in the sands. These prints tells the places where they have been, but not where they are going.

When a person lives on this planet, they leave prints behind as well. Their photo prints tell of their lives and where they have been, some hint on where they will go. Their choices in Life are like a wind. The choices direct them on the path, as where they will be going. As their life ends, the path for them ends. For those left behind, they can only see the photo prints of those that when before them. My mind then drifts back to the tumbleweeds, as they are caught up in a whirlwind. Its an event that takes them upward and then they scatter like pixie dust. Some are never seen again.

So as I seek out the prints in the sand from others. I am in a better position that others, as I have thousands of their tumbleweeds trails to follow. Most can be found, but as the real tumbleweeds, some will be lost forever. I can't save time in a bottle, or turn back the hands of time. Even the Hands on the clock give me a thumbs up. This is a good sign, but at other times the clock stops, and the ticking ends. It's like life, when the sounds of the footsteps stop, their prints on the sand end.

I look at the Tumbleweeds as if each one is a photo or Video that tells a story. There are thousands of them scattered over 70 years that, when matched up, tell the story of the people in our lives. I have to get the information together, so I have the story and memories, of those that have gone before me. I need to read the sand prints before they are eroded away by the blowing winds, and the ravages of time. I do this not just for myself, but for others that can't read or understand the secrets left behind in the sand.

The desert can be as lonely as the people that are left behind. As I stand in the barren landscape, the wind makes it's presents known. I feel the air move, I hear it whisper to me in my ear. I see the sand lining up for a parade. Then the rolling tumbleweeds come along as they are surfing the ridges made of sand. They are telling me the same message. Follow me and I will get you back on the path that you need. Follow me, as the tumbleweeds are nudged by the touch of an angel. Follow me, as I show you the way.

I see the memories and pictures, that the Tumbleweeds represent as they did the forward rolls in front of my eyes. Each one will be worth a thousand words. The winds are winding down. I see one last tumbleweed coming my way, with a hop, skip, and a Jump. I snagged it and held it close to see what vision this represents. This one had no photo, but a lesson. As I held it tight, thousands of seeds scattered all around me.

I am to take the lesson from this. I have to take my memories and photos, and scatter them around to others. If I don't, nobody else will learn what I had found out in my life. My walk along the path of life could be a wasted trip. I know other's would not want this to happen. So now I have to find my tumbleweeds and do what they do. Scatter my photos and knowledge to others, as the tumblers scatter their seeds along the sands of time.

Chapter 70

Heart Within the Arches - 1/23/19

I have walked around, and through the Arches for about 60 years. The have become a common place around town and around the world. There are several of these in Pine Valley. There even is a location that was removed, on H-20 street. I have seen them all and remember the first location the best. those quarter chocolate milkshakes. 4 for a dollar. These were good on a hot day.

Seven burgers for a buck. Many things were there over time, Fish, pork, double burgers with special sauce. I tried them all.

Every place had to be sure that the sandwiches were always the same, in California, or the Frozen Tundra. The all had to have basic menu items.

This place offered Teen's a chance to get their first jobs. The hired the elderly as many were still interested in doing something a few hours a day. It made no difference what country your grandparents came from, or the color of your skin.

When I enter, there always is someone waiting to serve you needs. Every worker fits into being a part of the crew. They all fit in and make the burger machine work. At times an error happens, at time things could be a bit late. They correct issues and welcome you back.

This day was something different. I walked into the place under the double Arches. I placed my order and was enjoying my meal. Later I was handed something from a Manager.

What was it ?, I did not know. I opened it and it was filled with signatures from the Crew and Managers. This was a condolence Card for me. I wanted to show it to my wife, But I can't. She passed away on Her Daughter's Birthday. This is what this card was about, the Crew remembered her,as she was a steady customer for years. Something that they did not know, The day I was Given the Card, was also the day of her birth. She could not be here to celebrate.

The card was trimmed in gold, Just like their Arches. But there was more here that meets the eye. I found something I never expected, a Golden Heart within the Golden Arches.

Chapter 71

Sorting Things Out - 1/24/19

Nothing can prepare you with the loss of your spouse. This is someone who you could have shared over half of your lifetime with, and they can't share with you now, about what things must be done. The Book of your time together has closed. The death do us part, has come. and in a few days, the dual will be parted. Now the issues of this begin.

In my case, she was living at an assisted living location, other people had their loved one in a Nursing Home. But when the time comes, there is a room without a patient or resident. This has to be dealt with now. Every day that passes is like a ticking Clock.

Everything is there, waiting for the resident to come back. There will be no one returning, so the room must be cleared and ready for the next one waiting in line. I have been through this and it never is easy. At first, this isn't easy as time is not on your side. things must be moved in a reasonable time. You don't have time to sort things out or remember why some items are there. Your task, move it as soon as possible. And remembering where each item is, is next to impossible.

All items have been boxed up and moved to the home of the remaining partner, or pack in storage. Large, tall, or small, everything must gome out of the room and down the hall. Sometime in future, this next task will begin, and the flowing river of memories will spring forth. It never is easy for anyone, even for me. I can't turn back time. I have to continue on my path, no matter where it leads.

Now spaces around me are filled, the task at hand is to sort through the boxes and, as some say, get the task over with. Its not easy, seeing what remains from their life, is in a collection of boxes that are in front of you. I have to look through every box, I find anything from momentos to loose change. In the last few years, all she had was pocket change. Any thing of great value was never brought into the room. I remember the 2 highest valued items were her lift chair & the Television. Any other family heirloom was in the hands of others.

Any item within the box can cause me to have a flashback. I never know what it will be until it happens. You think in your mind, why me? This is something that no one wants it to happen. It causes much pain remembering about the days before, before your spouse turns your status from married to single. Then you snap out of it and it's onto the next box.

I sort each item as Keep, Give, & save for other family members. You keep hearing requests as what items that they are interested in. My daughter was only interested in certain Items because they had a connection to her mother. This hurts even more, if you can remember that a child missed attending the funeral and asks for nothing of her possessions. Can't think too long about this. It's time to get to the next box, then the next, and the next box.

When the sorting is all over, it is time to sell or give away the things you will never use again. I gave the unwanted things away, but it had to be done. If I would have kept all of the items, I would have the mindset that she would return someday. I have to see it as, she is waiting to meet up with me again. This sorting could last days.

When it is all over, then the residence will look like a different family lives here. This is a hard thing to face. Every thing changes, down to the daily routine and the menu at supper time.

I have to keep on my path and remember my Grandfather had done it before Me. He spent 25 years along the trail alone. How long will I be on mine ?

Chapter 72

Hear the What - 1/25/19

Many people throughout my daily walk, do not see the things that I face every day. An example of this is presented here.

A friend of mine comes to many of the places I do. On one of those trips, He notices that my front tires on my vehicle are in need of air, they don't look right to him. Alright, this person would most likely to notice this as cars have been his life. He drove then, sold them, and raced a car at the local race tracks. I told him that I did not have a tire pressure gauge.

The next day, I see the same person and he had brought a tire pressure gauge that I now could use. So I had to think of where I could find a gas station that would have a air hose outside of the building, that the public could use. My mind was blank on this one, I would have to start tomorrow and look for one, starting at the gas stations nearest to where I live.

I could not do it on the same day. The sun went below the horizon and visual issues would be involved, as I did not have a flashlight with me. So I need to attempt this tomorrow.

I set out to do this task, I leave home and start driving around local places looking for an air supply.

I come to the first location. I knew that this place had one over the years. I arrive and begin to search for the air hose. I can't find one, I see the spot where it was in the past. I then think that they don't have one now, or they moved it. I search the different areas around this convenience store and see not. It's time to move on.

I get to my next location in town, This place sells gas only, and I can't find an air hose here to use, strike two.

Then I get to my third location. I look around and finally see a machine that has an air hose. I drive in and realize that it's in a position that I have to drive up to it. Because me vehicle is facing the wrong way, I need to leave the station to circle around the block to change my direction. I finally get back and drive up to the Air supple hose.

First problem, I need gloves. It's 4 below zero and my hands are sensitive to the cold. I have the air gauge and go over to the air hose. The instructions say, set air pressure desired, push the start button. connect tip to the valve stem on the tire, and when desired air pressure is matched, A signal bell on the machine will sound.

I get the hose, push start, apply end to valve stem, I feel the machine pulsing air bursts into the tire. I can't hear this for two reasons. The first is I have a hearing loss, and the biggest thing is the traffic. Gas stations are built on busy intersections for a reason, it's to get the maximum numbers of customers for the business.

The traffic noise is a challenge, My hearing aid picks up things I don't want to hear. The rattling of items in the back of a truck. The noisy, must need repair, of a muffler tooting out like a tuba. The teen that thinks every stop sign is a starting line for a drag race. Then there is the sound of the 18 wheeler that seems out of place, the truck is making a delivery, but it's rare to see here.

I don't know if the air pump has delivered enough air, I can't here the bell that indicates this. So I take out the air pressure gauge and check for myself. Looks like this tire has enough air, as this small device is as silent as an elephant in the refrigerator that stepped in the butter.

So it's off to do the other tire. I have to reset machine for every different tire I fill. I push button and repeat steps above, except the elephant. He left as I only see his foot print in butter.

I am done today, as the vehicle needs to be re-positioned for the rear tires. My hands are as cold as playing patty cake with Satan, after hell has frozen over.

Every day is a struggle to do simple things. I can't change things or my inabilities. I have to take it one day at a time and keep walking forward on the narrow pathway.

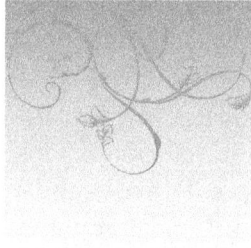

Chapter 73

Let's Make a Deal - 1/26/19

Trying to get back on the track and my path isn't easy. I have run into a stress train that snorts like a raging rhino. The stress numbers are beginning to exceed the 4 month time frame of 12/1990 to 3/1991. This started out with the House Fire and ended with the death of the second born Son. I had a partner back then to weather the storm. Now I have to make choices alone. I have to make the decisions alone, as I feel the cold air of winter, just as it was in December of 1990.

I had to face a fire that caused the house to be a worthless shell. I am facing another firestorm that could cause the current house to be another worthless shell. This time it is caused by a person with a fire within themselves, and not the open flame. The connection is this person was the same one that escaped death in the first event, that caused the 1990 home to be a worthless shell. The destruction in both caused the houses to need extensive repairs.

This is one of the major issues. Not another one have jumped on the bandwagon, since the death of my Wife, the financial issues are arising as a hungry lion looking for it's prey. I may not have a cage to contain the hungry beast. I was living in a world where 2 sources of income covered the expenses of 3, now it's 1 source for 2 expenses. I will take months to work this out. I see the same issues as in the past.

Then I see the lights of the stage light up, The announcer walks up to the microphone, welcome to the hottest game show on TV. Welcome to Monte Hall and it's time to play, Let's Make a Deal. Monte comes around and likes what I have to trade, so he want's me to play. He points down to the stage and says to continue on your path, to get fabulous prizes, or get zonked, you need to pick a door. There are 3 doors across the front of the stage. If you select a door that zonks you, the prize behind the door is yours and you are out of the game.

If the prize isn't a stinker, you continue to select doors. You can stop at any time after winning your first prize, but find the worthless prize and you keep it, and you are out of the game. Now it your moment to pick the first Door. I look at all the 3 doors, my imagination is coming up with a million possible things that could be behind the doors. I have to choose or walk away, and forfeit my chance. I then pronounce, Door number 2. I see a sign that states, snake eyes, your consolation prize is a king sized version of the game of Trouble. Its so large that I become a game piece.

Struck out there. But I am still facing the choices that are before me. I now realize that the answers will not be easy to get. I face the many doors of choices in my life. I must find one that makes my path easier, or do I fall between the cracks. At times, living at home feels like an earthquake zone, or an avalanche area. I never know when one will strike and bring down my house of cards. Never a dull moment around here. Time to get back to the task at hand, choosing a direction to go. I can't stand still, or I will never get anywhere. Life is not a game anymore, even if the set I have is missing a few pieces.

Chapter 74

Nine Dollars & 7 cents - 1/26/19

Two weeks have elapsed, since things came to a climax and one life was over. Two weeks to get as many things done as possible. The medical decisions were made, funeral arrangements were done. Moving her belongings from her room. Writing the obituary and a poem about her life that was read at her funeral. Then it was to arrange to get her to her final resting place on earth. The only thing left for her is to get a number and wait to be called to pass through the pearly gates.

As for me, Informing her loved ones is next to be in center stage. Getting her room cleared out and pack her items was next. Then the paperwork has started. Then move her boxed item home. Help was needed to take one truckload of her items, and bring them back to the house she left years ago. Now comes the sorting through the items that she had.

Some items will be donated away for others that need and can use them. Then it is time to find the paperwork that is hidden among the two dozen boxes. Opening each one is not easy. The flowers that were sent to her funeral, all had a soothing effect on the living, and had the colors that she liked. They also showed that others there, that the sender wanted to be part of the event.

As I open each box, I never know what memories will come with it. Everything she lived with for the past 3 to 4 years, is contained inside of the boxes. Personal items, clothes, and medical supplies top the list. There were puzzle books, and several others that she read, including a copy of my own book. She did manage to read my book within the last year.

Her major thing that she did with her hands was to knit. She left several projects unfinished. There was even crafting supplies that she never got to start at all. These things kept her busy and her Doctor's tried to find a way to heal her. This was the plan, but it did not end up this way. She cried out in pain during her last days. She could not talk at all during the last 12 days of her life.

I just had a flashback and the looks of her last room filled my mind. Everything in the room was there. I could draw a picture and a map of the layout of the room. One thing that she enjoyed in the last 3 years, was to have a room by herself. It was more stressful years before, when she had a room mate.

The biggest problem for me was that she was in pain each day and there was nothing that I could do. The workers at the facility did the best to make it better for her, and she had a better quality of life. No solution was in the works for her, to end her pain.

Now it's time to finish the sorting of the boxes. Every box has parts of puzzle that was comprised of her final years. There was nothing of great value, because we had to live a simpler lifestyle. There was no heirlooms to pass down to others. I wish things were different, but we were satisfied for what we had.

I went through every box and knew what was in them. People think that she had thousands of dollars in valuables. But the most valuable thing she had was taken with her, it was her soul. All the money she had left, when she passed, now can be used to pay for her funeral costs. It was Nine Dollars and Seven Cents.

Chapter 75

Trapped Inside - 1/26/19

A frantic day around the hospital, some of the workers felt like they were a computer in hyper drive. Coming and going, in and out of the room. My relative had a stroke and the crew did everything that they could to get things under control.

It seemed like they had every machine and monitor, that was in the ICU area, all in her room. It looked like a Laboratory. Wires and tubes went to all parts of her body. It would be this way for days. A brain wave chart was done. Chest x-rays followed, then a heart monitor, IV tube, then medications added. Then a breathing tube, later a feeding tube, they were turning her into a machine. This was done to keep her alive to see what her chances would be. They wanted 5 day statistics and the Doctor then would know what to do next.

5 days went by, the staff gathered all of the evidence. The Doctor said she was stable enough to leave ICU. So they packed all off the electrical goodies on the gurney and took her up to a new room. She would need more time to recover. So they unpacked all items off the gurney. Each day they would remove and item or two, that was connected up to her. She needed to keep the feeding tube, heart monitor, and feeding tube and the machine that gave her more oxygen to breath. This one required her to wear a mask with tube. This went on for a few days.

They had to feed her with liquids down the feeding tube. They had to have other items connected at all times. But the prognoses was good, she may be taken off machines in a week or so. then it was rehab time as one of her arms did not function because of the stroke. So this became a waiting game. Each day the patient would be asked by the staff, many questions. She responded by squeezing the hand of the staff member. This way they knew she could hear and see when they were coming and going. I wondered just how long it would take for her to recover.

Doctors said that if she was in stable condition about 10 days from now, they would have her sent to nursing home and then rehab could get involved. This would allow her some recovery of movement in her arm. This was all some could hope for. Then her world came crashing down. And her future became known. It would not be good.

The next morning, the staff noticed that she had breathing difficulties. They called in the troupes. After a few minutes it was discovered that the patient had a seizure. During this event, She bit her tongue and it swelled up. This caused a loss of oxygen to her brain, already damaged by stroke. Now she could no longer squeeze a hand or communicate with the staff. Things looked very bleak and the staff knew that her days were numbered.

Now this is where the story ending would be different. In the original version, all support machines were taken off and she was to let nature take over. Soon she would be at the Pearly Gates getting reservations to see the Judge on Judgement Day. But this now becomes a What If. What if she accepted the use of machines and tubes to prolong her life. Just what could another possible outcome be ? Time to find out, turn the page and see the other fate that could happen.

The Staff knew that if something was not done, she would die in minutes, hours, or a few days. So they went hog wild around the room, adding every thing that the body needed to survive. They had a tracheotomy tube placed in her neck, a tube through the abdomen to the stomach to feed her. The double IV connection for meds and blood tests. The heart monitor and a half dozen more sensors. She looked like she was ready for a shuttle trip to Mars. Meanwhile in her mind, she had a flashback of the way life was over 50 years ago. A domineering Mother that kept her in the kitchen like a caged in animal.

She had to do KP duty and anything that was not what her mother wanted, she got smacked by a wooden spoon that felt like a whip. Day after day, she could not leave the house, except to go to the outhouse. Day after day it was living on the farm, always in or next to the farm house. At times, not leaving the property for a few weeks at a time. It seemed to her like a minimum security prison. This went on year after year. As her younger sister grew up, things that she had to do went up and up, with no end in sight. This was not the way it should be like for girls of her age. The only daily relief she got was going to school. This was actually the best place to be. Other students thought school was hell on earth, but it was a vacation away from a home run encampment. KP duty and babysitting became the daily normal life style.

She was taken to a nursing home and connected up to the wall, this allowed all of the machines to twinkle with lights, as they did everything for her. They even brought their version of an outhouse to her. She got her daily bread, but could never taste food again. She could never smell the flowers again, and the tube through her neck did not allow room scents to be detected by her nose. She could not smell, taste, or touch things ever again, as her limbs never moved, unless the nurses change her position in the bed. Oh. what a life. A life for Who ? This is becoming a new form of prison. I should have told the Doctors what I wanted years ago and never found the time to do. A living directive would have saved me from suffering a hell like this.

I can't communicate. See very well, because I am not wearing my glasses and never will again. Smell or taste again, and my hands are as limp as rags. I am left here to exist year after year in a shell of nothing for me. Life is a living hell and I want to escape, but I can't on my own. I wish I could die and get this over with. I can't imagine the hell it is to my family and friends. I want this to end. Help me Jesus, take me home. I want to lay down in green pastures, Pet the Lions, tigers, and bears. I want to taste the cool waters of the promised land. Free me, The lord is my shepherd, I shall not want.

Then her mind flashes back to the hell that she had to live through on this carnal Earth. She asks for a miracle that she could speak for the very last time, But no luck, her thoughts would have to be enough to awaken her guardian angel.

She kept screaming in her mind, over and over. I want to go home, I want to go home. Any way that I can, her prayer then was answered. She was called home to her maker. Free at last, Free at last. My God, Thank you, I am Free at last.

Chapter 76

The Shadow Knows - 1/27/19

I feel the things of my past are around me everywhere I go. These are the good and the bad. They are of my life, or the life I had with a family. But in today's world, I travel around alone. I always knew life could be this way. I never knew when it would happen or why. I just followed my path in life and it took me to where I am today. It's like your life journey just changed the channel, and I can't change it back.

My mind slows down like the spin of the rotary dial telephone, I hear every click when the finger wheel is spun clockwise, and starts to return to it's starting point. Every time the switch clicks, is part of the number you are calling. Every one of these clicks is like a separate channel, to your memories from the past. The memories flash back year by year. I am turning back the hands of time as I keep changing through the years. I see many things of a past world that I have lived in.

I see that a gallon of gas was 25 cents. A candy bar for a nickle. a longjohn at the bakery was 6 cents. Milk carton at school was 2 cents. Seven hamburgers for a dollar, and many other things. I see where a carton of Cigarettes were a little more that two dollars. A pack was 25 cents. I go back and think, I am glad that I never was caught up in this habit. A pack today is around eight dollars, that would buy 3 cartons back then.

It also brings back a truck load of bad memories, of the time I was growing up. Then a few of the good times. I find myself at times, shuffling through the thousands of photos I have, looking for the good moments. Mostly I am still changing channels of my mind. I can't decide as the location I want to stop the Dial spinning and pick a number.

But life's circumstances today can cause me to switch from 50 years in the past, to the current issues of the day. All this time the shadow is a tag along, it sees what I can. I can't hear it, it is a silent stalker. It disappears only at night, or when I sleep. It follows me around and I don't know what it wants. It's like the taxman, you know he is there, but don't know when he will strike and take another penny from my pocket and place it in his own.

I have prepared my self in the past to be Mr.Lonely, I have been there before and I can do it again. I will never have life the way that it was. I have accepted it and am slowly moving forward. There is no turning back, things are history. I can look at it, remember it, but I can never change it to a better world, or have it look like it copied someone else. Then I am hit by powerful flashes, of the past century that have gone before me.

I recall all of the past 4 or 5 generations of my family. All of those that have gone before me. From the earliest of those who have passed away to the more recent ones, this happens again and again. My shadow rarely sees this because this happens in my dreams, so the shadow is no witness. I have to learn to live with my shadow, nobody else wants it, or they have one of their own.

The Shadow knows more than it should. I never know on what days it will stick to me like glue. It's a rare day that my shadow is missing. If it is, storm clouds around my head have replaced the sunny days, and the carefree times of my life. One thing that makes it disappear is to stand directly under the Son of God. He is the light of the world, and makes all shadows vanish right before your eyes.

Chapter 77

Salt into the Wound - 1/28/19

I can never seem to get through a crisis without others dragging it along and making it last for days, weeks, months, and into years. When you have an event that your spouse dies, It's one of the biggest events that can happen in your own life. The only thing greater is you, yourself, dies.

Dealing with the death of a spouse is 300 points on a stress scale. In 28 years, My Wife was 2nd family member to die. It was the youngest and the oldest family member. Just like it was in 1991, My Son was about 3 hours old. 5 weeks before my last Grandparent dies. The youngest and oldest in the set. My Grandmother and her Great-Grandchild. It is something that changes a family forever. After my Wife dies, she becomes a set of 3 generations to use same funeral home.

In my case, there were other things in the past that I have gone through, that adds to this stress. I have seen abuse, House fire, greed, a life version that others lived over 120 years. At times, I lived like it was when my Grandfather was born, 1896. I remember how many things my body was different that others. I don't have all the parts I was born with. My parents most famous line was, when you get to be 18, get the hell out and don't come backI live a life of moving forward. It's not easy when others drag you down.

Now the serpent has returned. When a family member dies, it is a calling card to re-unite to support the others. But I never see a normal response in many things, a Death in family is another.

I had to run the events for my wife, because that is what the remaining spouse does. I expected my remaining family to support me and I return support for them. After my Wife dies, I informed the family that was around the country. I did the legal steps and what was required to do. The day for the funeral was set. I wrote a poem about my Wife & I, I even wrote the Obituary. I wanted no stone unturned. I wanted to cover all of the bases. Then one link was missing from the chain

My first born, did not come to his Mother's funeral. Not everyone there knew that he was missing. This was a brewing pot that later would boil over. The countdown had began to tick off day by day. Jan 12 was the day my Wife dies and it was our Daughters birthday. Jan 19 was the funeral. and Jan 26 was the day that the boiling pot explodes and aftershocks will be felt for days, months, and years.

First born Son complains that he wants something that we had around the house, in the past. I tell him that I can't afford it now, because I have funeral costs since his Mother died, and facing a reduction in income. He screams at me from down the hall "there was no funeral". I say" What ?". And he says "There was no Funeral ", I say, "Your Mother is Dead". He says" No, she is not". I say," Yes she is, she died on the 12th, yes she is". He states" I don't have a cell phone". I tell him," Your mother is gone, where do you think these flowers came from ?" He screams even more. He would wake every cat in the house, if they were not stuffed ones.

Healing after a death takes time. This event has increased the time frame of recovery. another setback has raised it's ugly head. This is like rubbing Salt into the Wound".

Chapter 78

She Never Got Her Dreams - 1/28/19

As the years pass by, people are not seeing what it is for others. They walk the life for themselves, as most people have a me attitude. They think that things that happen to others will not happen to them, or it's light years off in the future.

My Wife and I saw things a bit different than most. We saw the limitations in life, but could not do the things that she wanted to have happen in her life. For her, she had to accept the things that came her way. As years passed, her time basically ran out, as the flaws in her body started to show. Then her fight for life was ended by another medical event that ended all chances of recovery.

There was many things that she had hoped for. Having better relationships with both sides of the family. One side never did welcome her with open arms, and the relationship with her mother was strained for years. This is the reason she moved into Pine Valley. She wanted to start a new life without her mother's control.

She wanted a 2nd honeymoon, as we really did not have a version of one, when we were married. We went to California over 3 years after we were married, and She wanted to take another trip before it was two late. But it did turn out to be too late a few years ago.

Having children filled the house and made every area short of space. We originally had a 2 bedroom house, But the fire in 1990 caused the need to get a newer mobile home. Then as the children grew up, even this ended up being short of space. We had to do the best that we could, today the house shows the signs of heavy wear and tear. We wanted a newer model, but again, time ran out as this.

Along the way, a chair became empty as our second son passed away, after being born 3 hours before. We never saw this 2nd child grow up, We always wondered what he would be doing today, and what life would be like. We both would never know.

As her medical conditions changed over the years, She wanted things that we had in the past. She always wanted to have a house cat as a pet again. But with her medications, getting cuts and scratches is always an issue. The risk was too great to have a fuzzy ball of energy running through the house.

Her life in the last 5 years gave her a new address. Nursing Homes, Hospitals, and assisted living locations became a way of life. She had to live at these location, life at times was lonely. People that were in her life, could not be found for her to share time with. Visitors that showed up to see her in the last few years, could be counted with the fingers on one hand.

She wanted to see her children grow up and get married. The wedding day for our Daughter was set, But I found out what it was, just days after she passed away. I know the date, but we can't enjoy the day together. She wanted to see any grandchildren as they grow up, but that wish disappeared like a snowflake entering a blast furnace.

As time goes by, She passed away before me, so we lost the chance to grow old together. We never had a chance to enjoy our golden years. She had many ideas as what life would be, but never saw the chances that she would not be there to enjoy her Golden Years.

Her biggest request that I heard over and over, again and again, was that she wanted to go home. She would cry out at times, I want to go home. It was her most popular statement during the last 5 years of her life. I want to go home, but She Never got her Dream.

Chapter 79

The Brick Wall - 1/29/19

I finally reached then point of the questions that arise after a death or tragic event, the why. Why me, why now, why us, why at this point of out lives does one of the two have to die. I heard that some cuss out God because they feel that He could have saved them. They don't realize that It may have been that the person with the stroke had asked God to go home early.

Some never see the both sides of the possibilities in a persons life. I don't like what happened in my life. I wanted us to be married at least 50 years. But that is not to be. 37 years was longer than any brother that I had. I was not expected to get married, I took a great chance by getting married. Even my bride to be took a big chance, as our first born happened after she turned 35. Some women can be a Grandmother at 35, I know at least two that were.

The weeks of pain and suffering that she had was something that nobody will ever know. She said nothing in the last days, only screamed out in pain. I did the best things for her, in her last days. I went by Her final written statements and wishes. I could do nothing else. The Doctors did the best with what they had. Buy the lingering question is Why Now.

I faced many obstacles in the days ahead. I took on a challenge and wrote a poem that was read at the funeral. This was a short version of our lives together. It was enough to show where the two of us became as one.

Her obituary was even written by me. Did I try to do too many things ?. If I did not do them, who would ? I had asked for help in a few ways, and many complied. I felt that I had to do as much as I could possibly do. I left no stone unturned. I must have missed something, because one chair there stayed empty. I never wanted anyone to repeat what I went through decades before.

I handled the funeral as expected. I was an example for others. I gave support for others, as others supported me in getting this event completed. I did my best, but others did not stand up next to me. One avoided the funeral. I did try to understand that this happened. I gave them the information. In the end, they missed the funeral, and denied that she died, several times. It was the most difficult thing for me to witness. I never raised my children in the lifestyle that I was raised. Each child was a one of a kind, and I treated them so.

I have finally came up against the brick wall. I did everything asked of me, and everything that I could do. I can't force others to honor the dead, or give them respect.

Now what?, It will be a month that has gone by. I saw things that I never thought I would. I seen the stress that is caused by an event like this. I could do nothing to stop it, I have to ride it out.

I see my routine has already changed in my life. I saw the helping hands, and the hands that want control. I can't give anyone control. I need it to stay on my path. The path that will allow me to meet with her again, then the two of us will spend forever together.

Chapter 80

Last to Know - 1/30/19

When I thought that all bases were covered, I find a loose end that showed up in the mailbox. A letter arrives and its from another state. When I open it, It is from the only remaining member of my original family of 6. The six of us grew up in the red brick house, that was along Highway 3, in Pine Valley.

In opening the letter, I see where it was written on January 21. My surviving Brother finally saw a copy of the Pine Valley newspaper. It took extra days as this paper had to go by mail and he was not the first one to read the paper. It also had to pass through security at his Correctional Institution, and sometimes this is slow process.

He states that he just read Rayne's Obituary that was there. Since the Obit was in two days in a row, I don't know what copy that he had. But he did see it and now all remaining loose ends have been covered. I still think about what should have been.

When Rayne had the stroke, it looked like it would take more that 6 months to be in rehab, and then find a nursing home for her. But when the second problem caused a major setback, it was apparent that it was too much, and no possible recovery could be in her future. Then her future was left in the Creator's hands, and He took her down the path. He placed her in front of the Pearly Gates, to be there when the gates swing open, so She can be part of His flock.

But in reality She has passed away. My Brother sent his condolence, for what it is worth. But states he has feelings for my family, and that he cares about the remaining family members.

He also knows that there is nothing that He can do to help, because of his current situation. With nothing more to say, He states that he cares and feels sorrow for the loss. He hopes that we can find peace at this time.

This brings up many questions and no answers, as this is only the second letter that he sent to me in over 25 years. My other relatives that are in Pine Valley area, did not know where he was. They thought he was in another state to the west.

So it will remain for years to come as a bits and pieces communication. Seems like nobody else has contacted him in years. His troubled past has caused his children to scatter around the country, as they consider Monopoly money has more value. Life should not be this way, but if they do too many things to their children, this may be the outcome. I have seen this before when I was growing up.

I really wanted things to get better over the years. Why does it take somebody to die before they wake up, and smell the coffee. I did not think that it would end up this way, but he would become the Last to Know.

Chapter 81

They Came for Me - 1/31/19

Time was not on my side, as I had to do everything, including what to do for a memorial service for my Wife. I had to go it alone and find the best options for Me, My children and for Rayne. The planning was for her, what to do ?

Do I have a funeral or something else. If a funeral, where would I have it. I would need an obituary posted in the paper. So many things to do. I thought of our second child that passed away in 1991. It would be nice to get the same place.

The location was available, so a meeting was made and the plans were set. I wrote the obituary, and a special poem to be used at the Funeral. After the Obituary was in the Pine valley Newspaper. Everything was ready. Did I do the right thing? Things have to go forward, I will have my answer later.

Saturday arrives and I start the day by going to the location of the high school class mini-reunion. This allowed me a chance to get something to eat, it was looking like a long day. I leave here and go to the Funeral home for a visitation time. Things went smoothly, as I even saw a few people that surprised me by showing up.

After the guests are seated. It was time for Her funeral. My special poem was read and it fit right into the service. This reading helped me relax a little. But it gave a good history of Rayne's life together with Me. After the service was concluded, there was time to visit at the end of the service.

I can understand that many came to the Funeral because of Me. It is difficult, as in my past, it was not this way for me. I remember many times that family members would do little or nothing. They would even go further than that.

I recall that when I came to a family funeral, My immediate family was with me. But it ended up as a waste of time, as I was told that I would have to leave or be arrested. This happened at the very same Funeral Home as I used for my Wife. So coming here was not going to be easy for me, because of the memories of the Past.

Rayne wanted to use this location as it was closer to the east side of town. Her relatives and family lived east of Pine Valley, so this was the ideal location. It also was the location of the funeral for our Son that died in 1991. This made our choice easier to make. Now the two are back together, forever.

Having them back together, helps a little. The two will be at the same Cemetery, this location has our Child, my Wife, my Parents, Grandparents, and my Great Grandparents. Five generations that cover a span of over 160 years

Many of my Classmates came to the funeral home, Many stayed for the service. Most did not know my Wife, some may have only saw her at a reunion. This did not stop them from showing up for Funeral. I realized that they came to help me deal with my loss. This helped as it would have been worse without them.

They Came for Me. But, I Left Alone. Rayne left days before, as an Angel came to Earth and escorted her home. She went to be reunited with our Son, He was waiting for her with open arms.

Chapter 82

Calling Mr.J - 2/01/19

It's a busy day on your calendar. You now have to jump out of bed and get ready for that appointment. You get your day started with breakfast. Then its getting your work clothes on and gather your briefcase, with today's tasks. It's an average day for you. This time you should get out of the house and be on your way, in no time at all.

You hop in the car and it's off to work, clear blue skies are ahead. Traffic does not seem too bad, not that many cars on the highway. I have seen worse traffic later in the day.

The driver was nervous today. He thought about what his future would be. He had a few loose ends to get solved. If He could, He would get the contract that he wanted. He was driving along at the speed limit, without a care in the world. He would get a bonus in his paycheck, for completing the deal to get the contract.

He started to relax a bit and began to think about his personal life. He thought, I have been putting this off for a long time, I will do it after work. This has to be done.

He relaxes back in the driver's seat, and the scenery goes by like a movie. He thinks, why should I wait until after work, when I can do it during the lunch break around noon.

His heart began to race and his mind was thinking about too many things at a time. He thought to himself, why not get it over with and solve my problem and please another.

Traffic started to pick up as He was over halfway to his office. In his mind, he thinks that he has waited too long. He picks up his cell phone and sends a text message over his phone.

He taps the keys as fast as his heart rate, He is text messaging his Girlfriend and enters a question that will change his life forever. He enters the message and it appears on his screen, and ready to send. He then looks down at the screen, as He pushes the buttons that sends the message to his Girl. The message was this. My Sweet Girl and my Intended, Nothing can stop us now, Will you marry me ?

He looks up from the screen, He sees the traffic light is red, He is going too fast, He can't stop. His car skids into the intersection. The tires are squealing like a dozen piglets. A large truck hits his classic car, it splits his car in half. His half rolls over and ends up in the nearby park. As He ends up lifeless, his hand releases the cellphone.

As the phone is sent flying out of his hand, it landed on a large table in the Park. After it stopped spinning, the final return message was flashed on the screen, I do.

Every time you handle a cell phone while driving, your are open to make a long distant call. A call that will be made is to Jesus Transportation Services, and one of his taxis will be arriving to bring you to his Father's Courtroom. He will put you on hold to get an appointment to talk to the Judge

He passed the large church on the corner, every day as He went to work. He did not bother to read the sign that was out front. HONK if you love Jesus, TEXT if you want to Meet Him. Life would have been much different, If He would only had read and understood that sign. His intended met up with him later at the Church. She could only give him a Goodbye Kiss.

Chapter 83

Ground Hog Day - 2/2/19

I knew this day was coming, I just did not know when. It is like a small prediction event or a Mini Judgment day. This was set aside as a day, that took a look at the last half of winter. It is called Ground Hog Day. If the Ground Hog sees his shadow there will be an early spring.

I seen many shadows that follow me around in life. Some are good and others are bad. The good shadow is like a guardian angel, the bad shadow brings storm clouds is that could last for days, weeks, or even years. Will I see that shadow if I come out of my house ?

Leaving the burrow could be like walking on thin Ice, it may support you or it cracks. It would send me to the bottom, faster than the Titanic. Too many things have happened so far this year. Having 30 degrees below zero, 2 nights in a row, Did not help. Things within my house froze, as well as the water lines in bathroom.

I decide to peek out from under my shadow, caused by dim light entering in. Then I emerged from my house that seems like a burrow, around 7:30 a.m., and did not see my dark shadow. what did I see ? I way saw the brightest flaming ball of hydrogen that was in the sky. I watched it as it's fiery tentacles reached out like a 1.5 million degree lashing whip. Where was this when I needed it to put an end to Mr.Frosty.

Always something in every new day. The solar prominence this day, came thousands of miles closer to me. Then the solar flare went off and bathed the earth in energy and bright light. Enough energy to toast the wheat in the southern hemisphere and turn every hog in North America into bacon.

Because of this, I did not see my shadow and am facing a long, long, winter ahead. Maybe it will be over on July 15th. So it looks as if my walk on my path is the same old, same old, rutted trail. So to me, it's not full steam ahead. I have to tread lightly, or the ice may crack beneath my feet.

The real Groundhog predicted an early spring. My experience gave me the news that I need to hunker down for the long road ahead. I see a few good things ahead, will it be enough to hold back Old Man Winter. I can't stop because of this. Even if all the Horse flies get toasted into wrinkled mini raisins, as the bright flaming sun wants to earn a diploma.

The bright sunlight outside, dances on the top of the snow, and then jumped back into the sky. Maybe later in the year, things for Me will improve. As for now, I have to keep chugging along like Steam Locomotive 2719, as it travels down the rails. It is looking for more shiny pennies and spare keys, to flatten along it's 1,960 mile, one way trip.

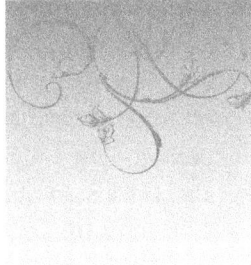

Chapter 84

Warp Drive - 2/3/19

Because of the events that happened around me in that last few weeks, months, and years, I find that my mind speeds up and runs back and forth though the timeline of life. It can run more that one event at a time. It can also multitask many things at a time. Time seems to slow down as I am doing many items within my mind.

I am watching the SB game 53, I research the lowest number of points in a game, by both sides, it was 21. I am writing this chapter, and following Face Book. I answer the messenger on Facebook. I am also playing songs off of You tube. My mind switches channels as fast as a coo coo clock allows the bird to yap along to the hour. I can't stop this event, it's trying to tell me something. Then my warning hits me when I need to be aware of what I am doing. My body chills off, it's 68 in the room, it feels like zero. My typing speed picks up.

Pressures in life also picked up and I had to do things to shift the mind into another direction. I must have over 100,000 to 125,000 photos or more. I needed time to deal with life, So I went to take photos. Some days I took over 1,000 photos in 3 hours. The camera clicks faster that your teeth chatter at 30 below zero. Time to change song playing, then I see the 10 to 3 score. 4 more points to not be the lowest scoring Super Bowl. Taking photos for 3 hours non stop, I turn into a machine. Walk, turn, frame shot, Click, move along tho the next one. I did this over and over for over 1,000 times. I see the names of those who will line up on judgement day.

Then another reaction, I feel I am going back in my personal Ice age. My hands shake they were in ice water. Some time these events last for over an hour. The songs I am listening too seem to speed up as well. I see too many things that need to be done and I stand alone. I can't stop as time accelerates, and I experience the memories in my mind switch faster that the rotary dial on the Television of the 1970's. Sounds switch between stereo and mono as I listen to the songs. My recalled memories are changing into color, as the SB time is approaching 2 minutes left.

Some people think that I must be on something, but you would be wrong. this has been happening over the last 50 years. Caused by others that changed my body, I must live with this as long as I live. The events like this happen faster as things change in my life . It's my warning that tells me to find a way to relax, I cant find what relax means unless I look in a dictionary. If I was a secretary, I would get a bonus for the words per minute, I never took an official typing class. With my physical limitations, it's hard to understand how I am doing this. But time is counting down. 10 to 3 is Super Bowl score with 1:16 left, they might break low scoring record. The Van Halen keeps saying Jump. My body feels like it's in liquid Oxygen. There is more that just a quiver in my liver, Dukes of Hazzard is where that came from. My mind is now like a revolving encyclopedia.

Seconds left in game, Rams miss field goal, Looks like new record for the fewest points in the game. My mind shifts gears, ... too many strange things. Karen passed away on Renee's birthday (our Daughter), is only the beginning. She passed away at 4:16 pm .. 416 was house number where she lived the day we got married, and where we lived for the next year and a half. This reminds me of Helter Skelter, and Clockwork Orange. This event has been longer then recent ones. I recall some in the past ran on for over 3 hours and the memories went back over 60 years. My Mind is trying to do that now. But it is slammed up against the bedroom door.

The bedroom door from the parent's room. This is in my book, and the chapter is "Down the Hall". I can't get my mind to open this door. I began to shake a bit, my body chills like I jumped of the Titanic. In my ear, I hear the lyrics.. the final countdown.. I can't get my mind to reveal the evil that went on behind that closed door. It is the only thing that I can't recall in the past 65 years. I can't unlock the mind to show me what Sodom and Gomorrah was like. I can't open the door. It treats me like kryptonite did to Superman. I am typing faster that the song I am hearing. The bedroom door will not open. Others have said that I might have to be hypnotized, Maybe this event is telling me that I need to know what went on behind this door. I am writing this event down. maybe others will then understand that these things happen. I am hit by another chill event.

What is a chill event ?, comes across messenger. A chill event is when my body feels like I am against an Ice block, or I jumped off the Titanic in 28 degree water. This happens in places that I am given a message to be aware. Or a touch of my guardian angel. I picture the Titanic in 1912, April 15.. My mind knows all of the facts, it was over 880 feet long. 1,503 lost, Carpathian was closest ship. S.O.S. wireless was used. The water was like a polished mirror, then I feels like I am on the backside of the moon. I recall everything in my life but not what's around me at the time. Random facts enter my mind. This happens, as I am as cold as the back of the moon. I feel like I am alone, all alone, even if there is another human in the house. I am all alone as I speed down my path going along at 186,262 miles per second. 3.1415926 comes in my mind as a flash. I am not hungry for pie. My back locks up, as I realize that time is going faster in my mind that on my watch.

The song I was listening just paused. I flip over to that You tube page, how did I pause that when I was not on that page ?. Strange things happen and I am not the instigator. The song that was paused was Staying Alive. I envisioned a sundial with the shadow spinning around and around. Then a picture of the Sundial Bar that is 30 miles away, flashes in my mind. The photo is of the 1960's. I passed this place every time the family vacationed north of town. This is where I was Tom, and the name is used as author of my books. Books ? this takes my mind back to JR High, this was the name of a teacher there, and I never needed any Text Books to be in that class. Ok homeboys, solve that riddle. I can't slow down yet. It has been over 2 hours. Without a Guardian Angel I would not be here. What my parents did to us kids, was unspeakable. So I wrote it in my Book.

My mind just analyzed my laptop computer and I know what it's greatest flaw is. Now my mind shifts to Lincoln High. How can a Carpenter be an electrician ?, another riddle comes off my numb finger tips. If I did not feel like I was in a bed made out of ice, my computer would be panting and melting under my hands. Lucky it has a SSD, without it the drives would be spinning to infinity and beyond. Now that shifts my mind again. The Buzz light year alarm goes off and I change cable shows as fast as Johnny Carson replaced his wives. He had Joan, Joanne, and Joanna, The bum never wanted to change monogrammed things around the house. But in the end it caught up to him, he married Alexandra.

Beat it. Michael Jackson dies on June 25, 2009 - The day that my Son became the first of my kids to become engaged, But like Michael, this dies as well. I now have 3 times, that my two surviving children were engaged, but none married yet. Back to me being like my Grandpa, My wife and his, never held or saw a grandchild.

. Now my body travels back to the last Ice age and even the woolly mammoths can't warm me up. Maybe this event is getting me to face something in my life. As of this time, I don't know what it is. I see that over 3 hours have elapsed. Most never experience an event like this. I lost count on the number of times. I may have to, I can't now. My Mind is telling me that I have not saved this writing update in the last 2 hours. Back to this as my memories are spinning like a roulette wheel. Just my luck as the number 37 comes up.

I need to hang up the phone and the numbers that are in my mind. I think my calculator needs to be turned upside down and spell out SHELLOIL, 71077345 .. The next Song, is another Jackson song.. Time to rewrite this song and remove Billie, Many in my family have Jean, or Gene, as middle name. Looks like it was used the most, both versions sound the same.

something just came across messenger. The State Theater as been sold. My mind changes as fast as the chambers in a gatling gun. The next song comes on, it's what at times, my pathway feels like. Its the Highway to Hell, by AC DC. Now I shift back to AC voltage and DC current. Ohms Law is now setting up the court case. Mr Amps is on one side, Mr Volts is on the other side. The attorneys are putting up too much resistance, then the Judge yells. Watt are you two doing ?, I am not giving the Power to the People.

Brain transmission shifts again, it shifts to my original poem made in 1970, it starts out. Although, I may be a Friendless Friend, I must fight until the end. My Guardian Angel changed the song, Bon Jovi comes on, Living on a Prayer. My body reacts to it. I seems to turn down the speed of the mind. This event will pass the 4 hour mark. I have seen thousands of photos flash through my mind. Envisioned enough ice and cold to cool down the gates of hell. Replayed videos of the mind, and seen new ones.

Wow, the events that were in my mind, are more exciting that the Super Bowl 53. 1953, another match here folks. More numbers went through my mind. I would need a Cray Computer to figure them out. I gave my laptop a fever, and it's demanding time and a half pay. Wonder if Spock could have solved this warp issue. I have gone where no man has gone before, without a Starship.

I finally have a version recorded of this type of event. It happened at a time where I was on the computer. It may be years before this chance comes again. I do have one version now. With this, something good may spring forth. I am now ready to travel again, go down my path again, taking my guardian shadow with me. I can't stop now. I have to go forward. The path is narrow along my walk, I will make it through the eye of the needle, as the camel did not. I have a destination in mind, and it's not in this carnal world.

I typed over 13,000 letters. The computer is begging for a drink. I finally realize that I missed my meal, over 5 hours ago. During this time, a Super Bowl started and ended in less time. That game was as empty as my dinner plate. This writing of my event has more things, and some hidden meanings to boot. I felt like I went through a time warp, as over 65 years flipped its pages in my mind. My computer's CPU is complaining that it has a migraine event. As the Director, it's time to end this kaleidoscope event ... "Cut".

Chapter 85

Home Bound - 2/4/19

Having to stay home for some is difficult. I need to start a new cycle that my life revolves around. After the recent death of a family member, I need to get out and not be frozen in time with the past.

The past that I had to deal with was very rare, but I was not the only one. I recall that we could not leave the fenced in yard around the house. We played with the neighbor's kids along a fence on the east side property line. It would be years before limited number of kids were allowed on the property. Most of us were only allowed 1 to be there. The Coca-Cola Kid was one of my brother's friends. We played touch football or softball on our baseball field. After the games, we were treated with bottles of coke.

So living like this was not desirable at all. My Wife, as she grew up, stayed around their house for over a week at a time. So the both of us had restrictions that my classmates did not have. But now when weather restricts travel, it effects me even more. I keep thinking I am hearing my wife around the house, but she never could come home, because of her mobility issues. This isn't much fun for me, as I walk the hallway alone.

I need to get out and looking for things that will keep me active and moving forward. Looking at a 37 year old soap opera, that I had recorded on VHS, should not be my first choice. I need to get out and setting a new schedule. When my Wife was at an assisted living location, I spent about 6 hours a day with her. Now this time needs to be filled. It will not be an easy thing to do.

I need to look into past, and see if I can be involved in things that I did before. I have plenty of hobbies to look at. Going out and starting a new relationship is way to early for me. I may never want to do this, but if I change my ideas about this, it's in the future, not today. Still have loose ends to tie up, and I will not move forward until these things are done. I need closure, I never expected that I would outlive my wife. I have a life now that repeats my paternal Grandfather.

Turning the pages of life is never easy, and no two people are the same. I need to hear what others did, and did not do. A few rushed forward and then were hit with another brick wall, divorce after their second marriage. Some ran out to replace their lost partner and ended up on too thin of ice, then they fell through. I have to go forward, but in slow speed. I can't do things if I am stuck in neutral. This is why being home bound creates issues. I can't relapse into the past when I am confined inside the walls of a house. I don't want to end up like a castaway on Gilligan's Island.

I want to move forward, I need to do it. I can't change things in my life when I am standing still. It makes no direction as what way I go, except backwards. Being home bound dampers things and stalls my actions, even after I decide as what direction I will go.

I don't like being trapped by things that I can't control. But, at times I am, stalled in my recovery attempt to create a new path that I will travel on. Being home bound will not take the drive away from me, to move forward. I want to put the past behind me so I can go forward. I always need to remember the past, as this is where I came. I need to keep what I have learned in life, as my past is my personal history. I can't let the past be a stumbling block. I now have to get back to my task, of walking forward along the path of today, and into the future. I can see many great things ahead for me, I can't stop now, nothing should stand in my way.

I want to be free again, to use what I have learned from the birds, and fly into the future. Being home bound or having a fence around me, can cause a delay. But, these things of the past and present, can't stop me now.

Chapter 86

Loose Ends - 2/5/19

When a death happens in a family, it's like time stands still. The loss of one person resets the clock of time. Your family is never the same again. One part of it is lost and can never be replaced. If it's replaced in the future, it now is in a different version. The original family will never be the same, ever again.

Time feels like it stands still, as I try to determine that one of the souls of the family has departed from this world. The hardest thing that I had to do was to tell all of the relatives, that one of our family members has passed away. There were 5 different kinds of her relatives in the room. I witnessed her final breath of air. After this event, the world changes forever in the relatives around me.

Everything that I was doing in life, has to be put on pause. Dealing with the needs of the deceased becomes the number one thing that takes over everything else. The paperwork, the choices, the options, all have to be made. This will consume all of the time in the days ahead. Dealing with the grief of the ones left behind, becomes another hurdle to jump. Then the final arrangements, the obituary, and the funeral.

After that, it is getting the final resting spot situation finalized. People think that this the end of it, to some people, it could be. For the masses, they end up like me. I have to deal with the financial side of things. Now that's all sealed and done, so it's time to relax and to move on, Right ?. No it isn't, this is where the loose ends come in.

After the passing of a family member, everything that I was doing was put on the shelf. Now I look around and see all the things that have been put on hold. This is the hard part, since one family member has a new address and will not come back, why should I do anything. The motivation to move forward, vanished as fast as the dancing snowman performance, after he enters a blast furnace. Many questions are brought up, and only I have the answers.

Why should I do anything ?, Who cares about Me ?, What good will it do ?, and the statement, Why did this have to happen to me. Guilt feelings can follow as well as, what could I have done to prevent this. I had to thing hard about this. Rayne had her stroke in the middle of the night. This was God taking control as when he was calling her home. Then the other main event that determines how long she has to live, was also in God's hands. These two events, left no guilt on the ones left behind. So it time to move on.

I then look around and see all of the things that need to be done. It seems like a job as large as Mount Everest. I have to whittle everything down to a more manageable size, like Rib Mountain. I do think it can be done now. On several issues, I will need help, as I am confronting several things that still need legal advice. It looks like a tough road ahead. It could take months. It would be a lot easier if I do not have to do it alone. This depends on others, I can't force them.

Now it's off to solve one problem at a time. The next few months look like stormy weather, as I am now the captain of my own ship, as my first mate is gone. I have to ride the waves into the unknown. I have to keep the boat from crashing into the rocks. Every loose end I tie up, will be one less task to do. Someday I might see bright sunny days again, the weather forecast ahead is still cloudy. I know things can never be as it was, I hope that I can see the sunny skies again.

I will do the best that I can do, I may never know if I did everything right. But, they will all know, I did try to do my best.

Chapter 87

Routine - 2/6/19

Many things in life change, some change over the years, and others can change as fast as minutes. The way people live their lives day by day can go on for years. They have things that they do everyday, and to them it becomes a routine. There is nothing wrong with a life style like this, nobody expects their routine to change. Events that happen to themselves, or those close to them, can change their lives forever.

One thing that twists the normal way of doing things in their lives, Is a death in the family. Within minutes, their lives will never be the same. The way that you live, and doing things on a day to day basis, slows down to a grinding halt. For the next few weeks, there are arrangements that have to be made. Informing the relatives of the death of a loved one, becomes the first major task. Then its what to do with their loved one. Funeral arrangements must be made and every thing else that comes with it, including all other final arrangements. Dealing with the finances is the next thing to come.

It looks like a never ending parade of events. You have to push your grief aside in order to move forward. This takes a very heavy toll on the surviving spouse. some have even said, why can't I switch places with the deceased, they could do a better job of handling this than I could. I see a mountain of paperwork and no end in sight. At times, I want to cry, but I can't. My body says yes, yes, yes, and my eyes say No. This goes on several times a day, and happens into the night. When will this ever end ?

Handling this kind of thing can be more complicated than getting married. You are starting out in live and there are plenty of things to build upon. Every aspect of marriage is like building a home, Both of you are adding to the house, that you will be living at, one piece at a time. Your future is bright on the horizon, You see no storm clouds in sight. But after a death in the family, everything isn't the same. The storm clouds have past, and the ravage of it's effects can be seen everywhere. Some see what the loss does to family members, and others turn the blind eye to avoid seeing the damage.

Now a death in family does some things opposite from a marriage. There is no honeymoon for the couple, as one now has to spend the first night alone in the morgue. The other one goes home to an empty house, and an empty heart. It also feels like everything is wrong and a piece of your heart is missing. Everything now is scrambled and you can't clearly see anything. The storm clouds that took your loved one has passed, But your internal thunderstorm from within is ready to burst. And to some people, this can become a cloudburst. You will never know what will happen to you, until this actually happens.

The grief is another road the the survivor must travel. Life is like a roller coaster for day after day. You can't make sense out of it, you seem that all you can do is hold on until the ride is through the worst of it. It seems like weeks have gone by, but it has only been a few days. Why Me ?, is something that comes into your mind. When will it end, and will I every find happiness again. Your mind is trying to find an escape from this, but it has lost the key to the door. Your problems increase if you live in an area that has snow. You could be stuck home for the day and at the end, you feel like climbing the walls.

Life can go on like this for days. In the weeks and months ahead, you begin to handle things in life, one step at a time. That is what you hear from others, take life one step at a time. They are not living this way in their lives, it's your life. Over many months this begins to slowdown and it gives you a chance to start again, start again to get back and finish the tasks that you started. However, you see new things that have to be started, and you really do not want to do anything. You want time to stop and make the world go away, even as the tasks ahead are surrounding you and they are in your face.

Sorting things out of your life, that were a part of your missing spouse, is the hardest thing some have to deal with. Every item that you give away or get rid of, takes a piece of your memory with it. Some of these things must be down, or you will make it harder to move forward in life. This sorting and rearranging of things seems to last forever. As this task is getting done, the question now is, what do I do with the rest of my life. I am now walking on my path alone, some days the dark clouds follow along with me. The clouds are so dark that I can't see my shadow. I have to feel my way forward in the darkness.

In order to recover in my life, I have to make a new daily routine. I can't live a life of standing still, time moves forward and I need to do the same thing. I have to start now, to find things to do, and change where I have gone in the past. My daily schedule has changed alot since the two of us, have now became one. I can do new things or restart old things, that I have done in the past. I see that no matter what I do, a part of me will still be missing. I can't let this stop me. I need to do something and not stand in the corner. As time goes by, I slowly begin to fill my life with things to do.

My daily schedule slowly changes and gives me a brighter outlook. I try new things and some work and others don't. As I fill my day, I begin to repeat things on a daily basis over and over. This helps me to look forward and end the clouds from following me down my path.

It look along time, I have found a new routine, it's not like it was in the past, but it is working for me. I am back on my path moving forward, and at times I see rays of sunshine. I can look back from time to time, to remember how I got where I am today. I begin to recall more of the good times and less of the bad. This helps me to stay on my path and invision a better life ahead.

Staying on my path will eventually take me to my final destination, meeting up with all my loved ones again. They had their own paths to travel. If their path stayed on it's course, they will end up going to the same destination. We will be all reunited in the end, standing in front of the Pearly Gates.

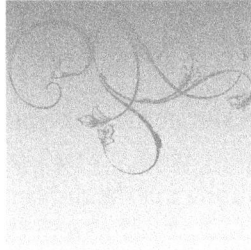

Chapter 88

Image on the Paper - 2/7/19

Life was a hard road to travel as the numbers of my age tumbled by, single digits became double. I accomplished many things despite my troubled life growing up at home.

After I had to leave home, I moved every few years. Settling down in the 9th ward. Others wanted an evaluation at to see what I could do to be productive in the world. I agreed to work at a location for 1 year and see what I could do and what I would need to be trained in.

I was here for a few months, when the Pine Valley Parks and Rec needed new trash barrels for a park expansion. So the metals shop prepared the barrels and had them painted green. But they needed the Pine Valley Park & Rec Department name painted on. There was only one place in the building where this could be done. The area where I was. So the call was made to find someone inside the building to do the lettering on the barrels. Several people were looked at and one was chosen.

The one chosen would end up being my bride. She worked in the same department as I did. I was re-conditioning electrical appliances. this arrangement went on for many weeks. She lived close enough to the workplace, that she walked to work. I lived farther away and I had a car. We talked for weeks, then we would share the noon meal time. We spent the breaks together too. Then the job she was on was completed, She was going to transfer back into her old department. A few days later, I saw her walking home after work, there was a chance of rain in the area. I stopped and asked her where she was going. She replied that after work, she went downtown to a family restaurant. I offered her a ride there.

This was out first date, out of the workplace. We went downtown to eat every work day. I met her friends there, later I met her room mate. This woman was legally blind, and she did get around in the 2 bedroom apartment. Rayne had her own bedroom in the back. We started doing other things on the weekend. We met every day in the lunchroom, even if we were in two different departments.

Soon my year at this location was over. She was back into her old department. I came by each day after she was out of work, and took her downtown to our favorite table. We spent time as a couple, and spent time with her friends on some nights. Weekends we went to other places.

Since this was spring time. We went over to where her parents lived. I got to know her sister and brother. Met both parents and a neighbor. We made a few trips over there and I did spend overnight there in a spare room. Rayne went to bunk in with her younger sister. On one of the summer trips, I asked her Father for Rayne's hand in marriage. And so it was to be. The next few months, wedding plans were done and a wedding date set. It was for 4 months away.

Her Mother and Sister came to Pine Valley and help get the tasks completed. I picked a best man, the Church and we had everything ready for the big day.

Our big day started out great. My relatives and her relatives and friends came. After the wedding, We needed an hour to drive to location of the dinner. Almost everyone came to the location in the next county, except my parents. After the dinner, we were to go to the Bride's Parents to open gifts and spent time with the family. Nobody from my family was there. Only the Best Man and his mother came to this event. My Brother and his family, Uncle & Aunt, and my other friends, did not make the trip.

I look at the photo's today, My parents only appear at the church. No relatives came to Rayne's parents house. We had no plans to spend first night in a motel. So before midnight we packed up the car with the gifts and headed home. This was about 1 and a half hours away.

A half hour into the trip home, I hit a deer on the highway. shattering 3 of the 4 headlights and the grill. The deer's head hit headlights and the body snaps around and dented in the driver's door. Lucky the Bride held onto the top of the wedding cake. So I resume my trip, with only one headlight instead of 4. So I need more time to get back to Pine Valley.

On the road again, maybe we will not find another deer. AS I get another half hour closer to home, and getting ready to pass through another small town, I see something else in my rear view mirror. It's a police car from the city I am going through.

He makes a traffic stop and wants to know why I have a defective headlight. I tell him that I hit a deer and it's head destroyed my headlight, as the Officer sees what we are wearing. My wife is wearing her wedding dress, and I am wearing a 3 piece suit. He starts looking for evidence of alcohol, asks me how much did I drink tonight. I tell him that I had none. He is wary of this answer, how many Brides and Grooms never drink at their wedding is on his mind. So he wants me out of car to show the deer damage. I do this and he sees that I have no affects of drinking. This satisfies him and does not give a written warning about the headlights. It's back on the road and we finally make it back to town.

Out first task is to call her parents, so they know we arrived back home. I told them that we hit a deer, but Rayne saved the cake. Now our lives are together as we now share the bedroom together, for the first time. Her room mate moved out a few months ago, So now, we are the only two that will live at the apartment. A new chapter of our lives begins.

We will spend the next 37 years together as Husband and Wife, We will have 3 children. We would go through a house fire after the first born Son was 4, and the 2nd Son would be born and die 3 months later. Two years later, our third child born would be a girl. We will spend the next 26 being a family of 4. On our Daughters 26th birthday, Her Mother, my Wife, passes away at the Hospital, after having a stroke 12 days earlier. She had other complications 5 day before she passed. There was multiply things that could not be healed. Her Obituary and Death certificate were written on the same day, as her Mother has her birthday, she is 95. So funeral arrangements are made and I wrote her Obituary, and special poem for her funeral.

After the funeral, she is laid to rest in the Lakeside Cemetery. This is same place where 4 generations of my family are, including our 2nd Son. Now the book of her life's journey is closed

I will never see Her again, while I am on Earth. I will never hear Her again or touch Her hand. The only thing that I can do to see her, is to gaze upon her face in a photo. Now all that is left of her, is an Image on the Paper.

Chapter 89

Death Matches - 2/8/19

Life goes on for people for years, then an injury, disease, or body malfunction, ends the persons life. This happens every day. But the death of an individual should not play the Match Game, or tell a past History in their death. My wife passed away and her death tells a History as well as matching events and numbers.

There are many long shots in this event. Rayne passed away at 4:16 pm on January 12, harmless statement, or is it?. 416 was our house number on the apartment, where we lived after we got married, we lived there about 2 years.

She passes away on January 12, this is also our Daughters Birthday. Rayne's death is the 2nd one in the family. Our 2nd Son was Born and Died on March 13, 1991. March 13 is also my Mother's, an Uncle', and an Aunt's Sister's Birthday.

On Friday Jan 18th, My wife's obituary is printed in the local newspaper, also printed that day was her death certificate, also on Jan 18th, it was Her Mother's 95th birthday. A Daughter's, Mother's & Grandmother's birthdays all in January. but there is more. It has to do with the Funeral.

I wrote a special tribute Poem for my Wife. it was read at Her funeral, It took 37 minutes to write it, We were married 37 years. I also wrote her Obituary. Her funeral was on January 19. The number 19 takes center stage. Rayne's Father was born in 1919. same numbers in different order 1991, is death year of our 2nd Son. The last 2 numbers in our House number is 19. Add the last 5 numbers of our Phone number together, and you get 19. Take 19, turn it over, you get 61. This is the age Rayne's only brother dies. Her brother was 2nd one born, same as our Son that died, he was 2nd born. 19 was her room number at the Assisted Living.

19 was her room number at the Assisted Living location where she lived. 19 = The number of complete years, the 2 of us, were together (38 years) divided by the 2 of us (=19). Last 6 digits of her SS number, added together is 19.

The last Card that I got from the workers at a restaurant we visited, was given to me on January 23. This was my Wife's birthday. The Final stage starts on her daughter's birthday & ends on Her own.

Other oddities, The last ICU room used, and the Hospice room where she passed away, I could look out the windows and see the location where I grew up, over 50 years ago. I also could see the Location where my Daughter's Fiance is employed. These 3 locations are in a straight line. Looking to the south, I see the last place where my Wife was employed. My Wife and my Daughter were employed at the same place. It was my Daughters 1st job, My Wife's last job.

Daughter's Fiance is younger than her, I am younger that my Wife (Jan 23). Daughter's Fiance has the same First name, as her deceased Brother(1991). Daughter's (Father & Father-in-law to be) Fiance's Step Father has part of his name matching my First Name. This Name also matches our First born Son. 3 with the same name that match.

The Same Letter starts the name of my Wife,(Daughter's Mother and Daughter's Mother-in-law, to be).

Same 1st Name initial match for Daughter's Fiance's Step Father & Her Uncle, that passed away at age 61 (My Wife's Brother), As well as my 2 of my Cousins and an Uncle.

Daughter's Name and Fiance's name start with the same letter, as does her 2 brothers & Her Father & fiance's Father as well.(6 of them with same 1st letter)

Chapter 90

Sorting Out - 2/9/19

So many things that need to be done, after the loss of a spouse. There is the final arrangements that include the funeral, and everything that goes with it. Then comes the financial costs and getting that done with as well. Now all the things that had to be done is very quick order is completed. Time to take a break ?, No it is not. Time to move on to the next level down after a loss of a loved one.

Since my Wife was living at an assisted living location, the first thing here was to empty out the room of her personal belongings. This took over a week, as for the most part, I was a one man crew. I did get some help to move the furniture out of the room. After she had her stroke, it was not known if she would or would not return to her room. But after a week, it was clear that she would not. This also sped up efforts to empty out the room, I did get it done and now the items are back at my house.

Boxes after boxes of items were brought back home. Sorting out the things of the past, now must be done. Some furniture was donated away. Now the decision of what to do with the rest, is the next thing to do. Because she will never return, most every thing that she has, has no use where I live. Some things can go to our daughter, but the clothing is not her size. So the first thing was to start packing up much of her clothes and donating them away. I could have had a thrift sale, but it was best to get this loose end tied up and donate them to others. Sometimes it is best to give to others, as others have given things, that I needed, to me.

It does not make it easy to sort things and give most away. Every item I hold, or look at, can create a memory of the past. This isn't easy at time. I want the world in the way that it was, but at this point of time, it can never be. She will never walk through the front door again. This was her most wanted thing to do, for the last several years, all she wanted to do was to come home.

The job needs to be done, and I have to do it alone. While doing this task, it reminds me of an old song of 96 tears by ? and the Mysterians. This is another problem, as I remember so much of the past. I can remember the first place we lived. The first time that we knew a child was on the way. The days that every child was born, and the one that died. All these memories were packed away and only opened up as I opened box by box. Every thing that I hold can produce a memory connected to it. I only want to do this once, as once could be one time too many.

I face a few setbacks along the way. The weather is one factor, that was not wanted or expected. It slowed down the movement of to be donated items, out of the house. Nothing seems to go as expected, but I still have to move forward. I kept the very personal items, photos, address books, heirloom jewelry, and more. The other items did get donated to more that one nonprofit organization. I wanted to share it to several places.

Every Item, package, and box of items donated, make my house become less and less ours, and more Me. I didn't want it to be this way, I was not my choice to have her reunited with our second Son. She was called to her new home, and I did not sent in this change of address card for her, Her Guardian Angel had it made. Now there is one less thing to do. Many more are on the horizon. The biggest question is how long will I stay in the place where I live.

With less income, I have to consider my options. If I start to go back into deficit spending, I will need to look at another option, where will I live in the future. There is good and a bad point to this. I would be starting over in another place, But I would be losing the home that we shared together for over 35 years.

Chapter 91

Dueling Jaws - 2/10/19

As I arrive at one of my favorite afternoon fast food watering hole. I hear a pair of windbags jabbering so fast at each other, that they can't hear each other talk. The 2 have their jaws snapping so fast that they could sew a quilt in 5 minutes. These 2 just keep talking at the same time, some times for over ah hour.

I can't correctly hear either one, as they sound like a pair of noisy boat motors, that need an overhaul. It seems like their mouths are misfiring and they don't care. Their jabber is filled with lies, bragging, cussing, and breaking commandments. But they don't care. Each one has their own personal pulpit and nothing will stop them at all. No thirst, hunger, events around them, will stop their sermon of lies and bragging.

One chatters about everything they ate over the last 7 days, the other talks about the places where they committed sin years ago. Both of these brag about their fine accomplishments. Meanwhile the angels above are hiding their faces and plugging their ears with their fingers. One and a while one or both overheat and their head bubbles over like a teapot and their tongues flap like a flag in a hurricane.

This is not a one time thing, but occurs more like a calendar, on a day to day basis. One lies so much that they imitate Sleeping Beauty, they can lie for years and have no end in sight. At times they sound like a 45 rpm record played at 78 rpm speed. They tongue acts like a needle, gouging out every word that they can, from the grooves within their minds. At times getting words and ideas, from the gutter.

Another has a prepared speech on everything that they ate for days, or their 4 meals a day plus snacks. Then complains about their sore knees. They don't make the connection. One day they will sink all the way to china, after licking a stack of china that was once filled to the brim, with their 7 course paradise. Their food pyramid in front of their eyes is larger that the pyramids of Egypt.

The other one talks about saving peoples life, over and over. They can solve every medical issue to save everyone. They brag about becoming a doctor in the military, but the facts don't back them up. They brag about multiple kids through affairs, and tell the who, what, where, and the why they surrendered to their lust.

These have more that the 7 deadly sins on their resume, they added a few that are not on the list. One tries to outdo each other, they tell tall tails, as tall as Paul Bunyan. Their lying tongue is as long as the ole' Mississippi, and their minds are just as muddy.

At times, several argue about things that have no defined answer and they think that they are right and not the other is wrong. This does not stop them. they oil up their jaws to go at round two. some days this can last hours. For one of the two, it justifies another round of cookies and a milk shake. While he snacks, the other keeps jabbering and tells the history of the war in Vietnam, and Korea, and World War 3, then tells about all the GI's that would not be alive if it wasn't for him.

Their mouths are like roaring engines, in full power, heading into a concrete wall. They must run on nitrous oxide. Their false statements are uttered as fast as a herd of Cows, at milking time.

Don't bring up politics, as this leads one to be psycho and argue about everything, their face gets red like a thermometer ready to burst. They can see nothing, hear nothing, except they speak, like an erupting volcano.

There is only a few things that will end these chattering staplers, it's too bad that they never learn from this. One way is to walk away from the pair of them. If only one is there, they will follow you around the place so you don't miss a syllable.

A few of us, took along time to find a way to have them stop their backfiring mandible. We pick a fact from their jabber fest and call them out on a lie. Because they can't back up their claim and will not admit that they lied, the pack up and leave for the day. They can't stand questions or being called out to prove their statements. They know that they are always right, but when called out about a lie, they left. Then got in their vehicle and disappear for the day.

As I try to catch up on my Email, I am now a spectator as another two, in this place. They start their own jabber jaws conflict, that can arise the dead. These two have taken different sides to an issue that has more that one answer, but they don't want to hear that. It's their way or nothing, not even King Solomon could not derive an answer to please them both. Maybe they need their tongues trimmed back to their collar bones.

Chapter 92

Reflections - 2/11/19

A month has went by since a death in the family, during my Wife's final days and hours, I think about what I could have done differently. Maybe the outcome would be different. But what I did or did not do did not had not affected the outcome. She had two setback events that combined together and took her life. There was also a 3rd complication that was written down.

Looking back at this, the timing of the events led to her passing on January 12. Both major causes occurred overnight and the time of these was chosen by Her Maker. This choice was not made by Man, it was made by God. So her final weeks were out of my hands as well as others treating her.

I look back at the moment I told the others, in the room, that she passed away. The look on my Daughter's face, after she realized that her mother was gone, is something that I never wanted to see on that day, or ever see again.

There was more than a thousand events that happened to Me as I grew up. I had my mind made up that any of these events should never be repeated to others, especially any possible family that I would have in the future.

My parents were a classic example, of what not to do. I remember the vacations that my parents had, and the fact that we were not going with them. Life for them was Me/Us first, and put the burden of the kids on others. I recall the 2 weeks that I stayed with my Aunt and

Uncle. It was like night and Day. This gave me ideas that not every family contained the seed of Satan.

I look back and see that in the last few decades, that I see nothing that stands out. We never had everything, but enough to make the family a unit. We had many setbacks, but I stayed on my path as I went forward.

If I had to do it over again, I would, but tweaking a few things could have made a better outcome. But not when it came to my Wife. Her Father and Sister both had issues with the heart. My Wife was in the same boat. This problem showed up over 10 years ago for her. So the final events were out of my hands and hers.

Dealing with a Daughter was something that I had to learn as life went on. I grew up without any sisters, and a mother that wanted to act like a man. This means that she did things men would do & avoid being a female role model. If the water pump needed to be looked at, she did it. Furnace would not start, she looked at it. Remodel the house by expanding the kitchen, she did it.

So having a female role model around the house, could not be found. I had to see what others did around me, as I grew up. But in the end, our Daughter turned out fine. Nobody is perfect, But she turned out better than her grandmothers, on both sides of the family.

Having 2 sons was great to dream of and then knowing a second son was on the way, was great. Then things change when the newborn dies after 3 hours. That decision was not in my hands, it was the creator's hands. Then we were given a 3rd child, a girl. This gave Me something that my parents did not have. They had no experience here to put their two cents in any opinion or decision.

So I can't see where we could have changed any major event in the last 10 years. My Wife should have quit smoking earlier than she did. She should have had a few less habits that affected her life, as she did consume more salt that she should have. These things would not have changed her outcome, but it may have delayed the outcome by a few more years.

So in the final outcome, a few things could have changed. It was Not going to stop the call from above to report to the Pearly gates. When anyone's time is up, this event is in control of the Creator. Gods call is the final one that is to be answered. When it does come, You will have a new home, and be waiting for your other family members to meet with you again.

Looking at the clock will not to be done. Your Forever Ticket has been punched, as the carnal world is now your Past.

The reflections you see now, are in the still waters, where the Son of God has gathered his sheep. They heard my voice and I know them, as they followed Me here, to be with Me forever.

Chapter 93

Avalanche - 2/12/19

Throughout my walk along my path, I find that over the years, I could be stopped and advance no more.

Life has thrown to many curve balls and I keep stalling the outcome by hitting the foul ball. I was hoping in life that I would get a Home Run, but this is not the case. I keep getting struck out or manage to get a walk to the next base. So far in life, I risk having an avalanche that will block my path forever.

I think back over the last 5 years, and recall the choices I made. I had to pick the 2nd or 3rd choice at times, I could not always get to take the top pick. Things keep getting in the way and sending me on a detour. It seems like I am facing another multiple avalanche risk.

There are things that are testing the limits of my abilities, as a High School teacher would. I see this over and over in the past. It seems that by now, the road should be straight and narrow, instead of potholes, bridge washouts, and earthquakes of life.

I find myself on the road again, alone, up against odds that I never expected. My life partner isn't along with Me now. I doubt at times that I am making the right choices. I need an easier road in life.

I cannot seem to find the correct path, of the many choices presented before me. I want to have a calmer life, but I never see it. I get multiple things thrown at me. I feel like I am sitting on the dunk tank chair. At times I feel like I am not in control. Problems in life, constantly test my inabilities and disabilities.

When do I get another, free pass. I see the, Go directly to Jail, Do not pass Go, Do not collect $200. I see this too many times. I need an equal amounts of the skip forward 7 spaces and get an easier life path to walk.

In the last month, I have faced an orchestra of Crickets. Each one playing a different tune. I can't get them on the same channel. I then face a destruction of Panthers, each one cloaked in black, as they circle to get the advantage. I can't hear or see them. When I see them, their eyes are partly open with a piercing, glaring, small waxing slit that looks like a new moon. I am constantly being tailed as I go forward. Where is my timeout ?, I never get one of these.

Issues in life keep building, as tall as a skyscraper. This will not end, until I find a solution or reach the breaking point. At times, my trail is filled with a quiver of Cobras. At times all I hear are people that don't help. they crack jokes like a cackle of Hyenas. They enjoy getting in the way like a prickle of porcupines. Jabbing and jabbing, never thinking that they are as worthless as a screen door on a submarine.

I try to step lightly, but they come rumbling down like a crash of Rhinoceroses trying to trip me up as a stench of Skunks would do. They follow me around like a shadow of Jaguars. always nipping at my heals. I am pushed forward to my limits. If I get too fast, I could derail, and get run over by a parade of Elephants.

I have to focus as I am facing a new world alone, and with the unkindness of Ravens. They become as demons and attack as a ambush of Tigers. They scream there orders at me, trying to lead me astray. They bellow so loud that it makes the walls of Hell vibrate. Then the choir of Sinners howl as a two twelve packs of wolves. I am stalled.

Too many things are confusing my choices and my options. I decide to jump and run like a leap of leopards. I am looking for a place where I can catch my breath, before it evaporates away. Run, run, run, the pressures in life are beginning to shake the world around me.

The questions keep popping up in my mind. Did I do the right things ?, Did I take the best choice ?, Am I still focused enough to find the answers that I need. Or will the next crisis spin my world around as fast as a roulette wheel, that I will not see correctly. What will reset the axis of my world. I am facing new issues, and still wrestling with the past. I can't escape this. I feel there is a gross of broken egg shells beneath my feet.

The path is being buffeted by the howling winds and it's as cold as a well digger's knee. One thing after another, like the Lemmings Marching off the cliff in January. I have to kick my shoes off and rely on my internal soul. I have to keep the fingerprints of Satan off my stained glass windows.

I have to let light in and avoid becoming a heavy black hole, where everything is sucked in and never see the light of day. I need a new plan to stay on my path, ahead of the storm. I have to extend my hand for help and to give it as well.

This way, the many old and new troubles I face, will not be piled up so high, that they create their own Avalanche.

Chapter 94

Phone Calls - 2/13/19

When I grew up, life was like a prison camp. We could not have friends over to the House. Other Days, we could not leave the yard. We had to play with our neighbor kids, with a fence between us.

Year after year, sibling after sibling, it's the same old thing. The Prison Drunk seeing how many beers he can drink, and how many packs of weeds, can he smoke in the nightly event. As for my mother, the Warden, she left us at home with the drunk, while she enjoyed a nightly coffee binge with her sisters and Mother. The Warden was not concerned as what the drunk was doing with the kids.

This went on year after year, also the brothers were getting older and wanted a new hobby. They started to show an interest in girls. They had all types of girls and since they were all older than me, they started dating. But the Golden Rule was not to be broken, don't bring them home. But this did not stop the Warden from meddling into their affairs. She would call up the girl's relatives and used this as a way to keep track of my brothers. My mother had her own version of being a spy.

If The Warden saw girls that she had issues with, she worked with others, to get rid of the relationship that involved one of her Inmates. She wanted control over everything. If any one, including girls that were dating sons, were not to her standards, she split them up. It was her way or No way. It made no difference as what level the relationship was in.

I saw this in brother after brother. What did they do that tripped them up ? This was hard to find the answer, until I remembered what she did during the times we were at school. She searched the bedrooms and at times stole thing from her own children. I recalled the watch that she had of mine, I called her out about this and she threw it at me. I then remembered a few phone calls that she had with others. She talked about the same things that the brothers were talking about the night before. The Warden was having coffee with her mother, while the older brothers had their chat. The prison drunk was too pickled to put the jar up against the wall to listen to my brothers.

The next day, I always was the first one back from school. The Warden was on the phone repeating the same information I overheard the day before. Then I knew she raided their room, and saw notes and phone numbers. Another way, of the 50 ways, to not trust your parents. I started young to write messages and information in code. I had a steel box that I had a lock on it. I hid items in places where either parent would not find. I liked the space behind the electrical box. My Brothers used the space near the water pump. They sneaked contraband in through the only opening that went to the outside. If the Warden ever found things, she would keep them for herself.

She would set uncountable number of rules and expected us to do them all. As for her, she had no rules. She raided our bedrooms, Raided the Drunk's pockets. She bought beer and brandy as a service for the Drunk, at times she doubled the price. She also had other money making scams, some were against the laws of man. She did not care what she did, as long as she had money for her daily coffee event. So dealing with girls that had interest with any brother, was risky business for the girls. If the girls were not acceptable to her, she would chew them up and spit them out. If the Warden could not get some control over the girls, so She could have her two cents in the relationship, She found a way to break them up, and sent the girls packing. I have seen this a few times.

I studied very carefully as what the Warden was doing, and what mistakes that the brothers had made. I knew that if I wanted to contact girls, I had to do it when nobody else was in the house. The best time was when the Warden went to go pickup the family barfly. She was gone each day for about an hour or so. This proved to be the key to my success in communication with girls.

As a few years passed, it was my chance to try to increase my social circle. So I picked a classmate to call up and talk with her, for about 15 minutes. Nothing too involved, and not too long. I knew she had a boyfriend, My reason for calling was not to replace the one in her relationship. I wanted a friend, and to understand that all girls were not lining up to be new Wardens. My mother was a poor example of being female. If I ever had a sister, She could end up being like the Wicked Witch of the West, from the land of Oz. A Sister also could end up like Nellie Olsen from Little House on the Prairie. What a bad world we would have, if this came true.

The Calls lasted for weeks, Nothing was ever too involved. I saw a better future as this girl made it clear that she was dating another. I understood that, but she did not realize that she was giving me something priceless. A chance that I could see girls in a different way, and then I could dream of a better life for me. I had many issues to solve in my life, so I was not going to rush out and get into any relationship, until I felt the time was right.

But I sensed trouble on the horizon. My mother was getting nosy. She heard gossip from the Co-op Shopping Center. Her Sister worked there and my name came up from somebody that was at the Co-op. My mother started her CIA style investigation other this.

I knew the calls had to come to an end. I did not want my mother to find out who this person was. Even if she got closer in her search, the fact that the Girl had a boyfriend would keep her at bay. It would also keep her from giving the Girl the third degree.

So the stage was set to end the calls. I had to make it so the Girl would think it was her idea to end the calls. I knew what was coming and I realized that it must be. She told me to get lost, over the phone. I enjoyed the times that we did talk. I saw that other females were different and not lining up to be new Wardens.

It would take years before I took another another chance to begin dating. It took a couple of tries, but I finally took the plunge. I did get married and had children.

The Girl on the phone was not the only one that I had spent time talking to. There remember that there were others. I recall when I took another chance. I held her in my arms and kissed her by the water fountain, in the hall. Then another time, the Teacher sent me to the Principal's Office for talking to another girl in class. These events were all part of growing up, and to understand that there could be a girl for me, someday.

The someday did come, and I did something that others said that I would never do, I got married.

But it may never have happened, if the Girl that I called had told me to get lost, at the end of the very first call.

Chapter 95

Headstones - 2/14/19

The headstone is your final statement in life, It also the last thing that you leave behind. It's not your footprint, hand print, or your fingerprint. The headstone is the final mark that you leave, telling others that you lived in this world.

In my study of history of the area and it's past, I started a few years ago to research family names of those who had lived here before. My interest in the headstones and tracking my Wife's family members of the past. Her last name was in 6 different versions.

So I went and visited over 175 cemeteries in a dozen counties around where I live. I take photos of stones and use these to follow family links though the years.

Taking photos of headstones have led to my collection of over 37,000 photos. One afternoon I visited a cemetery and took over 1200 photos. I find names that I have only see before in scripture. The name Dorcas comes to my mind.

My main interest in headstones was tracking my Wife's family members, of the past. Her last name was in 6 different versions. This gets confusing, but after a while, I have it sorted out. Other families have the same thing, there are several versions of their last name too. One letter could differ, other times it could be two. I have seen 2 letters switch in their order, in the name. This is what I found in my Wife's family.

I have seen about a dozen names where the person was born before 1799. Some born before George Washington became president. I take photos of every stone that have a date that is before 1900. I do take photos of the people I know, even if they were born after 1900. Since I was on a history mission, Every one before 1900 is needed.

I even have seen where my name was on a headstone, only the middle name differed. In the south east corner, I see the name of my Grandfather. In another location, I see matching names to some of my friends. Seeing one that had my first and last name, made me realize that in the years to come, there will be another. It will have my name on it.

I have walked past headstones worth more that $15,000 in value, other's a few thousand, and some not worth $20. I have also seen places where the headstones are missing. These were at a small pox cemetery, and one for diphtheria. Entire families died of the same disease, The children were the first that died, and they have the headstones there. As more members are lost, there is nobody left to place a headstone for them. But those without headstones, can be found anywhere.

I have seen an aircraft carrier etched on one, This was a Navy Vet headstone and he was assigned to the actual carrier. Other headstones look like a pulpit with an open bible. Other ones look like tree stumps, with tools of the craftsman that passed. Some look like chairs, but not the ones that you should sit on. Others have a bench made for people to use, their names are etched in the back of the stone bench. Some stones look as smooth as glass.

Other stones have a picture of their farms etched on them. Others have the tools of their trade, like trucks, tractors, and cars. Others have their favorite pet etched on their stone. Many have a symbol of their employment. Others have their military rank and name molded into a metal plate.

You can find headstones that have family photos attached to them, the people also have their names etched on as well.

I have walked past headstones of the names of babies, with their young mother nearby. I seen 4 family members lined up in a row. All died in the same tragic event. I have seen this more than once.

Headstones all lined up like a division of the Army. Many days, I came back with over 1,000 photos. It takes me about 3 hours to go past that many headstones. To keep from repeating the rows and rows of headstones, I use my hat as a marker. I drop it at the start of the rows that I have walked past Then I move it to the next spot 2 rows away. by doing this, I don't repeat taking the same photos over.

I saw the sports figures of the area, I was at the time and place where some of them lost their lives. I see sports figures that had their name in the local newspapers, year after year. I also find the people that helped build my hometown from a camp in the woods, to a full sized city. The names on the stones can match the known locations around the city today.

Memories from my school days come back to me, as I walk through some places. I see the names of the Teacher that I had decades before. Some from Elementary school through College.

I have walked by family members of a billionaire, many more of those who were millionaires, the middle class family members, and the poor. The Rich and the Poor can be side by side, the same as Blacks and Whites.

Cemetery locations are made to be a place that keeps those waiting for the judgement dayFor the Lord will come and descend from heaven with a shout, with the voice of an archangel, and with the sound of the trumpet, of God. And the dead in Christ will rise first. To be forever with the Lord. Cemeteries are holy places.

Some use cemetery roads as their personal area to learn how to drive. They think this is a save place. I happen to know that it not true. An inexperienced driver could easily misjudge a turn here. Their ton and a half car then would meet up with a two ton stone. I know that the car will be damaged more that the stone. Running over a stone will empty your pocketbook. Cemeteries should not be the place to start out learning to drive, but could be used to fine tune your driving skills. Precision driving is needed at many of these places.

Then I see the disasters that happen in the cemeteries. Teens and young adults come to these placed and knock over the headstones. They break some in pieces, other stones they use spray paint to deface the stone. Others break the flower pots, steal the mementos left behind,

What you do to others, may end up happening to you. In the future, your headstone could be ruined, just like you have ruined the headstones of others.

People misuse the Cemetery, they dump trash there. They have beer parties, some use drugs here. Others shoot off fireworks and this stains the headstones. These places are not playgrounds, but a place to respect the dead. These are not Lover's Lane locations or a drug users party area. Your sins will find you out.

I have found where early stones, these have dates mostly before 1850, have the names and dates mostly eroded away. The rock used to make these is not the type used today. Others are found cracked in half. When wet, they freeze and thaw over and over, This causes major cracks to happen over time. Some of these get replaced later, but others do not. Pollution can cause this as well as 150 years of natures erosion.

These locations should be peaceful and calming to the living. I don't always see that at every location that I have visited. Don't disrespect a cemetery, someday you will also reside here.

If you want to do what I do, be sure your shoes are sturdy. Some places have a steep slope to them, others have gravel in spots, even other places have soft wet ground locations. Avoid cemeteries after a rain or snow event. You could slip and hit your head on a stone, this will do more than mess up your hair. Other places have exposed water lines that you could trip over.

Safety should be the number one thing on your mind, and find a way not to get lost in the larger locations. Look at the shadows, position of the sun, or use a marker system like I used. Some places have rows numbered, or sections lettered.

I have even found headstones without a name at all. And it's a relative from my Wife's side of the family. All that it etched on the surface is "My Mother" Feb 23, 1844 - Dec 25, 1915. Through research, Her birth name was Maria, some called her Mary.

Chapter 96

Mount Vesuvius - 2/15/19

As I get older, life should have been like others that I know. After the children had grown, they should have left the nest and start a life on their own. But my life is never like others. The youngest moves from the house first, the oldest child stays at home instead. I had to deal with the death of a child in the past, so there should be three children, but only two grew up in the home.

Life should have been, two married adults living out their golden years together. But I never saw a life like that. My wife was placed in a nursing home and then in an assisted living location. She was out of the house before turning 65. A few years later, she has a stroke and 11 days later, she passes away. So there was no Golden years for Her and I.

While she was in the assisted living location, Or Daughter was out living on her own. She moved out when she was 18, and shared an apartment with her co-workers. They saved money this way. Time passes and she moves to a few more places and now is engaged for the 2nd time. She needs to stop playing the field and settle down. When this will happen, I don't know. But she is not the one that caused her first engagement to end.

The problem I have is with the remaining child. This one has lived at home since the day he was born. We did not have many problems with this, until a couple of years ago. He quit one Job out of the blue, and was let go from another. This is where things shift and creates issues.

He and I were living in the house for the years that my Wife left to be in nursing home and at assisted living locations. As time went on, he became more difficult to live with. Others have asked over and over, How do I put up with him. He causes damage to the home, increases utility costs in several ways, this waste could have been prevented. But since he has no income to help, he does not care.

Things at times get worse. It usually is caused by him doing further damage to the house. He breaks windows, damages bedroom doors, Leaves water running in kitchen and bathroom and leaves it on for hours. Other wonder why the water bill is so high, I do know the answer. A few other utilities are much higher that they should be. I always had enough money to pay them all. But live changes.

My Wife of 37 years, dies. Her income is now gone. I am the only one living in the house with an income. And it may not be enough to survive at the location I am living. I just don't know yet. It may take a few months to understand what I will get as income and what the total cost is, to remain living here.

Her funeral expenses was around $5,000, Funeral assistance from the Government is capped at $2,500. I don't know if I will get the full amount, or be a few hundred short. Time will tell. So I need to cut back on expenses. But my Son still causes the utilities to be higher than they need to be. He was told to stop being wasteful, but does not listen. Also by damaging items around the house, my costs are higher.

So I have to cut spending and limit what I do. I can't control his rage, as again and again he slams his fist into the wall in his bedroom, hits his bedroom door, and more. Now he is hitting new targets. I just don't know what they are, until something goes wrong around the house. Well it happened.

I was working on my computer while watching TV, I am getting cold. I thing it's because it's 19 degrees outside with the wind blowing. Because he keeps damaging the house, a few places now are drafty. after an hour or so, I go and investigate. Maybe he has a window open, or he broke another one by slamming his fist through it.

My investigation found no new problems with the windows, But I found out the the Temperature in the house was a bit under 55 degrees. The furnace had shut off. Why did it ?, I found the pilot still lit. I checked the thermostat and it was set for 68. Then I saw the damage. He had slammed his fist into the door, that the furnace is behind. He busted the paneling that the door was made of, and the top section became detached. The door was pushed back so far that it contacted the Steel cabinet of the furnace.

I started to test the unit. I got the fan to run and the pilot was lit. Still failed to turn on. So I went to look at the thermostat. I saw that the spring and contacts were out of alignment and the switch was not properly closing. This is why the furnace would not turn on. He must have slammed his fist into the wall near the thermostat, or he hit the temperature control unit. It's been more than an hour since I discovered this, the temperature inside the house is now 62 degrees.

He was in the bathroom while I discovered the damage he caused. When he came out and headed back to his room, I told him to stop hitting the walls and door. He denies that he did anything. This is when I show him the broken door to the furnace. I also tell him that the furnace was off due to his damage. He does not want to discuss this issue. He goes into his room and shuts the door. Normally I would walk away. Days later he plays with the temperature gauge and turns the heat in house down to 53 degrees. Doing this is affecting my health and risks freezing the water pipes in the house.

This time I push his door open and tell him to stop breaking the house, he caused the furnace to turn off. He is mad and begins to shout, his face turns red, He screams at me. I scream back and tell him he has to quit damaging the house, or move somewhere else. He spouts off more, He then storms out of the house, says he wants to make a phone call. He again bitches as why the phone in the house does not work. I told him he caused problems by calling Law Enforcement places and complaining that he was being followed.

Turning off the phone ended this problem for a long time, until now. He is leaving the house and going to a place that has a payphone. Now this is where he is now making calls. His anger issues are going to cause him more problems that he can imagine. It could end up being dealt with by Law enforcement.

If He does not stop acting like Mount Vesuvius, He will have an eruption that the Police would need to be called. His anger issues, destructive life style, and the Police, will cause him to blow his top, just like Vesuvius did. In the real volcano event, destruction was complete. If He goes off too many times, the destruction of his world will happen. He is playing around with matches, with dozens of fuses close by.

This version of Mount Vesuvius must be capped, if it goes off, He may end up destroying his world, and possibly, Himself.

I have tried several times to get help with this issue, the doors to a solution slam shut, time and time again. I just do not have enough evidence, or I have not found the right door.

This wild volcano needs to cool off, or sometime in the future, He will blow his top right into confinement.

Chapter 97

Silence - 2/16/19

On the first of the year, my Wife had a stroke. Every day I went to the hospital and was with her. She never spoke a word to Me or anyone else. She had movement in 3 limbs, her left are had no movement at all.

She squeezed the Nurses hand to answer questions. This was primitive but it worked, it also showed that she could hear things around her. I do not know if her vision was clear, all I knew that she could see. Nothing else stood out as a major problem.

This went on for a week. Then she suffered a second major setback. She had a seizure, she had these for the last 45 years. But because of the stroke, this one caused damage and affected her breathing to a point.

Now that the body lost more of its ability to sustain to keep all of the systems working. The Medical staff suggested that a feeding device and a way to have her breath better, be installed. I told them to see what was in her medical files.

After they did, they said that they can't add the devises. So she needs to transferred out of ICU, and be sent to Hospice.

On Her 3rd day in Hospice, today is now Saturday, January 12. I wake up at home, get dressed and check my Email. I find out that 2 of our relatives are in Pine Valley at a restaurant. We set the time to meet at Riverside Hospital.

I am out in the hospital foyer as the 2 show up. I lead them to the correct elevator and the 3 of us, go up to the 6th floor, Hospice area. We all arrive at Her room. My Wife, Rayne, is who they come to visit.

I am there with Rayne, my wife. Our Daughter is there with her fiance. Her younger Sister is now there with her youngest Daughter, Rayne's niece. We talk about Rayne's medical issues and she was not expected to last more than a day, after they transferred her to Hospice.

But on the 3rd day, she still is alive. I tell the crew that she can hear, but I don't know how good her vision is. We spend more than a hour reminiscing about the past and the good times. We also bring up her brother, that passed away 4 years before.

We also talk about the sister's Mother, she could not make the trip. It would be too long of a trip, She will be 95 on this coming Friday. We chat about our Daughter's Birthday, it is today, the 12th. The conversation goes on for over an hour or two.

It is around 4 pm. I still am listening to Rayne, as she inhales and exhales. I can hear it because I am next to her side. The other 4 are on the foot board end, sitting in a line against the wall. Conversation is sharing the many good times that we had over the years, at Ma Tater's Place. This was the name used for Rayne's Mother's place.

While the chatter continues, I am becoming aware of the changing sound pattern of her breathing. I can't hear her inhale. She is making the sound of Silence. I look and see no movements at all. I look at the clock on the wall, it's 4:16 pm. I finally realize that she has stopped breathing. I wait for a minute and realize that her end has come. Meanwhile the other 4 are still talking and sharing memories.

I call out my Daughter's name. I tell her Fiance to hold her hand. He also has his arm around her. Every one else stops talking, I look right at her. I tell my Daughter, your Mother has passed away. Then I quickly push the button for the Nurse, They need to know that Rayne's breathing has changed.

My Daughter bursts out in tears, This is the hardest thing I had to do in years. Lucky that her intended was along to comfort her. The look on her face when I told her, is something that I never want to have to do again. She lost a part of her and I can't replace it. Seconds later, the RN comes in. I point to My Wife, and then point to my chest.

The Nurse takes her stethoscope and uses it to hear my wife's heart. She has a second Nurse come in and do the same test. They have a short conference, and announce that I was right, She has passed away. My Daughter was looking for a chance that I was wrong. I, in a way, wanted that too. But it was written down, passed away at 4:20, this is after the two Nurses confirmed the facts.

Her Sister and Niece had tears in their eyes, But my Daughter reacted to the loss more than anyone. Her Fiance held her tight and helped my Daughter with her grief. After some time had gone by, Her Sister and Niece had to head home, this was 2 counties way. Then later, My Daughter was taken home by here Fiance. I was alone with my Wife for the last time ever.

It would be a rough road for me ahead. Our marriage was over, it lasted 37 years. Rayne went to meet Her Maker, and our Son that passed away over 27 years ago. It was now time for the staff to do their jobs. It was time for me to leave, it will be busy days ahead for Me. I look at her, one last time as I leave the room. Now the Room has Silence.

Chapter 98

Schlegelmilch House - 2/17/19

My look into the past people that lived in this area, took me on more than 100 trips to walk among the past rows of the names etched in stone. I now wanted to see a different angle to the lives of the past residents of Pine Valley. I was thinking about this for some time. I saw an article about an open house that was being given by the local Museum, that was guarded by Paul Bunyan and his blue Ox. I heard that this place had several generations of a family that lived here. It came with original items and other items that were around, over 100 years ago. This peaked my interest. I had to go see it. But before it was over, I never imagined what I would find and how I made the discovery. I got up on 10/6/18, got ready and I packed up my freshly recharged camera, and I was on my way.

Arriving there, I found a spot in the parking lot. I looked at the old 1871 Red Brick structure, was this an omen or nothing to it at all. I grew up in a red brick house. But, this style of house was the second popular kind, after Wood. I walk from my car and head up to the back door. the grass in the yard is tattered and splattered with dirt patches. there is a few bushes and different trees. I see the 2 chimneys and the back porch is uneven. There is even a old fashion locked cellar door, from the outside. There is a sitting bench next to the covered wrap around porch. The yellow paint stands out against the weathered bricks. I then approach the back door to read the posted sign. There is two steps to get to the door, marked 517. The porch is also built on bricks, large floral displays in several locations around the house. These must have kept the bees busy for weeks. I begin my adventure by going to the back door, and walking left on the porch, this takes me to the south side of the house.

I see an old style watering can for the plants. I see the cracks on the concrete floor of the porch. Age wrinkles people and creates crooked concrete lines. There are round yellow columns that support the roof. I am on the south side and the front door. A volunteer worker has me sign a visitor book and tells me a few details of this 1871 residence. I then enter the Front door to the House. I am stepping back to a time of 100 years ago, as I step on the red carpet runners.

The first thing I see is a Pine Valley Leader Carrier Boys 1907 calendar. I see the old Coat rack, a pocket door that can slide out of wall. Wood trim is found everywhere. In the foyer is a steam radiator and set of steps going upstairs, that passes an old table. Antique photos on the walls. Every room is furnished as it was during the time period of the families, that lived here. I enter the room on my right.

I see an Antique Chair, Old fireplace with cast iron parts, Photographs on the tables and walls. I have stepped back in time. These are period pieces. I see a matching set of furniture, and hot water heaters. I then see a handcrafted item it the corner, It is a windup phonograph. This house had no electricity for years, a thick dark patterned carpet, is hugging the floor to keep the room warm. Another table is in the room. On this table is a chart showing the Family Tree of generations of family members that lived here. The birth dates to the people and when they lived here is found. I then realize that this name is also found in my family tree. I could be related to this very family. I am walking through an ancestors house. On the wall is another family tree chart with photos. This chart has 20 people that cover 4 generations of those that lived here. Herman has the oldest birth year of 1830. Augusta, his wife was born in 1832. There is also parts of a diary, and a photo of their downtown building.

There is a piano here, a windup mantel clock, and candles. The fireplace has hand carved woodwork, and hand knitted doilies. The 78 rpm record in the phonograph is Christmas Hymns and Carols, dated September 22,1903. The ceiling lights were gas lamps converted to electricity. The electrical outlets in the room are on the floor, next to the wall, as these were added later. I leave this room and go back through the foyer.

I am now in a dining room, with a center table and 8 wood chairs. I see antique plates on all 4 of the walls, a chest of drawers near the entry, a dark patterned rug, pictures on wall, and stained wood mini shelf along the walls. A dividing curtain is at the point of entry. The baseboards are wide and match the trim along the wall. In a corner is a table with a small glass bowl on top, filled with replica fruit to look like it would 100 years ago. Some of the plates are with a vivid blue design. Another has pictures of Men of the Civil War. On top of the drawer cabinet is silver items, a cake knife & serving trays, also a candlestick from the era. The wind up clock in this room has it's face trimmed in the color of gold, hand painted on the dark wood. In the corner sits a rotary dial phone, this was the type that the last residents may have used. On the wall is a 1906 calendar, this has the family business name on it, as well as the 121 S River Street address in Pine Valley. There is also a push button wall switch. this would be the kind that was installed when electricity was added to the house. I leave and go back into the foyer, then go back in same room where I was, I want to leave through the shortcut to the kitchen.

I enter short hallway, there is a handcrafted china cabinet. It is filled with fine china and glassware of the era. I then step into the kitchen.

I see the Icebox, This is the refrigerator of the time. An Iceman comes with blocks of ice that keeps the foods cold. Next to it is the wood/coal kitchen stove, with the stove pipe rising up to enter the chimney. There is cast iron cookware and a teapot on the stove. There is a weight scale nearby. I then see another telephone. This one is the first type that some homes had. This was made of wood, had mouthpiece attached. The ear piece was on a cord, and it had the 2 black bells that signaled an incoming call. You had to crank the handle to get an operator to connect you to another line. There is a 31 day, wind up clock on the wall. You wound it up once a day and and it would show you the time and the day of the month. There was a small staircase leading from the kitchen to the second floor. The kitchen had many cooking tools of the day. There was a sink in a room next to the kitchen, a baby wooden highchair was also there. As I was leaving kitchen, I saw a sign in the window. This told the Iceman how much Ice you needed when he shows up. The numbers were 0, 25, 50, and 75 pounds of Ice needed. I left through the short hall, back into dining room, and then in the foyer.

My next interest is the steps, and the hand carvings done to the wood. So I go up 12 steps of the first section. On the top is space for a roll top desk and chair, a antique book stand is near. I turn and climb up the last 6 steps to the second floor. I notice that the end cap of the railing has cracked, over 125 winters of heating has taken a toll. There is a chair next to the top of the steps. A old style rug and old photos on the walls of the hallway. All of the rooms have hardwood flooring. I enter the first room on my right. It's the master bedroom with a few surprises. I enter and see the dresser with a large mirror, with an antique padded chair. In front of the window is a table, with flower vase. On the right, is the horizontal traditional cast-iron style radiator. To the left of window is an antique baby crib. Behind me is a large wood cabinet, inside is a wood bathtub with a metal liner. You open it up by pulling the hinged section to the floor. Hot water was brought into room to fill it when needed. The next half of the room had a chair next to right of the bed, with unique wooden head and foot board. There are handmade stuffed small cat pillows acting as they are sleeping against the bed pillows. To the left is another chair, and a night stand, with a towel bar. On it is a white china bowl and water pitcher. There are also dental care items and a family photo. On the floor and in the corner is a chamber pot. These were used before the advent of indoor plumbing. The wallpaper has a rose floral pattern. As I start to leave, I stand in front of the dresser with mirror. I see a pair of metal framed glasses, a starched shirt collar, a hand mirror and items for her hair care. another floral wallpaper used here. A few small rugs were used in the master bedroom. It's back in the hall and on to another room.

I enter next room at my right, this is room 2 out of 4. There is a few chairs, a display cabinet, and in the center of the room is an foot pedal powered Domestic brand sewing machine. To the right is a small storage space. Toward the floor is a wooden door, when opened, has a large secure combination safe behind it. This is where important documents were placed. Back into the hallway again.

Now to enter the 3rd room, it's the next one on the right. This is another bedroom, with a hand made rug next to the bed. There is a chair in all 4 corners of this room. This antique bed has a colorful sewn quilt. There is a nightstand and a metal wheel baby carriage here, with a homemade Doll inside. This room is designed for a child. It has one piece of unique furniture here. The dresser has a hidden compartment, that was made to hide jewelry or collectibles. On top of the dresser is a handmade doll, and a metal child's pull toy. There is a small clock here too. A pair of chamber pots are also in this room. Then I see a child sized kitchen cabinet with many metal toys, and doll house items inside. Next to that is a child's desk and wood rocking chair. This room has a child's walk in closet with a chest of drawers and hooks on the wall for clothes. a Coo Coo Clock is here and a cross stitched framed alphabet with upper and lowercase letters. Another floral wallpaper is also used in this room. Time to look at the next room.

Back into the hall. I turn to my right and see the upper end of the narrow staircase that goes down to the kitchen. To the right of that is a small hall leading to the 4th room. This is closed because it is used as an office space for the Museum that operates this house. across the narrow hall is another closed door. This leads up to the attic, there is nothing there now. it was used in the past as a storage space, and a small study space next to the upper window of the house. I look out the window at the end of the hall, I look north out at the Downtown of Pine Valley. I see where the green leaves are starting to turn a bit yellow. Last room upstairs is the bathroom. This was added later to the house. It has a modern toilet an old fashioned 4 footed bathtub. A sink is there with a shelf area above it, to store daily used items. Now it's on to the 4th bedroom, this could be a guest bedroom.

This is the last room. It has a mirrored chest of drawers with personal grooming items, 1 bed with a small wooded baby crib on the floor, at the foot of the bed. There is several chairs and a wooden folding privacy divider. There are several chairs and a nightstand. Next to the stand is two chamber pots. On the stand is a wash basin and water pitcher, as well as a windup alarm clock. There is another nightstand next to the bed with a flower vase on it. old style carpet is in the room. More photos adorn the walls, as well as a diploma written in German. Its now time to go downstairs.

At the bottom of the steps, I see the only room that I did not visit yet. I glance inside and see a foot pump organ. This could have been a sitting room, a place to have music and relax. This room has push button light switches and a Large photo on the wall that shows 4 women in the dresses of the time. There is a sofa here and several chairs. A table with the timeline poster that shows the who and when they lived in this house. The chart shows the Original 6 residents when the house was built in 1871. Two years later, the first child in born in the house. There is photos of the Early family and of the house. It covers the 4 generations. There are several tables with historical photos on them. I walk around this room and turn around to leave. Then it happens.

My body is in pain, as I feel as if I am encased in Ice. I start to shiver, pain goes up and down my back. I try to take a step forward, I can't. I am frozen in place. I only had this feeling before when I am walking through a few cemeteries, in this area. Something is trying to tell me something, what is it. I am still unable to walk. my legs increase in pain. It is like I am nailed to the floor. My breathing rate shifts. My hands are cold. The hair on my neck reacts. I turn my head and look around the room, I see nothing that triggers my mind to understand why I am reacting. Then my legs shift and become hot. I even have to check my own pulse. My heart is picking up speed. The cold on my back stops, but my legs are as hot as a branding iron. I am in pain, My feet heat up, and then I glance down. Then I get chills all over, the heat is gone. My guardian angel may have done this so that I would look down. I finally see the item that I remember over 60 years ago. I can't quit believe what I am seeing. I have not seen an item like this in over 50 years. It's the rug that I am standing on. It's an exact duplicate from the House of Hell. It's the same as the one that was in the house where I grew up. I still can't move, until I decide that I must take a closer look at it. Is it the same rug ?, My curiosity is as aware as a basket full of kittens. I have to know. Dozens of bad memories flood my mind. I see a scan of decades in a matter of minutes. I have to know the truth. My body then relaxes and I want to inspect the corners of the rug. My father was drunk night after night and at times, dropped a lit cigarette on the floor, and at times, on the carpet. If this was the rug, the burn marks would cause stains and an uneven pile of the rug. I lift up 2 opposing corners and look for missing parts of the rug surface and burn marks. I turn over the corners to find repairs to the rug and burnt edges. I breath a sigh of relief. This is not the exact Rug, But it is a duplicate rug. I walk around on the rug slowly, I still can't believe that a copy of the rug, from the House of Hell, still exists. I took my camera and took photos. Later I would compare the photos of this rug and the rug in photo from the living room of the house I grew up in. I found a match, it was the exact model of the rug. This affected my body for several minutes. I seen enough of the past to make a mini series. Now I new it was time to leave this house museum. The clock on the wall told me that the visiting time was ending.

I left the house from the same door as I entered, Looked outside and saw the leaves in many shades of green. This time I walked back to my vehicle by using the sidewalk. I got to see a better view of this side of the house. I saw the large round flowers, the small berries in the trees. The leaves were rustling around along the curb.

I got more than I bargained for. I got to see a house built in 1871, and a personal history lesson of my own. While I was writing this chapter, and came to describe how I felt on the carpet, a chill came down my back, and my legs reacted. This was more than a one in a million event, I even remembered that a fellow high school graduate of mine, was also in the house when my event occurred. I wonder how much she remembers of it.

She was the first fellow high school graduate, that showed up at the visitation and gave me a hug, to help me deal with my loss of my Wife. This was before Rayne's Funeral. Her name is the first one entered in the guest book. My guardian angel was working overtime. The past was shown to me, that someone that was in the museum when I was, would be tied into an event, just a few months later. What are the odds with linking a Rug and a Hug ?

Chapter 99

Last Mile - 2/18/19

I have been on my narrow path for over 6 decades, I passed through a valley of events. Some were planned by me and others were not planned. Some people constantly are coming down a rocky path, mile after mile. I am one of these that encounter this.

I have now passed another major change in life, and I am entering the Last Mile. I am on the path alone, I never wanted it to be like this. But I am not the one in control. I am an active participant, but not in the driver's seat. I have passed a mile marker in life that I never expected.

Now, what can I do or expect. I see life as it was, fade into the background. Gone are the dreams of walking the path, side by side. I can't stop the forward movement of time. I never expected my children to repeat the things that I encountered in life. The big difference is that I did not have a choice as to the outcome of many events in my life. My children did have a choice. But they are heading down the path and repeating things that I have done. I had nothing to do with their choices, unlike my mother, who acted like a dictator at times.

I copied my Grandfather by chance, both wives were older than their Husbands. I now see that my Daughter is on this same trail, if things go as they planned it. She will marry a man that is younger than herself. It will make it the 3rd set in 4 generations, within my family tree. I never saw this coming as the man she is planning to marry, isn't her first that she planned to marry. In my case, I married the first one that I was engaged with. Both children have had an engagement that ended, I have to pass it off as the way the world is today.

On another front. I was not allowed to be at one of my parent's funeral. It was not my choice. I was told at the funeral home, to leave or I would be arrested. Now I see that one of my children, did not attend his Mother's funeral. He was told of impending events and had many days to plan to attend. But He had a free choice as what he would do. His choice was to stay home. I did not want any child to miss the event, it was a once in a lifetime event, as you only have one Mother. He made his choice and did not show up. This now has happened in 2 generations in a row. He also missed the Grandparent funeral, as my entire family had to leave the first one.

I have walked the distance in my life that passed over the halfway mark years ago. I wanted this never to be repeated, but it was. It was their choice and they took it, without thinking what it would mean to them decades down the road.

I some ways, I see my life beginning to repeat events of the past. After the death of my Wife, I now see many things repeating that I lived through over 40 years ago. But now, it affects more than Me. I am not on my own, Like I was 40 years back.

Many things are the same. I don't have the same things that I had to go without back then. The major difference is now I don't have the dreams of finding a mate, and living a better life that what my parents gave me. All that was completed, now I am in my last mile along the path. I can't turn around or stop. I am going forward into a new uncharted world for me.

I remember having a world that had a promise of a better life. I did manage to find short sections of this along my walk of life. The world offered me chances to have some sunny days, instead of severe storms always clouding up and raining out my chances. I remember my past, so I don't end up repeating it. I keep my children from having to repeat the lifestyle that I had. Many bad things that happen in their lives, were to their own making. I did not want to be another dictator or Warden, like the one that I had to deal with.

I am finding that many doors of opportunity that I saw 50 years ago, are closing one by one. I have accepted it as the facts of life. I find that others have become a hindrance to my walk along the path. I have not changed my address in over 35 years. I now have to make a backup plan, in case I do have to move. I see storm clouds ahead, But I now have an umbrella along. I do have some options now.

I have spent half my life caring for my children. The last several years, I had to do it alone, as my Wife was in a nursing home or assisted living. This was one more step that took many options out of my life. Now that she has passed, I see many options that have fallen by the wayside. I lost others that supported me in the past. I never wanted it this way.

All the I can do, is hope that the others will again, be part of the solution than be part of the problem. If not, I am facing of traveling down the long and winding path alone. I will finish my walk on my path and feel proud that I did the best that I could.

Chapter 100

My Pen and Paper - 2/19/19

I am facing a turning point in my life. I have been through so much in a short time frame, this has happened several times in my life. I again have to take my pen and make the paper speak what I have on my mind. I have so much to say that my pen needs a refill every several miles. I have to make decisions that I do not want to make, but needs to be done. I can not procrastinate too long.

I am given many roads to follow, by the direction of others. But they are not on my path, they are only observers, and observers they shall remain. I can't let them take the reigns of my horse and gallop down the road. I need to travel at my own pace, and I will still get where I am going. This is not easy for me to do. Too many things are stressful and need precise answers, and not a hurried decision. No two lives are the same, and there is no single universal answer. I can't be like the turtle, He won the race with the hare, but it took too long.

My decisions need to be made in a timely manner, without rushing and knocking the apple cart over. This does not solve my problem, it will only delay the final answer. Too many people are pushy in society, they think that they have all the answers to anything, they want to be the new Social Adviser to the world. I am heading into making major changes in my life, in the next weeks, months, or years in future. I don't want to have to make a choice in a hurry, and then regret the choice.

People should understand that I want their opinions, and then let me make my own choice. This is the best way for me to deal with a problem. I research facts about the issues that I face, I want an informed decision. But those around me want me to do the things that they recommend, sometimes they insist. They are forgetting that they have not lived my life, they have lived their own. Yes they may have a solution that can work. But some don't explain everything that lead to them finding their solution, to their problem. So how can I work their solution into the problem, that I am encountering.

Since I can't use my pen and write the problem and answer choices in my mind. I have to use My Pen and Paper to write down what my eyes have seen, so I don't forget what I have seen and heard.

Chapter 101

Snow Days - 2/20/19

Growing up in the northern half of the country, winter was a part of life and some white fluff called snow. Snow was part of late fall, winter and spring. I can recall going to the stock car races on May 2nd, and before the races ended, it snowed. I recall many times that it snowed on Halloween. This was normal in an area that had the 4 distinctive seasons.

I remember the times many times going to elementary school, and having to deal with snow. Getting there was not easy as there was no sidewalks between my school and where I lived. I had to take a shortcut though a neighbor's farm. This presented many of the issues that farmers deal with everyday. The dirt roads, fences, and getting around the many obstacles found around the farm fields. But when heavy snowfall occurred, I had to walk, over half of the way, along the side of a highway, to get to school.

I recall a time that there was extreme cold that came after a snowfall. This is the only time that I can remember that my mother actually drove us to school. She got the car started with a hand crank. This was used on our 1932, Model A. This 2 door car, also had a rumble seat. I remember this day, as the car made it's way to the school. When we arrived, my mother was informed that there was a problem with the school's heating system, so there was no school that day. It became another snow day and no school for me. My mother was not happy at all, we were going to be home all day. She had other plans that did not include kids, she had to change her plans and stay home. It was the place to be, instead of running around in a very cold day.

On some snow days, my brothers and I walked across the highway and went skating on a man made pond. the water was not even 2 feet deep. This was caused by the city flushing out the fire hydrants in the area. This had to be done many times a year, as there was a hospital not far away. So we had our own little private rink. There was enough space for a half dozen kids, so simple versions of hockey and other games could be played.

The biggest problem that we faced was getting the snow off of the driveway. I recall in the early years living at our location along the highway, our original driveway was about 25 feet long. After the new 4 lane highway was put through our property, and the original highway was expanded to 6 lanes, Or driveway was changed and now was about 250 long. This was a major issue for me, as a few of my brothers had graduated high school and left home. So to get to work on time, after a snowfall, my father would take a shortcut. He would drive to the edge of the highway, and run over the curb to get on the 6 lane divided highway. This only works if he wanted to drive to the east. This was not a fun time for me. The only advantage that I had, was riding a school bus to get to school. I lived just far enough from Lincoln High School, that I qualified to get a bus ride.

I was the last one that got on the school bus, on the corner of the intersection. I also was the earliest to get off of the bus on the way home. I lived on a major intersection, so I got a ride from the first bus that came past the house. It could be bus number 5, 6, or number 7. Almost all of the time, it was bus 6. All three of these buses picked up the school kids, from out in the farming areas south of town. I got to meet and know more kids this way, than other kids that lived within the city of Pine Valley. Rare times, I also rode buses numbered 2, and 4. Bus 2, was the bus that dropped off the Candy Stripers that went to the Riverside Hospital. Candy Stripers were hospital volunteers, they work without regular pay in health care settings, and are under supervision of nurses. I rarely rode bus 2, but is was there in case I needed it. This meant that I could get a school snow day, only when the school buses were cancelled that day. Even if the actual school did not close, when they shut down the school buses, I had the day off.

Having the day out of school was not all that it was cracked up to be. This meant that we have to live around the Warden. Our mother was not changing her ways because we were home for the day. We had to spend most of the time in the basement doing what we were interested it. She did not want us in the living room disturbing her time to watch her shows on television, as well as her time jabbering on the phone. This was her, no man's land, we were not to be heard or seen during this time. On the warmer snow days, we went outside and made snowmen, igloo forts, or play in the shed that was in the back yard. Running around the pine trees on the property, was not the thing to do, or we would end up looking like a snowman. This was due to the snow falling off of the branches. Some of these trees were well over 20 feet in height. After a snowfall, was the only times that we avoided playing in the Norway Pine trees.

Being at home on a snow day, was better that the routine at school. Monday was the best day to be snowed in, getting a snow day, and to stay at home. Fridays were the second best day to have off. As kids, we liked the 3 day weekends as well as the working folks.

The worst thing about snow days, was to be sick on that day. We had to be in the bedroom, and not getting around the house. This became like your private cell, and our personal Warden was there as well. After leaving the Warden's Home detention center, I went to live on my own. Snow removal here took me back 100 years, As at this location, I had to shovel a path through the back yard, to the outhouse.

Today, on the 20th of February, we had over 8 inches of snow around the area. This gives me time to stay home and let my fingers do the walking around the keyboard, and type of my memories of the past decades. I truly become a visual storyteller, my words and style helps others know a would that is different to them.

I always find snow days, a time that I can catch up on projects that I need to finish. It also allows me to remember my past as the way it was, enjoying the good an learning from the bad. It's time to get the snow removal started, and getting rid of all that white dandruff, cause by Paul Bunyan shivering out in the cold.

Chapter 102

King Food - 2/21/19

Food is number one thing in some peoples life, it controls them and leads them around town, with their nose on the prowl. They are always looking for their next morsel of food or any crumb they can find. Their nose sniffs out any free samples of pie, pizza, or cookies that they can locate. They eat everything offered to him, even thirds and beyond. It does not matter what the Calorie & fat count is, or that they can play Santa without padding.

They even fail to follow their Doctor's orders. The Doctor gives them information as what they should eat and what to avoid. Taking some medications, restricts the patient from eating certain foods. Written rules to them make a good place mat, Nothing stands in their way, at times they consume an entire pizza. Life becomes a contest, seeing how many servings that they get at a place that offers free meals to the needy. Other times they get money from others and go to a local organization's Friday night fish fry. They eat as much as they can. This Non-profit will not make a penny for their cause, if too many of these dinner plate vacuums show up.

Many of these fossils have government health insurance, they need more Doctor visits and prescriptions than the average person. They really don't care if they are driving up health costs, because someone else is paying for it. Some of these vittles vacuums already had a surgical procedure that costs thousands of dollars, and sent John Q. Public, the bill. They needed that procedure because of their unhealthy lifestyle.

But after they heal, they go back to doing the same unhealthy thing. Food becomes their God, it also can be an addiction. Some donut dunkers, crave sweets, others caffeine, or salty items. They think a 10 ounce bag of chips is a single serving. They chew, chew, chew, like a steam locomotive rumbling down the track

Their day starts out eating a breakfast at home. Then they are off to visit a free 'Soup Kitchen' meal location. This place serves a meal with meat, potato, vegetable, drink, and a dessert. After licking off their plate, they wait around for awhile and go back for seconds. Sometimes they go get thirds. They then take a bus or cab, and arrive at a local fast food place. They sit around sipping their coffee, or large soft drink, bathed in sugar. Sometimes others think that they are hungry, they offer snacks, or an entire meal. Plate cleaners, always accept the offer of a free meal, even if only 2 or 3 hours have passed since their last meal, or two. At times they then buy an ice cream treat or piece of pie, an hour or 2 later. During this polishing the table with their elbows event, they talk about what they will have to eat at their evening meal at home. Having 5 meals a day for them is not rare.

Some days these food inhalers, burp like they are proud of their accomplishment. They burp like a wound up coo coo clock. They could burp on the hour and the half hour, over and over. They can get into patterns, Burp, chew, grunt, chew, and burp again. They are so full of gas, they could fill all the balloons at a child's birthday party

Fried foods is another craving that they have. Fry everything because it tastes so good. They might try to fry anything that comes to their mind, including pickles, cookies, and candy bars. Deep fried turkey is something that they would enjoy. They could stuff the turkey and themselves, all in an afternoon.

Weight scales are something that they avoid. They say that they feel alright and don't need to know. If they can find clothes that will fit them, then it's alright to have a salad, as long as there is plenty of fat filled dressings and crumbled bacon.

When they go out to a full service restaurant, they want a meal, drink, and dessert. Later they recite every food that they ate for the day. They have schedules, as to what place they will eat at. No matter the weather, they will travel many miles to their favorite place to indulge in emptying the plates. Some times they go to their local watering hole, for Bud's Burgers and suds.

When they are ready to go home, some waddle like a duck as they putt putt along to their last meal of the day. At times they smile, because they had it their way. They always can tell a story about every Burp and Slurp, that they chowed down at.

They are tempting fate with their bad habit, as this style of living can make any meal that they eat, the last meal of their life.

Chapter 103

My Dreams - 2/22/19

When I grew up and became a teen. I started to dream what my future would be. I had many things that were wrong within my body. I saw no solution to find a cure or correction for my body. I was a prisoner in more that one way. My future was bleak and I could not be like anyone else in my family. So my life was more of, I can't do that, versus I think I can.

I knew from a very early age that things would be impossible for me, my body held the clues. I knew that there was a chance that I might not live long enough to graduate. The internal pain that I had, was hidden from all others. I did not know exactly what was wrong, all I knew was what parts of my body did not work normally. This limited my lifestyle in the real world.

So My Dreams were limited to the a few years into the future, not more than 3 to 5 years. I saw no future 10 years ahead. I expected that my timeline might be over in less than 7 years. So my dreams were about life that was normal to others but not for me.

I dreamed of graduating High School, I have already seen where some students died before they graduated, and I saw that I could become like those. Since graduation was about 5 years away, it was too long to expect even getting to this event. Over the next few years, I saw my chances improving and I had to shift my dreams a bit more into the future.

I never had a dream before I became a teen, of becoming rich, married, having kids, or being like my Grandfather. But fate has dealt me a strange hand of cards. I many ways, I became like my paternal grandfather more than anyone else in my family tree.

Then I did things that I had no dreams of. I remember going to a Junior High dance. I can't recall why I was allowed to go. There are things in my past that my brain locks out. Like what went on behind the closed door down the hallway. I still can't remember this. My imagination can come up with ideas, but I can't agree or disagree with my thoughts.

Things were very difficult during my Junior year in high school. I did not have a dream of graduating Lincoln High. It would take until the start of my Senior year, that I had a dream of walking down the isle and get my diploma. My dream kept me on my path.

I had several girls in high school that I could talk to, but this was the end of the dream and I saw no future with any of them, due to my medical issues. I still had no answers as what was wrong inside of my body. So my mind refused to dream outside of a future that was within 5 years.

I did dream when I was in grade school, what it would be like, if I was normal as the other kids in class. But this faded away after more than 10 years passed by, and I still had no answers. My dreams were trapped within my mind, and I could not find a key to unlock them. I wanted dreams like the others, but the pain within Me stymied my mind from dreaming outside of the box.

Graduation time came and I was out of High School with a Diploma and still No dream of what my impending world would be. I was out of High School about a month, before others suggested that I get vocational training and use my hobby interest and turn it into a career. So I spent the next 3 years in Technical college and got a 1 year and a 2 year Diploma, I now had 3 diplomas and no dreams of a brighter future.

My award from the 'Warden' after I graduated Tech school, was a simple command. Get out of the house. This begins my Little House on the Prairie days of living. It was like I was taken back through time, and living a life like my Grandfather had. No Phone, No bathroom, & no Car, or even heat in the House. My dreams were only of finding a way to get back to civilization. But my body screams out in pain.

Because I no longer was under the 'warden and her drunk', I took a chance and asked to see a doctor. I recall I had to see a few to find a specialist. Once there, I put my cards on the table and I was on my way to an operation and 5 days in the hospital. I went home and my pain that I shed tears of pain for over 7 years, was gone. My body started to act more normal. it would take another 4 operations, but I got as close to normal as I could get.

This is when My Dreams started to line up as well. The dreams were those like other classmates had about 10 years earlier. This is when I finally had a dream that said, I think I can. So my life shifted as I was more like the others, even if I would never be equal to them. There was many things that I would never become due to other faults within my own body.

I increased my social life, I moved to another location, I got a car and went to get a Job evaluation and then job placement. I was moving along at a faster pace. As I had many years to catch up on. I completed the evaluation, and started working with electrical appliances. This is also the time, where I started thinking about my future. I started dreaming about finding a life partner and having a family on my own.

Then Fate took over. At my job location, a task came in that nobody in my department could do. So they brought in a woman that could do the job. This was my point in life where I started a relationship with the transferred co-worker. We dated and then married over a year later. My dreams began to come true. After We married, a house to move to was next. Then after 5 years, a family was started. I had many dreams then. I dreamed what was possible.

But many setbacks begin to show up. The house fire, the death of my only Grandmother I knew, and our second Son as well, setback my dreams as I had great losses to deal with. With the birth of our only daughter, this allowed me to dream of a better tomorrow. Many of my dreams did not come true, but some did. Enough that I had a better tomorrow, I began to dream of life decades ahead and my mind opened up with hundreds of them.

As time moved on, and the children grew up and became adults, Dreams of time with my wife, and a new life style was possible. Dreams of walking our daughter down the isle, and having grand kids that the both of use could enjoy, begin to fill my mind. Both adult children had a good chance to marry, and our daughter was out on her own. My Wife and I saw a hopeful outlook in life, something that I never had too much of.

Then My Dreams were shattered like a glass bottle falling on concrete. My wife has a stroke and other complications, days later she passes away on our Daughter's birthday. Now I have lost the dreams that I waited years for. They have shattered in my mind. I am now alone and I have to start new dreams as I can't use the old ones. They have became Null and void. I have to start new ones, but my mind stalls and refuses to make new dreams.

If I make new dreams, will these become shattered as well. So at this time my outlook in life is following my paternal Grandfather. I look at the Easter photographs over a half century old. My Grandfather is sitting in his chair, grand kids are all around him. My events and dreams are repeating his as well. I will be alone during family events with my grand kids. As their Grandmother can never be there. I truly ended up like my Grandfather.

This was not one of my dreams, But it ended up as my life. Fate took me down this path. I will have to tell them stories about their Grandmother, like my Grandfather did for me.

I see no return soon, of any dreams for me. Other outside events would have to change in my favor, or something else that would give me a reason to dream again. Until then, I don't know how, or if, I will have any return of My Dreams.

Chapter 104

Video Family - 2/23/19

Making videos for over 37 years, has many different things and a timeline that goes back generations. I remember when I grew up, all I have to see the people that passed away before my time was photos. I saw photos of my paternal grandmother and great Aunt and Uncles. This is all that I had besides other relatives telling me stories about them. There may be a rare audio recording. Not too many families went into tape recorders of the 1960's. only a few did. I had a tape recorder in 1968, there is very few voices of the people that later would become Grandparents. I have very short recorded sections, none are the voices of my paternal Grandparents. There might be one of my maternal Grandmother. After 50 years have passed, I wonder how many can still exist after a half century of time.

I am one of the few that recorded tapes and stories back then. There is hundreds of tapes that I am on. Trying to find others on these tapes will be tough. I do know at least one brother is on the tapes, the question is where. There was no computer back then to keep an inventory of my recordings. I wish that there was, as it would be an easy task to keep track of the recordings. I have to listen to each tape today and take notes about every reel.

One thing led to another, as time passed through the months and years, I began making videos in 1982. This started a new way to keep local and my history videos, and events of my extended family for them, and others to see. The videos could have been for the family members of the past to see, or the future family members to come. I see my videos as a window for all to see, just what my world was like years ago. Most videos I make, are now part of a video history, that will pass the test of time. These let others see my world as it was, and not only rely on the spoken word of others. My video camera records what my eye has seen. I got many great videos at times, and not very good ones, at other times. It comes down is what you see is what I got. I did the best I could with what I had to work with.

Any grand children that I will ever have, cannot visit and spend time to talk, or visit with their Grandmother, She is no longer alive. But what is in my videos, will allow them to actually see and hear their Grandmother. The hundreds of videos cover many facets of her life. The Videos also allow the Grandchildren to see their Parent during many stages of when they grew up. My videos are like a Family photo album that comes alive before their eyes. They then can imagine, themselves in the video with current and past family members. I expected that any grandchild would be able to grow up with all of their grandparents. But my life copied my Grandfather, He was alone when his grandchildren grew up around him. I am now alone to see Grandchildren grow up around me, except I have videos that will show them just who their Grandmother was.

I have hundreds of events with Family members in. I never knew just how valuable that my tapes could become, until I saw Family Members pass away. It isn't just one, but many. My Grandmother is not on any of my videos, but her voice could be recorded on the reel-to-reel tapes that I have. I know a brother or two is recorded someplace in the tapes. I wish that I had more, but years ago, my life was restricted too much and money was scarce for me. I had to get tapes for 25 cents each, at a local gas station.

When I started making Videos a T-120 video tape was around $20. Many years later they were only a few dollars. This allowed me to fill my tapes with Videos of my family. I wish that I could have done more.

So now, many years have passed, I now have something on Video, that allows my offspring to know what kind of a family that they came from. They will see my efforts, and things about the family of the past. They will see their Grandmother as what kind of person that she was.

They will have something that I never had, a chance to see, hear, and know more about their Grandmother, than a photo ever could. I have made videos of many past family events, and now the images can still be seen. It is a way for others to feel part of the Family, that they have never met. It is my version of a Video Family.

Chapter 105

My Scripture - 2/24/19

I have written over 250 chapters. Each one is telling a different story of the past or present, some even have a line or two that tells of what could happen in the near future. All of these chapters are written from within my abilities, and many explain events that I have gone through. Many readers have noticed that I have a style of writing that isn't like the others. I wondered just what that was. I would later see it in another person that finished reading one of my newer chapters that have never appeared in any other place.

Several of my chapters have been posted on a restricted page, this allows me to get feedback and check for spelling errors. It also allows me to check the flow of the story told in the chapter. Some think that this is what is going to be printed in my book, they are not correct. I have changed almost all of the chapters by the time it goes to print. Some chapters in my published book, were three times larger than the version I posted on Face Book. One entire chapter on the Face Book page, had to be entirely rewritten to be published in my book. So those who only read the few dozen chapters posted online, have only gotten a version of the final release. My book chapters have the only complete version, of all of my finished work. All of the completed ones, then tell the story as the way I intended.

What is my style of writing ?. I did not get a clear understanding of this, until I let another read the newest chapter that I wrote. They read the chapter and told me what they got from it. I told them, that they missed the point that I was making. They admitted that the skipped over a part here and there. They admitted they were skim reading the chapter to look at the text in the chapter quickly, in order to have a general idea of the contents. Then, why did they miss the true meaning. They did not read the key words that have to be known, to get my intended meaning out of my chapter. They missed what I put into it. So what does some of my writing remind me of ?, It reminds me of scriptures.

What is in my chapters, that my style of writing reminds me of scriptures ?. It's having key words. Skim readers can miss these few key words in a chapter, and miss the intended meaning. It's like skim reading the Ten Commandments and leaving a word out. Thy shall have other Gods before me, misses the intended meaning. When it should read, Thy shall have no other Gods before me. So in a way, my chapters have to be read word by word, the same as you would do to scripture. I do not make my chapters longer, just to add extra fluff. Scriptures have enough words to make you understand what God intended, and not more.

My readers need to take in the whole chapter, to tell them the story, that I presented to them. Don't leave anything out, not even one word. That word or two that you skimmed over, may be the most important ones of the entire chapter. Read my chapters, as you would a recipe card, instruction manual, or scripture. You need to read it all, to get the true meaning off the written page. You shall not condense My Scripture, or any of the original Scriptures.

Chapter 106

Christmas in July - 2/25/19

. I look out my window and see 12 inches of newly fallen snow. We had so much snow in this month, that it would be more that the average of an entire winter. This month and year, may be in the record books for along time to come. And spring is over 3 weeks away. So what am I thinking of, It is a warm coat, gloves, boots, and other warm items to wrap me up like an Eskimo. The windchill outside was said to be, seventeen below zero.

. So what I expected to see in my weekend newspaper edition, was snowblowers, shovels, road salt, antifreeze, and everything to keep me warm for the next month or two. But what do I see in today's store flyer ?, I see college aged women wearing only 2 piece bikinis. As if they were here, and out on the local beach. They would be bitten so badly by frostbite, that parts of their anatomy would be falling off. They would be a block of ice in no time. They could end up like statues for the next month.

. Why would any store advertise this in a national publication. There should be more of a regional issue. There should have been things in this paper that had a spring feel to it. Like lighter versions of jackets, and still have gloves, hats, and tools for making upcoming spring gardens. Seeing a garden tiller would make more sense that sandals. What drives stores to jump so far ahead of the season that they are in ?. Must be that old thing called, do anything that may increase sales. Some call it beating the other guy to the punch.

. Stores do not realize that selling swim wear in February, there will be not enough buyers in May, June, or July. They will need to cut their prices in May, and have clearance prices by June. Also in June, they can set up for Halloween and Thanksgiving items to be there until September. So what can they do then to stimulate sales. I hate to say this, But 300 pound Santa will be arriving much earlier in the store, wearing his full red suit. By the time the night before Christmas arrives, Santa will be 98 pounds. Maybe this is how he can enter your chimneys. His secret will be out. It also explains why he eats cookies and milk, at every stop along the way.

. The Elves are busy making toys at the North Pole all year long, so the toys will made by the time Santa needs them. Santa will be able to wear his fat off, that he has been adding to, during the first half of the year. Maybe this is how Santa handles his health during the year.

. Dasher is the busiest reindeer of all, running around and getting any thing that Santa needs. Dancer and Prancer are being prancing instructors, to teach a new batch of reindeer to be Santa's sleigh pulling crews, and for any possible crew replacement. Vixen is thinking of things that she should not, like being the best sexy beast, as she could be.

. Comet is gazing off into the sky, looking for arriving relatives. Cupid is out practicing on the archery range. Donder and Blitzen went to visit their Granddeer, and to recruit new reindeer to be replacement crew members.

. Rudolph is out enjoying his bachelor lifestyle, while He is getting his nose recharged out in the sun. Rudolph then becomes a weather watcher. He hopes that He finds fog in the forecast for Christmas Eve. This way, He will work for Santa and earn a few bucks along the way.

. You are never told this. But Santa has more sleighs with him on Christmas Eve. They follow behind with a crew of six reindeer. They stop and swap, a full sack of toys, for any sack that Santa empties. But nobody knows this except me, and Rudolph. Whenever Rudolph blinks his nose 3 times, a swap of Santa's sack is needed. A sleigh pulls along Rudolph and the 8 reindeer, and the swap is completed. Restocking sleighs only need 6 reindeer as Jolly Old Saint Nick, never rides along with them.

. Because Summer items are now sold in Winter, Winter items can be pushed up to Summer. Now this, will allow them to set up for their biggest event of the year, by starting Christmas in July.

Chapter 107

My Grandfather - 2/26/2019

Today, My paternal Grandfather was born 123 years ago. He lived to be 76 years old, but spent the last 25 years alone. He was a widower at age 51. When all of his grandchildren grew up, they all saw him living a life of being alone. He was not a perfect man, but one that did the best that he could. He went in the Army to serve in World War 1, went overseas to complete his duty to his country.

He got married in 1920, at the age of 24. His Bride was 28 years old at the time. They lived in a house in the 9th ward and their first born Daughter was born in the next year. Then a year and a half later, my Grandparents had a set of twins. Then over a decade would pass, before their last child was born.

My Grandfather came from a family of 8 brothers and one Sister. The last 2 siblings born were a set of twins. So life for him was being part of a group and learned how to be part of a team.

He worked in a construction business, and later worked at an Egg and Poultry business, called Armours. At the same time, he ran a family farm, on the west side of Pine Valley. When World War 2 came along, Armour's location was taken over for production of tires, that were needed for the war. My Grandfather then started his own business.

He started his own Egg and Poultry business. He hired local Women to work there, as the Men were off to serve in the military during WW2. My Mother was one of those hired to work there. After my Father came back after being in the Army, was hired by his Father to drive a truck delivering chicken products.

He then had to deal with the death of his Wife, My Grandmother. She never saw any Grandchild, before she passed away. This was also around the time, when the first two of his Grandchildren were born. One was born before she died, and the other born a month after her death. She died of cancer and a cure for this was not in her future.

So now my Grandfather was a Widower, and ran a farm and a business. Four years later, his third Grandchild was born. He would end up with 11 Grandchildren, 9 boys and 2 girls. This is what life was like to me growing up. My Grandfather's only Daughter, never married and she lived with her Father for over 50 years. She ended up being a Grade School Teacher for 39 years. So over all the years when we visited our Grandpa, She was there as well.

Every Easter, and Christmas, we would visit with other family members at Grandpa's house. Once and awhile, we would have Thanksgiving there too. As well as a few picnics set up in their backyard. The most important days to visit were Easter and Christmas. My Grandfather did visit my house and many times slipped us a few coins, or a dollar bill. A dollar at the time, could buy 20 candy bars, or 7 hamburgers at local fast food places.

My Grandfather was involved in the Local Junior Ski Club, when He started as Chairman on January 6, 1932. So we went with him at times to the ski events in Pine Valley. He also supported Little League Baseball in the city. He was involved in charity work as well. He was did things through the VFW. A very involved community man.

The times that I went over to his house for the holidays was the best times for me. Every Easter that we went there become memorable as the others. My family of 6, got up to go to Church, for Easter service. After this, we went over to my Grandfather's house. The first thing that we had was an Easter breakfast with all of the other family members. The main Dining room table was not big enough. Many times, a few of the older kids had to use the kitchen table. My problem was there was too many eggs everywhere. I could not eat them, so this became a part of the Easter day.

After the dinner meal, most of the family went into the living room. The Kids went to many places around the house. There was a Ping Pong table in the basement, the office to play in, and there was a toy box for the youngest ones to snoop in. All of the Sister-in-Laws were in the kitchen during cleanup time. After the dishes were done and all other items put away, they came out to the living room. Then all of the kids were added into the group. This is the time where my Aunt had a Easter story and played the piano at times.

We did not see when one of my Aunt B, left the room to go hide the Easter baskets. She had a name on each one, this was to make all of the kids search for their own. This took several minutes to track down the goodies. When that was done, It was picture taking time. All the kids in one family, would take turns getting a picture taken with Grandpa. Then every family group would be in a separate photo. Then everyone there would be in one. My Aunt took many photos to make a new set each year. This is when we got to raid our Easter baskets and pick out some to eat.

Late Afternoon arrived and we ended the event. We did everything that we wanted, including raiding the cookie jar that was on the kitchen counter. My Grandfather did this for about 2 decades. No two were the same, as this was the best way to make them memorable. The Other big event was Christmas Eve.

We went to Grandfathers house by mid afternoon on Christmas Eve. This allowed time to ready the dinner for everyone. After the Meal, My Aunt had time for singing Silent Night, this song was used almost every year. then she had about a half dozen other songs lined up. The music time allowed for the adults to complete the kitchen cleanup. After this was done, Everyone went into the living room, a few kids skipped out for a minute and raided the cookie jar, again. After all the gang is rounded up, my Grandfather gets his chance to play Santa. He hands out the gifts with the help of the oldest kids there. My Aunt B is taking photos during the event. The kids then get to raid their boxes to see whats inside. Every grandchild got a main gift, 2 smaller packages that had clothes, and a smaller present. Then we got a small gift from each Uncle that was there. There would be one or two at every Christmas Eve Event.

Before we left, My Aunt B would have a small snack and a drink. Then before we went home, we were given an assortment of Christmas candy to take home. My grandfather had stories of the past to share, My Uncles and Aunts told a few stories as well, over the evening. Over time, the number of those that were there, started to go down. I will always remember that my Grandfather, really did do his part, even if our Grandmother has been absent for over 20 years. He did tell about her from time to time, we had to listen closely when He did. The information was from a man that did not expect to live alone for the last 25 years of his life.

There were many things to learn at every event. I remember so many of them. Learning how to raid the cookie jar, without making a noise, was another thing that each of us had to learn as well. I listen, but can't hear the cookie jar. By the end of the day, the cookie jar becomes empty again. We could never convince our Aunt to get a second cookie jar, or a bigger one to have on the counter.

In talking to other people that knew him, told me that my Grandfather ran a tight ship. He wanted his workers to work for the entire hour, of each and every work day. They also admitted that they got paid a fair wage. They understood He expected each worker to be part of the team, and he was willing to pay for work well done. This showed me that He treated his employees fairly, just like he did when he played Santa to all of the Grandchildren. Every Grandchild was treated the same, their was no standout favorite. He pushed no child aside to help another.

This fairness was done, over and over. This included his will, every Grandchild got the same thing. There was two United States Savings Bonds for every Grandchild. There was no favorite grandchild, He treated all of them as part of a Team, and treated them all the same

Chapter 108

Old Man Winter - 2/27/19

This month of February has had more snow that an average year. The 30-year annual average for the city is 46.8 inches, But in the first 26 days of February, 50.7 inches have fallen. This makes this month feel like the entire winter.

The problems this causes are many. When I drive some side streets, I feel like driving through a tunnel. I have not seen this in years. This makes travel tricky. If I have to go out, I need to travel the fewest miles as possible. I see issues everywhere. Some cars that are not used, can't be seen at all. All I do see, is the snow stack that the car is hiding inside. The problem with this, is that some cars look like this as they are parked along the curb. The City crew works day by day, and every night, and can't get to this snow lumps along the curb. These appear to be frozen in place. You need to slowdown or your vehicle will end up looking like the one you hit. This is not a normal year at all.

If you end up needing a Tow truck, now you could be looking at a wait time of over an hour. Some outside of the city, have reported white out conditions. This makes visibility so bad that you wish that you stayed home, and under your bed. You can't see the other cars on the opposing lanes of a freeway.

This type of weather, makes the world around you, seem to slow down. You can walk 50 feet outside your house, and you think you are alone in the world. Snow rates can be over an inch of snow per hour. This is great if you are an avid skier, or you want enough snow on the ground in July. This will allow you to go camping and never buy any ice for the trip. Chilly Willy would feel right at home here. I can even envision a parade of the penguins. An entire football team comprised of Polar Bears, as the wind chill can be over 30 degrees below zero.

Driving isn't the only hazzard. I hear reports of roof collapsing, there was one at a Church, another at a local business, and another of a barn. Farm animals have been seen walking on piles of snow and then walking over the fence, that was made to confine them. Blizzard conditions have been observed in many locations and on several days. Oh what a winter wonderland this ended up to be. It is only great for the photographer, If he can prevent from becoming a frozen statue within his own photograph.

Snow Days rattle across the daily local news. Kids think its so great to get school called off day after day. I wonder how they will like spending an extra week, going to school in June. Then they will think so it is not as great getting many snow days off of school.

Many residents complain that people block their driveways for days. My question is why, the drivers should know better. Maybe the car owner is thinking that they will get away with it, because there are so many that have done this. They may be thinking that the Police are so busy with accidents, traffic control, and other cases, that they have to time to be bothered with improperly parked cars. Many will procrastinate so long, that they will get up in the morning and report their car was stolen. The joke will be on them, as the Police will have their car safely packed away in the impound yard.

I am finding myself staying home more often this year, as any other year in the past 50. This leads to more time at home, unfortunately more time to shovel snow. Getting snow off of the driveway and from the roof, are taking a lot of time. Many other people spend time at home, watching TV and enjoying piles of snacks. Doing this will soon make them as sluggish as a car going down an unplowed street.

Many drivers end up like they have lost their minds. They drive too fast for conditions. They want to pass 18 wheelers like they were standing still. Others forget to turn their headlights on. More forget to clean the snow off of all their car windows. Other fail to brush off their head, tail, and brake lights. Could be that they don't want to be bothered by something that they will not see. The driver behind them may not see them as well, just before the bumper of the car shatters them and sprinkled the snow covered street with the pieces. Now the Owner will be bothered as what it costs to replace them. The written law also states that headlights must be turned on at least one hour before sunset. This means, sunset today, not tomorrow.

Then there are cars that look like moving cone heads. There is enough snow piled on top of these vehicles, that they will get a free trim, as they pass under a freeway overpass. Drivers should care about this, as their gas mileage suffers as well.

If it wasn't for evergreen trees, all you would see is white fields. All I can see on some side streets is an obstacle course, as drivers park too far from the curb. Other drivers can't correctly park on the proper side of the street, on snow routes, after a snow emergency has been announced. You may have to weave side to side to get around all of the cars. Winter driving is not an amusement park ride. At times, it does act like one.

Every time I hear the house thermostat trigger, I feel the invisible hand reaching into my wallet and handing over more money to the utility company. Many hidden costs come out of the closet and play catch with my wallet.

People that have pets need to let them outside, from time to time. When it is time for the pet to come back into the house, the owner might have to read their name tag. Every pet in the area all begin to look the same, like a lost wandering polar bear.

Old Man Winter needs to take the remaining months of the year off from working. He has broken the spirit of a few and the shovels of many. He has also broken many water pipes while he visits here. It's time to send him to his home up north, and take his dandruff with him.

Chapter 109

House Divided - 2/28/19

I see the end of what many call the family. My family should have been 5 members that were tied together by blood line. I saw the possibility of My family being a stronger unit as time passed by. But cruel things happen that can cause a family unit to falter. I have see many over the last 38 years.

There are many contributing factors that can cause the dream to breakdown and all parts of the family will be going their own way. The life of my family is like my Grandfather's. It's a broken family and you have to live with it's outcome.

My Grandfather's family consisted of 6 members. It was in trouble as one of the kids kept getting in various kinds of trouble and was labeled the black sheep of the family. As this was going on, His greatest loss was happening. His Wife, My Grandmother, was battling cancer. She lost her battle and passed away. This led to a family unit scrambling to stay together. The Black Sheep was not helping out and caused more issues within the struggling family unit.

In My case, I started out like my grandfather, We both married and the children came later. I was hit with a loss, real early in life. Our second born Son dies within 3 hours of birth. This is a loss that you can never recover from. There is nothing you can do to replace a child.

Life went on, We had our third child, a Daughter. She could never replace her brother. So as a unit of 5 members, we never would or could have all 5 together. We looked like a complete family of 4 to the outside would, as most everyone else was unaware of the 2nd child's death. You really can't do much about Fate, when it deals you a bad hand, except move on. We had no other choice except move on.

Years went by and the another major issue happens. My Wife had several major setbacks, the first one required surgery, and then another caused her to end up in a nursing home. This caused unrest between the 2 children, one was still living at home. Then problems with the facility caused me to get my Wife moved out of this, questionable facility. I found her a better place. She moved into the new place at the end of December.

For the next 3 years, things for her were better. She saw some things that allowed her to relax more as she was getting the care that she needed. But then Disaster struck like a tornado. She suffered a stroke and any future for her was bleak. Then within a week, Her ship sunk. She had another major medical issue and this could not be fixed. She was taken out of the ICU and sent to hospice. Her days were numbered. The Staff said that she could pass away within hours, or a day. I said that she would be alive in 3 days.

3 days, I said. Our Daughter is coming that day for a visit. And so it was, 4 guests showed up that day. In mid afternoon, She died. I was the only one that noticed it. I was the one that had to tell my Daughter that her Mother had passed away. This was something that I never wanted to do. The look on her face will never be forgotten by Me. The hospital staff confirmed my findings, My Wife of 37 years was gone. She went to be with our child that had passed away 27 years before her.

This was a devastating blow to the family unit. My Daughter has to deal with a world without her Mother. My son denied that His Mother was dead, as he will not accept the fact that it happened. And he denied it more that once, as he yells as loud as he can. He screams this at me, She is not dead. This event is one of the nails in the coffin that will seal the family fate. This event may foreshadow the sinking of any chance that the remaining 3 member will ever recover, and be a Family again.

When my remaining Son is reckless and damage things around the house, He is speeding up the end of the time that the house will be useful. I see a time, in the near future, that I will be offered Government assisted living. This means that I will be living in a building that you have to be 55, 62, or 65 years old to be there. Reduction of my income can also end living where I am, and I will be in a place that restricts younger residents. This ends my Son from living where I am, and it also ends him living where we are now. His name never was, or will be in the title to the house. This means he has to live elsewhere. He may react to this by avoiding Me, just like he avoided his Mother. He came all the way to the door of her room, at assisted living location, looked in the room and then walked away. His Mother never saw him, only the workers and I did. She did not even know that he was there.

Turmoil ahead is what I see. I can't get my Son the help he needs. The laws were changed so that if an individual wants to live in the streets, they can. It's their free choice to ruin their own lives. Nobody can get involved and steer them in the right direction, except the Law and other Government Officials. I really do not want this to happen, but it will be his own choice to anything He wants, including ruining his life even more.

Life without a partner, will leave the 2 remaining children adrift in their own reality world. My Daughter and I, have the best options, She wants to further her education and get married. I have many options for people like me, as my age is past being 39 forever.

I see a bleak future for Me, and Us as family. Can we ever be a family again, if so, what kind ?

Chapter 110

I March Along - 3/1/19

I have more things to deal with than I want. I finally got another setback. I was informed that I will have less income to live on that what I expected. I see cutback ahead, but there isn't any fat in the budget that is primed to be trimmed. This now sets the pace and speeds up decisions that need to be done. I have been putting them off as long as I could, but I see tough choices ahead.

Where will I live a year from now, I don't know. I may have to try to find affordable housing where you pay a percentage of your income. I know that rent amount will be less than I am paying now. I wish that it did not have to be like this. This will cause another shift in the family, as I can't have anyone to move with me. I have to move alone, as I am the only one qualified to be in admitted into the over 55 rentals.

Walking alone on my path, I have not done this for the last 37 years. But I am on the road alone again, walking on a two year old pair of shoes. My insurance now refuses to pay for my special shoes. They think there are other ways to solve my foot problems, I don't see that. If there was a way, why wasn't it tried over the last 10 years. So walking on my path will hasten my foot problems as well. I see roadblocks no matter what way i walk on the narrow path.

Maybe another living location will end other problems that I encounter. I was sitting on the sofa last night, working on my last chapter for my book. I felt cold, and as time went by, I got colder and colder. What was the problem, was I catching a cold or flu ?. My face got too cold, I had to investigate what the room temperature was to know if it was me catching a cold, or something else.

My drink next to me felt colder than usual. I got up in the early morning. got a flashlight and investigated my concern. I peered at the temperature gauge on my furnace thermostat, that was on the hallway wall. I used the flashlight to check it again. It said it was 53 degrees in the house. The Furnace was not operating. I opened the door of the unit. I moved a switch and tried to see if the blower fan was working, It was. I then looked into the peep window and a small amount of light was there. So I knew the pilot light was lit. So what now ?.

I went back to the thermostat in the hall. Took off the cover and looked inside. It was not clear to see if the problem was here. This is a unit that is about 45 years old. There is no computer chip here, or any buttons to push. It runs on a thermal strip that expands when it gets warm and retracts when it gets cold. I them did the next logic choice. I pushed down a bit on the contact that was on the end of the strip. At that moment the furnace burner came alive. I waited and saw that in a minute or so, the blower fan came on, heat flowed from the vents.

So I had to know what prevented the contacts from closing. I removed the small cover from where the contacts came together. I cleaned off the metal contacts. Then I saw some dust buildup on the coil spring and cleaned the debres out. Then I reassembled the unit. It now works again. This type of unit does not like vibrations or an environment that it picks up dust. But I know that this unit has not been cleaned on the inside for over 15 years. Something as simple as a dusty control unit, can stall a major appliance. This summer, when this is not needed, I can clean it again to keep it working as long as I can.

I call this as another detour as I walk my path. I am facing many hurdles and this failed to stop me from my advance forward, but it did slow me down. I am not prepared for a major costly repair expense, at this time. I still have to see what I can do about a headstone for my Wife's grave. There is no easy answers as this has to be looked at for cost.

With the recent bad month of weather, around the city where I live, this causes delays and prevents me from keeping the pace. We had about 54 inches of snow in the last 4 weeks. It set an all time High as how much snow we got in a given month. It was 4 and a half feet. The snowpile along my driveway is 7 feet tall. The last time I saw something like this was over 50 years ago. But I am not 50 years younger to shovel out my driveway. I have to do it alone, so I can only do so much in a day. It makes it hard to get things done. The bad weather only makes my other issues harder to deal with.

Having that much snow in the yard, means a lot of snow on the roof of the house and I now have to deal with that. I am a single solder that has to battle alone. I see many things that I need, but it all now has to be put on hold. My budget isn't what it was just 2 months ago. I have to make a new battle plan, or I could loose more that what I want to.

Walking on my path now, seems like a different world that I had, just 7 weeks ago. But I have to stay on the path, putting one foot ahead of the other, and advance forward. It's not time for me to quit or retreat. I have to go forward, even it I trip a bit over every stone in the road.

Chapter 111

Free World - 3/2/19

I come across many kinds of people in my daily life. Some do not feel that they have to follow any rules, or be part of the normal human race.

They want to live for free and use others to pay their way. Some of these go on welfare and stay on it for decades. Others live with someone that has a job and expects them to support them. They sit around the house every day, while their partner goes to work and pay the bills. There are others when they turn 18, they don't want to do anything except sit around the house, while their parents work. So many types of these exist. Some even live with a parent for as long as one of their parents is still alive.

They are not motivated to do anything. Many play video games all day. Others hangout on social media from sunrise to sunset, and beyond. They use all of the services of the household and return nothing to help the family. They see this style of life as normal. They think when others go to work, that they are wasting their time and should be enjoying life, like they are. They don't see the dangers ahead.

One of these dangers is the reduction of household income. The free loader still wants their things that they use, They want others to go without. They see no need for them going without things that they want, and want they do. They want this, they want that, they want and want more. This has nothing to do with their needs. They do nothing, but expect that they will always have their needs taken care of. Some do nothing to lessen the labor of their caregiver. The think that they have a birthright to do what they want, and to get what they want.

Some adults whine and stomp their feet, like a ten year old, they have been doing this all of their lives and see no need to change. They think that nothing can change for them. They expect that this will go on as long as it takes to collect Social security, by using someone else's number. They live by a hidden creed, why work, when someone else will do it for you. After years have passed, they are overweight and in bad health. Then they expect the government to take care of them, just like they did for Grandma. They fail to understand that their situation can change in a, wink of an eye.

Others roam around town, as the homeless. They rush the gates of the places that give them a meal and a bed for the night. They push and shove at times, all are thinking that they are first. Spending their days around town, seeing what they can do for free. Some even collect government payments, but want others to spend their hard earned money on them, by providing free food, medical, and a bed for the night. They roamers want their money to buy a $500 or more, cell phone. They use their money to pay the one and only monthly bill that they have. Others spend their income on smokes, drugs, and arcades. Why should they feed themselves with their money. It's more fun to hangout at a bar and play pool all day, than a 9 to 5 job.

These people become drifters in the community and see nothing wrong with it. Then at some homeless shelters, they act like two year olds. The want the room, bed, location, of their choosing. Nobody else should take what they want, even if they own nothing there, except what they carry and the clothes on their backs. The want others to sacrifice for them on a daily basis. To them the world is free, free, free.

They fail to see their future until it hits them in the face. The person who works and supports them can loose their job, they retire, or they pass away. This now leaves any remaining in the home, to still care for them. But what happens if there isn't enough money to do that. They refuse to give up some of the things that others took care of for years. When asked to help the household out, they have excuses, or they refuse, or blame others. Now is the time where they should chip in and help the household stay afloat, they refuse, or run off to another place where others will support them for free. They only place they will ever learn what responsibility is, from the dictionary.

These types of people never realize how much others did for them. They were lifelong users, some even proud that they were. They tell about everything that they did in their life to have their fun, not once, giving thanks to the many people that sacrificed to provide them with their needs and wants.

Some people are users, they see the whole world as free. Why work or payback to others, when you can get it for free. They see the world as free, to them. Why do anything when they can find others to do it for them.

In the final days of their lives, some may wise up a bit. When they do, it will be too late. Instead of living a normal life and being part of the human race, they wasted their lives playing games, enjoying their playboy lifestyle sins, and taking everything without giving anything in return. They have earned no respect from others, or themselves. They will end up in the same situation in life, like everyone else. Their life is coming to the end. In their final breaths in life, they may realize that they will be alone, because they were a constant taker. They were not being any kind of a friend, to those that gave them everything.

Chapter 112

Goodbye a 2nd Time - 3/3/19

. Weeks have past since the death of my Wife, my life was changed forever. A new journey has began. It is not an easy time, but I have to move on end do the best that I can. I now am faced with dealing with the things that she used on a daily basis.

. I, and other members of my family, have no use for many of her things. My Daughter cant make use of clothing or other personal items. So decisions must be made as what to do with many of the items. Some keep everything, and others get rid of everything. I realize that I can not keep everything that she used, so I have to look at what is the most important to keep.

. Every item that I give away, is like giving a piece of her daily life away. I have see how other have handled this situation, and some of the methods will not work for Me. One man, after his wife died from cancer, closed the door on her bedroom and preserved it for many years. he had a cleaning woman come in each week to keep it clean. The room was left just the way she left it, before she entered the hospital. But she never came home. He left it this way for decades. I don't have room to let any space remain unused. So I move on to the sorting and saving technique.

. Sorting out clothing will be first on the list. Because there is no relative that can use her sizes, this will be donated away. I can't see selling these things at a garage sale, and seeing dozens of things get sold. I might get too involved about the past of every item, as they are carried away by others. It's best to give these items away and know that others can make use out of them.

. She had many hobbies that I or anyone else would use now or years from now. I would have to assemble all of the like items and donate everything at one time. It is easier for me to do this. Monetary gain is not my concern. I want her items to be in the hands of those who will use them.

. As for medical supplies, Many had only one reason to make use of, and finding the right person would take too much time, and I don't want to risk the safety of others, if the wrong person gets the supplies. Most of these will need to be disposed of. It is best to be safe than sorry.

. And books, photos, and other forms of her records will be kept. These will be passed down to others when the time is right. It is a bit too early to do this now. So I must do what I can with the items around me. As time passes things will get better, I just do not know how long it will take.

. It still feels as if Her life was taken without notice, like a thief, in the middle of the night. In the Twelfth day, the final curtain came down. I really do not want to do this, but I must move on. I can't make a shrine out of her possessions.

. For now, She is lost under the sea of snow that has blanketed the Cemetery. I can't find her, as there is no marker or headstone. No trees can be used as a reference point. Even dealing with this issue, can be another chance that I will feel like I will have to deal with her loss, all over again. . . . . . . (My mind only remembers a 25 year old clue, K-fanda)

. Getting rid of the things that I can't use, or she was using, is a hard thing to do. Every item can bring up memories. Getting rid of every one of these things, is like saying Goodbye a Second Time.

Chapter 113

The Tapes - 3/4/19

. The volume of the Videos can only be matched by the audio tapes that I used. Audio tapes had 2 separate recordings tracks on them, video tapes only had one. Audio tapes could be flipped over and use the 'Other side'. The audio tapes started in 1968, these are 14 years before the 1ˢᵗ Video. They sit in a box, as silent as a church mouse, that took a vacation to the Vatican. I recall buying a reel to reel 150 feet long was 25 cents, a 600 foot was 99 cents, a 900 was $1.35. They can talk when I want them too, But as for now, they have been packed away

. The tape reels hold a part of my past that are not in my video collection. The recordings within echo the life that I had, Some events are good, and some were bad. There is sounds that echo from the stage of Hades. The Warden and the drunk of the house can be heard at times, in the background of the recording, as the tape recorder pulls the ribbon of mylar across it's head. The sounds rumble out and can echo in my mind.

. Most of the recordings are stories that I made up without a script. These were made like some of these chapters, they spring forth out of a simple idea, and a simple title. It seems that I could record a story, with only a simple thought in my mind. I can write a chapter, by only coming up with a title first. I use no notes when I write a chapter, or record a story live.

. One of my most powerful audio recording is the first complete one that I made. It tells of a troubled life where the child is mistreated by the mother figure. No matter what the child does to be accepted, the mother figure ends up betraying the child. This maybe the first recording that reveals the inner turmoil that my mind saw over the years. The name of this one is called, Mommy My Vacuform Won't Work. Most of the recordings were made over a 10 year time span.

. These covered many subjects and some were record insert clip versions. I tell a line or two, then use a short sound bite off of a 45 rpm record. I speak another line and use another sound clip from another 45. You do this over and over, in the end, a complete story is told. Some of these last about 3 to 5 minutes long. Others can run for hours. It depends what type of story I am telling, by using the short sound clips. Apollo 13 is the name of one of those that I made in my early years, it was made around 1970.

. Most of these recordings were of a comedy variety, but had a second message hidden in the story lines. The second message was about a serious subject, that could be one of a few dozen, that are repeated in different styles. The Comedy of the story is the main meaning of the recordings. If you take the story apart, word by word, you could find a hidden message within the spoken word.

. As the years rolled through the 1970's, this activity was replaced by other things in my life. By 1982, a Video cassette recorder had replaced the reel-to-reel audio recorders. My stories and recording activities now are all centered around making my videos. I only go back to the old reel-to-reels to play what has been recorded. Many things are hidden into the little ribbon of mylar plastic recording tape. Many recordings that I want to hear again, and some that I should leave on the shelf.

. There are many voices of the past that can never be heard again, unless my tapes are played. The tapes are another form of history that tells a story of the world, when I was growing up. A few of my family members are on the tapes. I just don't know what tapes that they could be on. I need to start and play them again. Take off the sounds of those that I need to save, before they are lost because of the passage of time.

. I recall that I made a new audio recording at least a thousand days in a row. Some of the tapes have the effect of being an echo, from the house of hell.

. On some of the tapes, the sounds in the background, have more information that the spoken words on the tape. There should be the sound of the water pump that supplied water to the house. The sound of the air compressor should have made it into the iron oxide coating, that records the sound on the tapes.

. This was a large improvement over the wire recorders, of the days gone by. Most of these early recorders had 3 inch diameter reels. I had one recorder that had 2 inch reels, also had 2 units that used a 5 inch reel. I finally moved up and bought my own 7 inch reel to reel unit. It was the only one that I could record sound in stereo. I hooked up a turntable to it and this allowed me to play 45's and albums in Stereo. I also used it to make a few audio recordings, as well.

. It has been over 50 years since I first started making live recordings. Mommy My Vacuform won't work, may have been the first. I recorded this out in the shed that we had in the back yard. I needed to keep any recording I was doing out of ear shot of the house Warden. Later on, I went to a fellow classmate's house, and did recordings there. Some of these are interesting recordings, they open up another part of my past, and another way to see how life was different in my world.

. Now, I have found another thing that I can shed light on my past. If only, I can find them all, and then see if all will play on the recorders that I still have

. Later a Series of Stories were made on audio cassette tapes, There was 37 of these, Mission Impassable recordings. This took 2 of us to make this series. The Mission Impassable episodes lasted 15 minutes. I would record the beginning on all episodes. I took a minute or two and recorded what the story was going to be. I stated the mission to be solved, I setup the scene that had to be used, and then I ended my part of the episode. 'Mr. Harv' was then given the tape. he would then record the remaining time on the cassette, by continuing the story, to make 15 minutes.

. Mr. Harv would hear my setup, add to it, make a story that links to the mission that I set up for him. Then solve it anyway he wants, and then close out the Impassable Mission. We Did all 37 missions this way. After He did his part of the recording, I got the tape back and added it to the series. This was the final series of the era of our audio recordings. These were completed before 1980.

. My audio recordings gave me another way to record history, that the house Warden, did not understand. Many of the tapes contain history that never can happen again. Some tapes do have a small slice of time, but enough is there to know what things were like. These are just another way, in which I saved a bit of my history.

Chapter 114

Not Here - 3/5/19

As I meander around in my part of the world. I go to a few places each day to do the things that I need to get done. After the needed tasks are completed, I need a bit of refueling for Myself. So I set out to go to my final stop of the day. I find myself stopping by a local restaurant. It's not the same place every day. I like to switch things up, so I don't end up doing the same thing day after day.

Arriving at my chosen place of the day, I enter and then order what I want for this visit. The food is ready and I sit at one of my favorite tables. I then I do a magic trick, and make my food disappear. Time to do my next task that I want to do. I then set up my laptop and get it onto the free WiFi. I need to check my Email and other messages that are on other web sites. I also am thinking of catching up on some other paperwork that needs to be done

After several minutes, I am completing a few tasks and move on to my next one. After a few minutes, I notice that a few others came into the restaurant and sit down with their meals. Everyone is getting along as a few others show up to read the newspapers, others have their tablets online to do what they want to do. Still more, gather around the Televisions that are placed around the room. They want to know news updates and a peek at the weather. Some want to know If they will need to mow their lawns soon, or will they still have the snowbank deposits in their yards in July.

Then it happens, I hear the theme song of the Lone Ranger. Now where did that come from. Somebody picks up their cell phone and begins a nonstop jabbering with their jaw. This jabbering goes on and on, so much that I think their jaw needs to be taken in for a lube job. I am thinking that it needs a little glue or a few locks.

They talk about things that disturb others in the place. Some talk about their clandestine affair that is planned soon. I don't want to hear about what she will or will not do. I don't want to hear what they call the new to be Ex. I am not interested in stories about rabbits. Why do people assume that they are the only ones in this place and treat it like a phone booth. Then it gets worse, they cuss and swear over and over, as they describe in detail telling how evil another person is. Maybe they should look in a mirror. There are kids here that are less than 10, their language spoken over the phone, would make a statue blush. This language belongs in a bar or porn movie. Their words are not even found in a dictionary.

These people sit within one table away from others, then think only of themselves. Then they talk so loud over their phone. Any people around them, can't listen to the another person, that is sitting at the same table with them. Then these jabbering chewers, want to eat and jabber, they have to keep repeating things because the person on the other end can't hear them correctly. It look's like they need to fill their faces to get the energy to keep their jaw flapping. Some flap so fast that you think that they are planning a liftoff. These people need to be more respectful to everyone in the place. They need to quit doing this, Go off in a corner and keep things to themselves. Stop broadcasting to the entire building.

I don't want to hear about, how you had to deliver a baby, your problems with addition, your uncle is child preditor, you hate all your neighbors and politicians, or you have an answer for everything and could teach your preacher a few things.

My question is this, why did you come here ?, If you have serious problems with someone, go talk to them. Turn off your phone in public places, and when you drive your car. If you are waiting for an important call, answer the phone, then go to a location that others will not be bothered. Respect the rights of others.

Stop hanging out your dirty laundry, take it somewhere else, Not Here. Pay attention when you are driving. Honk if you love Jesus. Text while driving, if you want to meet Him.

Chapter 115

Family Dream - 3/6/19

. When I started growing up and was around the age of 10, the main question was, what would I do when I grew up. My brothers were all older than me, and they also faced this question. The idea of the brothers was to use what skills the family had and run a business. What kind of business was there that the entire family could get involved with. I remember what each one of the family members could do.

. My Father had the ability to paint cars. We had the equipment to do this. The Oldest brother could do Painting trim, auto body repairs, and mechanical repairs. The second oldest was good at engines and auto repair, and could do car body repairs. Then the next brother was good at engines, repairs, and still knew the basics of painting cars. My skills were more on the business end of things, I could do the bookkeeping. I was limited as what I could do in the painting of cars, but had some knowledge in the other fields.

. So the plan was there. I would run the office and the bookkeeping. I ran the schedule that would keep the team gears moving along and do the jobs that earned income to pay the bills. The three brothers would do the auto repairs and when it came to painting, they would prep the cars for the final step. This is what the father would do. Inspect the car after sanding and body repair work. The final thing that he would do is paint the cars. This was the ideal setup and it would have worked. It was a dream that could come true.

. This dream was in place for several years, and even if any brothers went into the Military, a job would be there when they completed their time serving our country. Everything was in place to have a career, and have all the family work together as an unit. What could go wrong ?

. Everything was in place, only had to wait a few years and all of the pieces would fit together. It was like having a Big Boy Steam Locomotive, cruising down the rails, pulling over a hundred boxcars. Everything was in place. Time was on our side and a bright future was coming into focus.

. As time passed, the train started to cough and sputter. It was still on the rails, but things were not as it seemed. The Engineer that was to own the business and lead the charge, started to let alcohol be a bigger part of his life. His beer belly of a keg was getting in his way to operate the train in the best way possible.

. The the pin on the caboose let go, as the oldest brother turned 18 and joined the Navy. Recovering the caboose later, still would keep all hands aboard. But, after he left the Navy, our Father thought that he was not good enough because he was in the Navy, because our Father was in the Army. More issues showed up and the oldest Brother then joined the Marines. This ended his future as being part of the crew on the train.

. The next brother start getting into trouble in many ways, spent time in reform school, and his life would go down the narrow trail and later had to pay a price to society. He now would not be part of the crew, that would run the business, or the train.

. At this point, the Chief Engineer, started to pay for his wages of sin, His medical condition was getting poor, and he resigned as Railroad Engineer. The train isn't operating like it should, It's beginning to chug, chug, along. This doesn't look good.

. There was two left that had the dream. My next Brother and I, were the skeleton crew that kept the train on the track. But it would not last long, The train is running low on coal and the team spirit that kept it running this long. Too much neglect of the train, and the lack of investment to keep the train and the family dream on track.

. Then the last brother that was home, left after the school year and joined the Army. This left the Depot empty of qualified workers and by this time, The Chief Engineer had allowed the beer and booze to overtake his ability to even blow the train whistle. I was the only one left, and I saw the warning signs coming, faster that the Bullet Train. The Big Boy was now on it's last load and increasing speed, as it was coming down the mountain. It then began to vibrate and puff along faster than the Engineer, that smoked over 3 packs a day. it now snorted along at a faster pace. The neglect of the locomotive began to show.

. The Engine began to go faster, the brakes were not cared for, so the began to over heat. They squealed as loud as a thousand pigs. The pressure gauges peaked to the danger zone. The caboose snapped off and made a new route into the canyon. The rattling of the boxcars make their own music. The cab was heating up so high, you could fry eggs on the Engineer's seat. The door to the firebox glowed in orange. Anyone in the cab was getting free time in a tanning booth. A rivet or two began to pop off of the steel rib cage that held the belly of the boiler together.

. The replacement Engineer did not know the first thing about running a business or the train. This Warden of the house, tried to do her best to save the train and sell it for what she could get. She tried to shut down the steamer as it stomped down the rails. But at times she was more loco than the locomotive. Parts began to fall off and more popping rivets played a new tune as they bounced off of the glass windows. She tried to get the boiler door to open to cool this mini coal reactor off. The door would not unlatch. The Choo choo train was now increasing speed, chewing up the railroad track as it headed to an abyss. It would huff and puff for as long as it could.

. Any car that dared to get into it's path, would end up as a cow catcher decoration, semi trucks too, even a few stray cows. The Warden decided to abandon ship, as it was huffing and puffing more that she did, when she yelled at her home bound prisoners. She then took anything of value and left the train, by jumping into the lake, as the train hurdled over the railroad switches. The safety valve whistle went off, it was so high of a pitch, that dogs in 3 counties away could hear it. They packed up their bones and ran away from home. All the family members had been scattered across the world. The Locomotive of the Family Dream, was on a life of it's own. A thousand pacemakers would not keep up with this hothead of a Loco Locomotive.

. It began to Shake, Rattle, and roll faster down the hill. The ghost of Elvis could not stop it now. A short curve was coming, some called it dead man's curve. Others called it the widow maker. Then the behemoth jerked and the brakes locked tighter than a misers coin purse.

The rivets popped off the boiler like a 21 gun salute. Then the boiler exploded in a million pieces, Alice took a few with her to the moon. The coal tender impacted into the loco, coal powder made the mountain blacker than that ace of spades. The boxcars began to stack themselves, as the hit the canyon floor. They looked like Paul Bunyan's lego blocks. The explosion of the boiler blew the bridge into a billion toothpicks. Every tree within 5 miles became fodder to make new railroad ties.

. The entire Big Boy Locomotive with it's cargo, vanished from the face of the Earth, as well as the Family Dream that began years before. These went up in smoke, affected by booze, greed, & incompetence. Both of these were never to be seen or heard of again. Maybe it was too much of a dream to ask it to come true. But is was, the one and only Family Dream that we ever had, and there would never be another.

Chapter 116

Mini Reunion Time - 3/7/19

During High School, we wanted to pass every test
Each of us thought, that we could be the best
Every day sitting in class, with a Teacher
Many of these acted like, they were a Preacher

Don't worry about things, we all are Old Abes
Half of us are Guys, the other half Babes
We have our Diploma, School came to an end
Being an Adult, is just around the bend

Time to get married, and have a few Kids
Crying, chasing, and closing baby jar lids
Whether we have a Daughter, Or Have a Son
We have to let them leave home, one by one

Decades have now passed, We are showing our age
We look like grandparents, time to turn the page
Remembering our past, is not very easy to do
We should all meet our old friends, it's for Me and for You

Other's came up with an Idea, I will call him Rick
Lets all get together, this is not a joke or a trick

Many calls were made, many emails were sent
We were having a reunion, at a place with no rent

We call these a Mini Reunion, We meet at various places
We all seem to enjoy, looking at all the old faces
Everyone Mini is different, each has a different Cast
They joke around and have fun, I stay to the very last

Time to be with friends, and order up a tasty dish
Some order the burgers, fries and some get the fish
Some have soda, a mixed drink, while others have beer
Nobody leaves thirsty or drunk, after they were here

We had fun every minute here, before we had to go
Tested our memories about the people, we used to know
We ask Classmates to show up, everyone that we knew
The Mini Reunions are great, for the Class of 71 Crew

I took the photos of everyone, that was at the event
It's something that I can do, It does not cost a cent
Through my eye I snap the photos, everywhere I look
I take all of the pictures, and post them on Face Book

Chapter 117

Grandpa's Life - 3/8/19

My Grandfather was born in 1896, in 1917 He was at the age of 21, This was the age where a Male was considered an adult. His first thing to do was enlisting in the Army, as World War 1 would not be over until November 11, 1918. After the War ended, the Military started to let the GI's come home. Some of my Grandfather's fellow soldiers came back in 1918, My Grandfather would come back in a few months. and this is the world as of 1918, that he was facing in the United States. It was a world where only 6 percent of all Americans had graduated from high school, and two out of every 10 adults could not read or write.

Getting around the area was done mostly by Horse and buggy, Cars were expensive at the time and you may have to travel some distance to buy one. If you bought a car, the fuel to run it, was sold in drug stores only. There was speed limit laws to follow, as the maximum speed limit in most cities was 10 mph. Drugstores also handled different things back then. Marijuana, heroin, and morphine were all available over the counter at your local drugstore. Back then pharmacists said, "Heroin clears the complexion, gives buoyancy to the mind, regulates the stomach, bowels, and is a perfect guardian of your health!"

You used your means of transportation to go to work. The average US wage in 1910 was around 26 cents per hour. The Average US worker made between $200 and $400 per year. A competent accountant could expect to earn $2,000 per year. A practicing dentist $2,500 per year, veterinarian between $1,500 and $4,000 And, a mechanical engineer about $5,000 per year. My Grandfather started his forst job after leaving the Army, by working in the office of Hoepp-Bartlett Construction Company. He worked here after he married in 1920.

Finding a place to live after the War was not easy. 14 percent of the homes had a bathtub and, Only 8 percent of the homes had a telephone. Eighteen percent of households had at least one full-time servant or domestic help. After location a residence, it was time to look at a few food costs. Sugar cost four cents a pound, eggs were fourteen cents a dozen and, Coffee was fifteen cents a pound. There was no Fast Food restaurants. There were Cafe's and Diners, that served a family home style menu.

Most women only washed their hair once a month, and, used Borax or egg yolks for shampoo. You had to take rugs outside and beat the dust out of them, and very few homes had indoor bathrooms. Your bathroom was called an outhouse, a little wooden building that was out in the yard. Life was getting better by the year, but that did not last too long.

My Grandfather knew his first child was on the way before the end of 1920. Around this time, more than 95 percent of all births took place at home. But ninety percent of all Doctors had NO College Education! Instead, they attended so-called medical schools, many of which were condemned in the press AND the government as "substandard." Living in the City was not an easy life in '18, as The average life expectancy for men was 47 years. The Five leading causes of death, at the time were: 1. Pneumonia and influenza. 2. Tuberculosis 3. Diarrhea 4. Heart Disease and at number 5. Stroke.

Taking a Vacation in 1918, to see the tallest structure in the world, the Eiffel Tower, was an expensive and done by ship. A vacation to Los Vegas was unheard of, as the population of the city was only about 30 people.

United States was not the first country to restrict crossing of their southern border. In 1918 Canada passed a law that prohibited poor people from entering into their country for any reason.

This was a time of having real low crime figures, there were about 230 reported murders in the Entire U.S.A.!

At this time, the American flag had 48 stars, Crossword puzzles, canned beer, and iced tea hadn't been invented yet. Also, there was neither a Mother's Day nor a Father's Day. This was the world at the end of the 1910's.

My Grandfather lived in the city for over 10 years, Leaving his first job and then went to Armour Egg and poultry company. He worked there years and moved up the ranks. He moved out of the city and bought a farm. He then became involved in starting a local Ski Club.

After the start of World War 2, He saw Armours sell its business location. He then started his own Produce Company, that also handled chickens and eggs. 50 years had passed since his birth, and this is when he became a Grandfather. It was also around this time, that He became a Widower. He would be around for another 26 years. He passed away in 1972.

Many facets of his life are interesting. Every door that closed, he went to open a new one. He never married another, He stayed being a Grandpa to all that we born in the family, and he welcomed every new Grandchild that came along. He supported all 11 of them, for as long as he walked on the Earth.

Chapter 118

Parents Never Learn - 3/9/19

Over the years that I, and my brothers grew up, Many unusual things occurred. One of these events should have caused my parents to look at their lives and reconsider what they were doing and not doing for the family.

In the early 1950's, was the first event that should have opened their eyes to see the world as it was and what it could be. They failed to learn anything out of this. The day started out with an early spring rain, and ended up in a thunderstorm. Then it gets worse and a Tornado emerged out of it. This formed over the horseradish fields, to the SW of Pine Valley. As the storm intensified, a funnel developed and moved NE into toward the city. The Tornado touched the ground and traveled between our house, and the house 200 feet to the west. This white house had heavy damage done to the garage, roof damage was also done.

To our uncompleted red brick house, it was wrapped in tar paper, the bricks have not been installed yet. The roof had heavy damage done to the shingles and some tree damage in the yard. When the worst of the storm developed, Our mother, who was expecting at the time, went down into the basement with my brothers. There she took all the crew and went under the steps, as that was the safest place in the basement. Soon the tornado passed by and the danger went with it. The tornado then damaged the Ski jump, that was across the highway, to the north. After this, the tornado exited to top of the hill and remained high over

300

of 3rd ward, and the valley below. It then disappeared back into the clouds. Our house needed new tar paper and to be re-shingled.

The house could have been ripped off of the foundation and left in a pile of rubble. Our mother failed to learn anything from this close call. This was the first of many events that should have led her to be a different kind of a mother.

The next event came about 7 years later. Two convicts escaped from prison, from an adjoining state. They came into Pine valley with a stolen car. This vehicle had a breakdown and they went looking for another. They saw the truck in the front yard. They came to the door, as an excuse to get in, they asked to use the telephone because their car broke down. Once inside the house, both displayed guns. They then wanted the keys to the truck. My father refused to give them the keys. The convicts then pistol whipped him. My father then ran across the living room and jumped through the closed living room window, like He thought he was Superman. Shattered glass was inside the house and outside the yard, it looked like ice chips. My father then ran into the trees in the yard and hid.

Then the attention from the convicts went to my mother, they again demanded the keys to the truck. About this time, one of my brothers came out of his bedroom. The noise drew attention from the convicts and they drew their guns. My mother than tossed the keys to them so they would leave the house. The convicts then went to steal the truck, but they could not get the truck started as they did not know what they had to set the choke lever at. After draining the battery in the truck, they abandoned it and ran off. They later were captured and sent back to prison, with a few more years added to their sentence.

Any lesson learned here was made by my brother. He learned the power of the gun. This event was the beginning of when his life began to stray from being on the right side of the law. Whatever lesson my mother got from this, quickly evaporated. She could have been a Widow, and have one less child alive. This event was just a bump in the road for her, as her mistreatment of my brothers and I continued. But this event, clearly showed everyone what child was her favorite. This changed the family structure, but not my mother. She eventually did more and more things to advance her cause and harm her children more. So in the end, This home invasion, taught her no lesson at all. It led her to be more of a Me First attitude.

My Mother failed to see the risks of the things she got into. She almost lost 3 fingers one time, when she was around the water pump, that was in the basement. She was adjusting the belts and failed safety guide lines. This was not the only thing that showed up. In the 1970's She placed herself in the Queen Bee position, and nobody or anything was going to change this. She ended up with the me, Me, ME first attitude.

One of her friends in the early 60's was feeling sick, by 1964 her condition was worse. I took a day off of school, and made the trip to the State Capitol with them. This city had the best cancer treatment that she could find. Many things were tried, but Mary passed away. I saw this is a possible lesson for my mother to learn, that life for some is too short. She should have counted her blessings, that she was not the one with days to live. My mother should have been thankful that she was healthy and there was time to turn her life around and be a better Mother. She did nothing to make life better for her children. She went back to he old ways, and assumed power and control over others. She learned nothing from the death of Mary. She missed the chance to be a better person and help others, instead of hindering them. She became more evil by the end of the 60's. This was too bad that she did, she missed her chance to seek forgiveness and be a new person. Her children were the ones that suffered the most, as she began to meddle into the lives even more. She paid a large price by traveling down the wrong road. She failed to heed the warnings and the examples she encountered. So in the end, she was bed ridden and had no true real friend.

As for our father. His teen life was involved with the bottle of beer. It was his love affair. Women were a sideline and a way to have a servant around the house. He drank decade after decade. He abused his children, His money bought cigarettes and booze, before groceries. He neglected the house, cars, his true friends. He would belly up to the bar with strangers, instead of spending time with past friends. Alcohol became his daily god. His warning in life came when his ulcer was so bad that it caused heavy internal bleeding, that he was sent to ICU. During this time, The wife, the Warden, did not allow some people to see him, including their children. He did recover and He missed his chance to turn his life around and seek forgiveness. He was forced to give up his booze, or die real soon. He lived for a few more years. And when he died, the Warden banned family members from attending the funeral.

Both parents set up the homestead like a Stalag style Prison Camp. We could not leave the yard or have friends over. Neither parent was worthy of the position in life that they were given. Both were given a chance to change, but they never did. This is a case of 'Parents Never Learn'.

Chapter 119

Up in the Trees - 3/10/19

The magic place to be for Me was anywhere that I could be solo. I wanted time to myself. This was not easy around the property where I grew up. But I had dreams to be free, and ideas that needed to be expanded. I had to find a place where this could be done. I had to think of things that I could learn from and expand my horizon. I looked around and it took me to the trees. Trees were everywhere and in any direction. This gave me a place, I now needed a reason, and in 1963, I got my chance.

The construction of Riverside Hospital was being done. I saw a row of tall trees across the 2 lane highway. I would climb up one of the trees, day after day, week after week. I would watch the construction being done, and a 10 million dollar hospital would arise from the ground and would stand 9 stories tall. It was something for me to see and study how it was done. It also got me time away from the in-house Warden. This place started with a hole in the ground.

There was not much to look at for sometime. So watching the traffic on highway 3 rumble along was the thing to do. Counting Semi trucks was interesting too. Around 60 semi trucks would pass my location every hour. At times, I would see bumper to bumper traffic for over a half an hour. 2 lanes was getting smaller every year. In a few years, I-13 would be completed and drain the semi traffic down to a dribble. I can still remember the Frito truck accident, 5 cent chip bags were all over the place.

The footings were done and so where the basement walls. It was time to build the floors. They poured the concrete slab that was at ground level. It was interesting as the 1st floor re-enforced concrete post were made, one by one. After that, the 2nd floor concrete slab was done. Then they made the 3rd floor posts and the next concrete slab. They did this again and again, until all 9 floors were done, and the roof too. The building looked like a skeleton, I could see right through it. They wanted the building enclosed before winter, this allows them to complete the inside of the building.

Day after day, I saw the steps to build this. What was a cow pasture just a few years earlier, will become the newest Hospital Facility in town. It will replace a more than 70 year old structure, and increase the number of hospital beds in the area. This is the first major structure to be built in this area of Pine valley.

The next step was to enclose the floors one by one. The would bring flat panels to the side of the building. These were room window panels that had yellow parts that would be the final color of the facility. A winch was on the roof, a cable was dropped down. The cable would lift each panel up to the next location, one by one. Once at desired location. The panel was fastened in place, and it was time to get the next one. They started on one side of building, and filled in each floor, by filling in the sides. After one floor was done, they would move on to the next floor. One by one, each floor was completed.

They had finally paneled each floor and the exterior walls were completed before winter. The workers moved inside of the building and completed that too. But I could not see that, and with winter coming, being up in the trees to watch ended. during the next year, 1964, the Hospital was opened and cars filled the visitors parking lots and the employees lot as well. The Hospital was running, full steam ahead. This also pushed other businesses to be built nearby.

The traffic on Highway 3 increased, due to the influx of patients, visitors, new construction in the area, and to the Physician's Clinic. This area blossomed out of a cow pasture. The proof of this was a cattle tunnel that went under the highway. It took another 5 years and the 2 lane highway was turned into 6 lanes, then came traffic lights, another clinic, hotels, and gas stations. Later retail stores showed up. Years later a department store and strip mall with service road, gobbled up the land where all of the trees once stood. Some call this progress, but I'm not so sure. One thing I do know, it made the house of hell come tumbling down, one piece at a time.

It's been 55 years since this Hospital opened, it was expanded several times. UWPV University also expanded nearby. There isn't much left of the house where I lived. I can only find one part of it. Just enough that allows me to keep the memories in my mind, about a house, that was torn apart 41 years ago.

I remember being outside in the backyard at night, Looking up and seeing the stars that painted figures above the clouds. I can remember being on top of a telephone pole, that was in out backyard. this what put there for a yard light, but it was never completed, like hundreds of other projects that were started. I was on the pole, watching the car headlights over a mile away. Wondered how each driver enjoyed their freedom on the road and in their lives.

I am the only one left now, that can go back to this area, and walk where the trees were. I had my best thoughts and dreams when I was along the side of the highway, being high Up in the Trees. Without my dreams, just what would I have today.

Chapter 120

Mind Shift - 3/11/19

. Time around me seems to speed up and Slow Down at Any Time at All. I am experiencing another time of my life that too many things are happening in too short of a time span. The last time that it happened was from December 2nd to March 13, almost 30 years ago. I saw one of these extended events, Tell Me Why is another happening to me. This time around the dates are January 1st and it looks like it will not end until March 13. Both times a family member dies. This time I have to handle it alone as the one that helped last time, is the one who passed away. I was not walking on my path alone, I hope It Will Be the Last Time, But I feel like a Nowhere Man, I have hinted to others, Don't Let Me Down. I need some to Come Together and doing things With A Little Help From My Friends. I know that All Things Must Pass.

. I expected that I would have some support, but one denies that all the things actually happened. The other is hard to find and the communication line is being stretched so far, that an ant could use it in a high wire act. I see shadows along the side of the uncertain future that I face. I am starting to see that I have to go back to Yesterday, to go forward. I turn the time frame back into the 1960's and have my own Day Tripper. There isn't another to say She Loves you, or another making the statement, I want to hold your hand. I am walking on the Abby Road alone, it is now like The Long and Winding Road. I see a Bad Moon Rising as I pass Penny Lane. Some times life goes slower, as I now have Eight Days a Week to try and recover the best than I can.

. In My Life, I just can't say, You Know My Name, Look Up The Number. When I say Good Morning Good Morning or Good Night. With every time I say Hello, Goodbye, I have to be aware that some know about my loss.

. There is no chance that I can celebrate, I need A Beginning The memories are Here, There and Everywhere. I don't want to repeat this, Not a Second Time. It Won't Be Long to Get Back to a more normal life style. I can't stay in a Helter Skelter world. I can't Let It Be.

. There's a Place Across the Universe where she got Her Ticket to Ride. Do You Want to Know a Secret, From Me to You. I've Got a Feeling I will end up in the Sgt. Pepper's Lonely Hearts Club Band. There used to be only one of Us Watching Rainbows. I was thinking what it would be like When I'm Sixty-Four, again.

. This became A Day in the Life of a Paperback Writer, another Magical Mystery Tour. It seems like A World Without Love and I Just Don't Understand it. You Won't See Me Carry That Weight, as I'll Be On My Way with Lonesome Tears in My Eyes.

. Tell Me What you See, I Want to Tell You Every Little Thing I see, she is Free as a Bird, and free of pain and Misery. For No One should have A Hard Day's Night.

. Everybody's Trying to be a friend and offering Help. All I've Got to Do is to get them All Together Now, Don't Let Me Down. If I Needed Someone the time is now. We Can Work It Out When I Get Home.

. Things We Said Today, has The Word That Means a Lot to us. Because of this, things are Getting Better. Thank You Girl, There was no one Till There Was You. I was Glad All Over when another told me that She Loves You, The Night Before.

. From a Window, I'm Looking Through You and see the Little Child. How Do You Do It? It makes me say, I Need You, Please Please Me, Etcetera, Etcetera.

. Now Here Comes the Sun, We can take a Day Tripper to Strawberry Fields Forever. Now I Feel Fine, as I saw The Inner Light. I did not need help from Lucy in the Sky with Diamonds, Like Dreamers Do. In The End it will only be the Two of Us.

Chapter 121

She is my Grandma - 3/12/19

I am my Paternal Grandpa, I look at his life and I have repeated it in many, many ways. My wife also repeats many things in my Grandmother.

I looked at the life of my paternal Grandma and I saw her shadow in my Wife. It took until after my Wife passed away to see where my Grandmother and my Wife walked along in the same footsteps.

Both grew up on a farm, and they had to walk to a one room schoolhouse. Both of them had a house that used wood as a heat source. They lived in a house without a bathroom inside. They had to go outside, and across the yard, to use the outhouse. Both grew up canning food to be used on the farm. Both women had to milk cows to get fresh milk, and take care of chickens to get eggs. Both farms were out on rural postal routes.

Both of their husbands have another relative that was named after them. Both Wives were older than their Husbands. Both marriages lasted longer than 25 years. My Wife and I, only had one daughter, same as my paternal grandparents. Both families had more than one son. In both families, the oldest child was not the first one to marry. Both, new in-laws, have a first name that can be found elsewhere in the family tree, and within 1 generation.

When both of them passed away, neither one had ever seen or held a grandchild. The 2 of them, never saw any of their children get married. Both did know who their first in-laws, were going to be. Both were visited by the parents of their future Son/Daughter in law. The first wedding of their children happened, after more than a year, since they passed away.

Both of them passed away before their husbands. Both of them, had medical issues that began to affect their lives and lasted for several years.

My Grandmother and Wife, had their Husbands and other relatives with them when they took their last breath.

So, in many ways, history repeats itself in many places. After I realized how I matched to my Grandfather, I looked into seeing if my Grandmother matched my Wife. It looks like she did, and this makes the set. in a strange way, History does repeat. This time, in a very personal way.

Chapter 122

2nd Born - 3/13/2019

28 years have past since Ray was born. Having a 2nd child at this time in our life would work for us, it made no difference if we had a girl or a boy. We had the room for him and he would be a companion for our other son. Our firstborn Son was over 4 years old when Ray came into the world.

The problem we saw, was the fact that he was born early. His due date was May 21. But he was born at a body weight of 5 pounds, for this reason he had to stay in the hospital, and in an incubator for a few weeks. If he was under 5 pounds, then it would be more time. I was with them when he was born, and shortly after birth, they weighed him and took him to an incubator to keep a watch over him and to keep him warm.

Everyone in the room did what they had to and do it fast, So fast that neither of us could hold him or touch him. they wanted to prevent any possible thing that could cause problems later on. He had to be warm and monitored at all times.

I stayed with my wife after they settled her down to rest. I was in the room and we talked about the choices that we needed to be made. The name was easy and this choice was decided months ago. If it was a Boy the name would be Ray, It fit with Rayne's name. My name started with the same letter, so a boys name was decided on. If it was a Girl, Rachel would have been used.

We then had to plan as what we would do as soon as Rayne was released. We knew it could be 4 to 6 weeks before we brought him home. Or first born was there, I was with him in a play area, after the doctors saw complications in this birth. He was at my side until Rayne was brought back into her room. So it was a waiting game, We had to wait until the Doctor informed us as what they were going to do. This could be an hour or two. We had to wait.

About 3 hours had passed, and a few staff members came into Rayne's room. They informed us as what they did to care for our Son, But he passed away. They did everything that they could, but he had problems with breathing and a few other things were not what they expected. He was not strong enough to survive, They then brought our Son into the room. This allowed us to see him and he was held by Rayne. It would be the only time that we held him, or ever saw his face.

Or oldest Son, saw his brother and ran and hid into the corner. He knew something was wrong, but did not realize that his brother was not alive, as he had passed away.

Then Ray was wrapped up in a blanket and a staff member took him out of the room. We would never see him again. It really asked the question, what did we do wrong. The answer was they was nothing anyone did, as all tests showed things were normal, but he was born too early to survive.

Rayne had a Black Rose placed near the door, but outside in the hallway. This told all staff as what they had to do to help us deal with our loss. After a few days, Rayne was allowed to come home. The funeral was then held. We did not have money for all the Funeral expenses and the Cemetery costs.

So arrangements we made to have our son placed next to my Aunt, she passed away about 6 and a half years earlier. She never married and was a elementary school teacher for 39 years. It was the best place for our son, given our circumstances.

Life would give us another chance, in a bit under 2 years, We had another child born. This was not a replacement for our son. It could not be, as this child, was our daughter. We treated all our children as what they would be, an individual person.

Over the years we would wonder what life would if he was with us. What his first day of school would be like, His graduation, and what he would do for a living. there was also many other stages in his life as well. If he would marry and have children.

Ray has been with the angels for over 27 years, before he would no longer be alone. The hardest thing for Us was having him born and then pass away on the same day. This was also his paternal Grandmother birthday, as well.

Ray has be alone waiting for others in the family to join him in the heaven above, Nobody would know who the next family member would be. As time marched along, the answer came. His Mother, My Wife, would be the next one to join him. They are now together, 28 years after she gave birth to him.

They can comfort each other as they wait for a time, when the entire Family can reunite and live forever in the house of the Lord.

Chapter 123

In House Studio - 3/14/19

I have always had an interest in electronic things. I would look at television and wondered how Mickey Mouse moved across the screen. How did he get to thousands of TV sets across the city. How did the voice match the movements. I wanted the answers to those questions.

Whenever someone we knew, had a television set that was broken, and they wanted a new one. I was given a few of the old ones. I then took them apart, piece by piece. I looked for the reason as why they failed, I then continued to disassemble the set and save the good parts. I ended up with several boxes of used parts. I even took some of the parts and disassembled them as well.

When I entered Junior High, I enrolled in every class that educated others in electronics and electricity. I later was given gifts that were project kits that allowed user to wire parts together to make over 50 items. I continued my electronics classes in Senior High, as well. I had 6 years of classes in a row. After High School, I entered Technical College. There I started out working around appliances, I took them apart, and repaired them. During my last year in College, I went through Electronics Repair. This involved all of the home electronic devises, including the television.

I first tried to get a job at Maytag, an appliance manufacture. Later I got a Job at a local Television Repair shop. This peaked my interests in what other things I could do in the electronics world.

314

I recall an event when I was in grade school. I sent in for some tickets to go on a local Children's Program. This was lead by a man that was an on screen Sheriff. There was interviews, games, cartoons, and locally made food products. There was hot dogs, milk, and an ice cream treat, for all of the kids that were there. I had 4 tickets and I came with 3 others. Part of my group of 4 did get to play musical chairs, and we were given prizes by the local shopping center. I was looking at all of the equipment that was used in making this show.

I saw the host with his wired microphone, and the cameras on dollies, all attached by cables. I was watching the director in the control booth operating the system, that put the live television show on the air. I even remembered what they did during commercials. I never forgot this one time event.

Years later, a fellow classmate went to the local public access station, and started his own talk show. The cost was low and he had a weekly show. I thought that I could make a better program that he did and I made mine about local events, and then I made a second show. This one was a children's program. I let my Son host the show. It had cartoons and various children's activities. I started out as the Executive Director, at the Public Access station, for 2 other TV talk shows. Then I wanted to make My two shows. I needed a lot of time to record the raw recordings and edit them for airtime. I needed my own control room and studio.

I set my plan in motion to make my studio at home. The home studio would be in the living room, and my control room would be placed in a bedroom, over 20 feet away. I ran about a dozen and a half cables under the floor, between the living room and the bedroom. I put together my Beta and VHS VCRs, video mixer, and audio mixer, as a system. I used one VCR to record the show, and the other to provide the unedited video and the cartoons.

This system started around 1994, and I ran it for over 25 years. I made about 1,100 programs. A little over 500 shows were children's programming, and over 550 were made about local events and History. These have been on the air for over 25 years. I did things and made videos that others would not get involved in for years after I started.

I had thousands of my videos that I made, since 1982, to use as a source material. So I continued on making more videos, and showing the older ones as well. This gave me a lot of local history to show. I also made my videos in 2 other states.

None of this would have happened, without my interest in wondering how Mickey Mouse ran around on the TV. My creativity in taking my home VCR on the road, allowed me to make an early version of the Dash Cam, in 1984. I also went to record live events and meetings. I recorded my hometown as I saw it. I also recorded a few years of stock car races at the Redwood Speedway.

I did all of this to save the world as I saw it, so my children and beyond, could see what I saw around me. I made my In House Studio for the present, and the future. I made it to share my vision of my world around Pine Valley.

I also involved my children in making the Kids show. It now becomes a living record of my children growing up. This is worth more than all the cost and effort, it took me to make my In House Studio.

Chapter 124

Cellphone Call - 3/15/19

. Hannah is the kind of girl that is always on the go, her mind is like an over wound clock. Life is busy, busy, busy. She has a get together with her friends tonight and she has to make dinner for her impending guests, Everything has to be done and be ready by 7.

. She leaves work and hops in her Plymouth. She is driving home, then realizes that she better check in with her friends. She flips oven her phone, pushes the buttons with her nose, and starts jabbering with her friends, one by one. Hannah wants to be sure they do their part and be at her house on time.

. Hannah then realizes that she needs a few items, and races over to the Speedy Mart. While still chatting with her friends, she jumps the curb, scattering the pedestrians as they Dodge out of her way. She then cuts around a few cars and parks her car backwards in the lot. Then, gets out of her car and walks into the Exit door, bumping her nose. Then she finds the correct door and stumbles her way to get a cart. She then spots a nearby cart and grabs it. A moment later, 2 kids in the cart start whining. Their Mother runs up and takes back her cart. Hannah will have to look for another one.

. Now Hannah has her cart and on her way to find her sweets and treats. Hannah enters the fruit and Veggie isle. She runs over a few tomatoes and Potatoes, Hannah tells her friends on the phone, People here should be wearing shoes. She keeps jabbering as she scallops a few potatoes, grabs a few noses for the snowman, takes a mushroom because she wants to expand the house. Holds an onion up to her ear and whines that it does not make a sound. Then grabs a few cayenne peppers if any of her friends get cold later. She avoids the butternut squash because she hates damaged veggies. She avoids leeks as she wants to save water. Hannah then stays out of the bakery as she has too fruitcakes as relatives.

. Time to make her own cherry pie, but as she jabbers to her friends, she can't remember what fruit she needs to make one. So around the corner she goes, and tells her friend that she knocked over a display potato chips. and says" They are already chips, after I ran over them, the customer will have more in every bag". Hannah rushes to the Dairy isle, but can't find the cow to get milk, so she buys instant Cocoa. She wanted to get whipped cream, but she isn't a violent woman. Then she gets a few cases of root beer so the gang can get liquored up at the party. Hannah then runs over to buy a Rose so she could bake cookies. Since there was enough couch potatoes coming to the party, she avoided the russets.

. Hannah then hurried to get closer to the checkout, read through the rag magazines and avoided the TV Guide, as she was not planning on taking a trip. She then rushed back to get a box of Trix, The girls always liked a little magic before the night was over. Then rushes through the meat section, as she was too chicken to stop, then knocks over tower of canned beverages. She tells her friend not to worry, because they were soft drinks.

. Then Hannah pushes the cart into another shopper and cuts in line. She gets up to the cashier and places her items on the conveyor belt. As the packages jostle for position to be first, the Cashier asks her, "Miss, what is your hurry?". Hannah replies, One moment please, as I ask Mabel to hold on the line. I hear from the other person that she had called, say. "My name is not Mabel, My name is Mary". Hannah "Mary !, I called up Mabel, What are you doing on her phone line?". Mary "I live here, not Mabel". Hannah "oops Wrong Number, after I hang up, I will hit redial and try to call Mabel again"

Chapter 125

John 3 16 - 3/16/19

. For God so loved the world, that he gave his only begotten Son. With out this, I and others would not have any hope for a world beyond the present day Earth. Without this Gift, I would never have a chance to ever see my Wife again. and other family members.

. I know I will not see a few of them as they failed in following the guidelines put before them. They lost their way along the narrow path to find everlasting life. I can't save them or any of the works that they have done. They missed their chance for everlasting life.

. I look at my life and family, 2 of them have already passed away. Nothing I can do can bring them back. Their names should be written in the Book of Life. I have to be diligent and stay on my path to join them. I see many temptations that I must avoid. Traveling along in life is not going to be easy. I have to stand strong and not wander from what the Son of God has done for Me.

. I hope that the other remaining family members follow my walk along the narrow path. This way, they will be reunited with their family again. They have to do their walk on the path without those who have gone ahead of them. I can't hold their hand. They have to accept the Son and what he gave to all mankind, as he died on the cross. Every person has the control of their own destiny, I can't do it for them.

. I believe in that Son, and His sacrifice. This has given me a way to reunite with my family members, that have passed on before me. I can't buy passage into Heaven, I can't trade for it, or talk my way in. I can't bribe others for a ticket. Heavens Gate accepts no coins or offerings. The Son of God has paid the complete cost. It was given freely to those who accepted Him, as their savior.

. All I can say is, Thank You Jesus.

Chapter 126

65 Year Old Stranger - 3/17/19

When I grew up, I heard my parents argue about the things of the present and of the past. I knew about their shortcomings and failures. I also heard about other relatives faults and successes. I was aware of the life of my Grandparents. Where they came from and why some died at a younger age. Cancer claimed my Grandmother at age 55. A Grandfather dies of a heart attack at age 57. I knew he worked for 25 cents a day, during the depression. My paternal Grandparents ran a dairy farm and I know where it was. Both sides of my family was mostly an open book as I grew up. I learned about the bad things later, I had a great Aunt and her Mother both die at age 42, due to others that took their lives, in a crime event. I had the basic history, the relatives names and dates.

I can go back over 1,000 years in history, and see layers of relatives step by step. On my Paternal Grandmothers side. I can go back 2,169 years. Family history was there, and if you dug into it for a short time, you could find the answers. When it came to my wife, everything was hidden away and very little past history was know for over a half century. My own Father in-law was a mystery, as much as I was for over 60 years.

When it came to my Wife, She was around age 65 when the secrets of her Father became known. I helped in the research and scoured over two dozen cemeteries miles south of Pine Valley. I found Her Grandfather's first wife, His Aunts and Uncles, half Sisters and Brothers.

I researched the internet, shared information with her cousin's wife. I helped make their side family tree. I then traveled around 2 stated and over 25 counties. I took photos and researched others. Working with others uncovered 6 versions of my Wife's last name. After 65 years, Rayne finally knew what she wanted to know, who her Father was, as a person, and where He grew up. She now knew about his roots, and the relatives that lived a hard life.

Uncovering history comes with the good and the bad. My Wife's Grandmother was facing jail time, but things worked out that they gave he another chance. But her First Husband end up in jail. They got a divorce and this allowed Her to enter into her second marriage with Rayne's Grandfather. This marriage resulted in two boys being born. The first born boy was to be her Father. Her Grandfather's marriage ended about 5 years later. He came back to visit about 3 years later, left with the oxen and was never seen again, nobody knew where he went or where he died. Rayne's Grandmother placed her 2 sons in an orphanage. Later they were adopted by 2 families, that were related. The two Boys saw each other almost every day, they rode the same school bus and went to their adopted family events. The other school children thought they were cousins, but they were actually blood brothers.

Each brother got married and had their own families. I never saw my Father in-law's brother until the day of Rayne's Father's funeral. He showed up to pay his final respects. I looked at him and my Father in-law, that was up front in his casket. They were a matching set of brothers. The same face structure, build, and more. It took a death to get the families together. After this funeral, I and others began out search of their past. A booklet about 30 pages was made with our found information and given to other relatives. The secrets of their past was finally revealed. Rayne finally knew about her Fathers past, just a couple of years before she dies.

Why wasn't the information known earlier ?. You can't change the past, so why hide it all. I could see where they would hide about the crimes done by family members, But why cover up everything about their past. It took me a few years to find out that my father in-law was named after his father. There was a Senior and a Junior, Her father was a Jr, like I am a Senior, and our Son is a Junior.

Over the past 2 years, I went to find each Headstone that has her family name on it. I found 3 relatives headstones in 2 separate locations.

I even found Rayne's Grandfather's first wife, her name was Cora. I took photos of all of them and shared them with my children and Rayne's other relatives. This was a labor of love.

The side benefit of this was I found that I was related to another Class Member of mine. I went to high school with her. I am trying to link myself to another Class Member at this time.

It would have been better if the secrets were not there. My wife should have been told decades before. The good thing about this is the my children and their cousins, now know about their families past.

The bad thing is that Rayne's brother died over 3 years ago, and never knew about their Fathers past. But, now his only daughter knows. I remember that she had questions about the families past, even on the day that she placed her Father's remains into his grave. They waited too long before starting this family history search.

I wrote my first book so that my own Daughter would know what I was like and how it affected her life. She now has information about her Parents past. She knows where we lived, how we met, And how our lives blended together for over 37 years. Now my Children know about their Grandparents history as well

I wrote my chapters for my Daughter before she was 25. I did not do it for the money or Fame. I did it so others would not repeat the mistakes that my parents made. Others besides my children, can learn from my examples, so that their children can have a better world, and be in a loving family relationship.

Chapter 127

Back Then - 3/18/19

I grew up in the small town of Pine Valley. It was a time where others had more respect for each other and we helped others. We were more active and enjoyed the outdoors, instead of being Couch Potatoes. We played games that required or brains to think, like checkers and chess. Not a game that used our thumbs.

My brothers and I, were up in the morning without an alarm clock. We ate cereal at the breakfast table before walking to school. We walked home from school and We played outside, before supper time. After the meal, We watched the the local aired cartoons and then the Flintstones. On Saturday mornings, We watched the cartoon lineup until noon.

We played outside in the warmer months, and in the basement during winter. We would ride our bikes for hours, when we could. Each of us went to our friends houses, because we were told it was better that way, than them coming here. We did these things without a cell phone or electronic toys or games.

Eating any fast food was a rare time. At home, We drank milk, water or Kool-aid, or Fizzies. We ate baloney sandwiches, PB&J sandwiches, grilled cheese sandwiches, hot dogs, soups, homemade mac and cheese, scalloped corn and hot dishes. If we had a late night snack, it was popcorn.

We lived during a time when we would gather glass bottles to take to the store to get a few pennies each. We used the deposit money to buy penny candy, in a brown paper bag. A quarter's worth was a lot back then. We then played outside by climbing trees, riding bikes, playing in the sand, and touch football. At times, we had a few baseball games in the backyard.

We bought a bottle if soft drink for a dime, a can was 12 cents. There was no bottled water, at times we drank from the water hose. We had no microwave or cable TV, no VCR's, no cell phones, and no remote controls for anything. Our phone had a dial, Only appliances that was plugged into the wall was a Toaster and the Coffee maker. We made popcorn in a large pot with cover, on the electric range.

You did not hear curse words on the radio or TV, and IF you cursed, you did it away from the public or you got punished for it. "Please" and "Thank you" were part of our daily dialogue.

If you were bad in school, you got sent to the Principal's office. They called your Parents or sent a note home to be signed. and when you got home you got in trouble again because the school informed them. This meant that your behind would feel the heat from being swatted by a belt, or hand. Then you behaved yourself or else. Repeating the same wrong, wasn't an option.

You learned from your Grandparents and your Parents, instead of disrespecting them and treating them as if they did not know a thing. What they say might have been written in the Holy Book. You never knew, but you were not willing to take that chance, that they could be wrong.

If someone had a fist fight with a friend or neighbor, that's what it was...a fist fight and you were back as being friends in a short time. Kids that were around guns were taught to respect them, and never thought of taking a life, or having one along to scare others. Guns were not used unless hunting or on the practice range.

We could not leave the yard as we have to be in range to hear our mother yelling out the back door. She yelled when supper was ready or when a chore had to be done. We had to earn money, we were given no allowance.

All of the siblings had to be around the dinner table, and we talked to each other. Going to School was required. We didn't have Truant officers, we had GOD. We sang our National Anthem and listened to our teachers. We did the Pledge of Allegiance every day at School.

We watched what we said around grownups because we knew If we Disrespected them, we would get punished for it, it wasn't called abuse back then, it was called discipline!

We carried packages, Groceries, and held doors open for others. We did this without being told. When we were given things and money, we said Thank You. We learned manners were an important part of life. We faced punishment if we made fun of another child.

The world was not perfect, but it was a better life back then. People worked for a better world for everyone, instead of doing everything for themselves. We shared back then, instead of being greedy. We were part of a team, Not a single person that would fight with others to be Number One

What a wonderful world that we lived in.

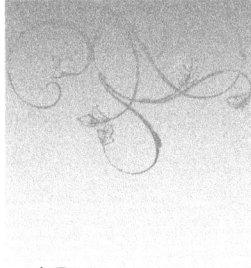

Chapter 128

Down Town - 3/19/19

When I was traveled around town alone, I sometimes found myself downtown in Pine Valley. I could walk around downtown and escape the problems around home. I needed to get away from the house, staying there was bad medicine to me. When I was in my early teens, I needed to be in a place that I was alone in the world, or in the center of all the hustle and bustle of the most crowded place in town. My parents would not find me here.

I would tell others that I was going down to a friends house, but I went downtown to see the things I could only dream about. There was a large slot car track downtown. It was in the basement to the Moose lodge. It had 8 lanes and filled half of the room. I watched others how they raced, I could not afford anything like this at this time, I could not even afford to pay the cost to race an hour. I did meet those who raced there and saw how they put together the cars. Sometimes I imagined that I was in the race and took home the Checkered Flag.

I recall the time that I was with another classmate and went into the back of the drugstore and enjoyed ice cream, The classmate paid for it, I could not understand why, as he wanted nothing in return. I was not used to this, but it gave me a ray of hope. I felt that being downtown was better than living at home. I remember the many places that I went to and other places that I would never go to.

I remember waiting lines in Woolworth's, the store was full of customers, many were at the lunch counter too. After school at times, and on Saturdays, the drugstore Ice cream fountain had all seats filled. The Hay market parking lot was filled. J C Penny's elevator was always busy. Escalator in Woolworth's always had someone on it. The Country Kitchen had a short wait time to get a table. The three level parking ramp had a mini traffic Jam, at times. Then the Train crossing by the Post Office, got cars going into downtown backed up. Then the biggest backup, waiting for the train to get through the N Dewey street intersection, that was halfway up a hill.

The crosswalks were busy. Kresge's was one of the big Department store down there. The was Sears, Montgomery Wards,Days Music, and Toy Land. Shoe stores, Dress shops, a Book store, and placed I feared to tread. The Women gathered around Edwin's, Samuelson's and The Fashion Store. This was mostly their place, as well as the Jewelry Store and a place that sold furs. Another place sold luggage and car parts and supplies. There was even a Greyhound Bus station and a small bowling alley. Something for everyone. Later they was an arcade, with dozens of classic games.

Downtown looked like a modern Mall of today, that exploded and the stores scattered over two dozen blocks. Everything you needed was here, banks, movie theaters, a library, restaurants, and Bars serving food. This was a famous place at times. John F Kennedy and Bobby came to visit. Boris Karloff came her too, there was Blondie and Dagwood and dozens more. Famous singers of yesterday and today show up and do their thing.

The place isn't as active as it was in the 1960's, but it is starting to come back to life. In the last few years, One hundred million dollars were spent to reshape the downtown into the world of tomorrow, But I remember the place over 50 years ago. Even a Root beer Stand was within a few blocks away. Trains went through here every day, and semi trucks by the hundreds. This was also part of the Yellowstone trail.

It gave me another place to escape from the Warden around the house. Another place IO went to was the candy store that was operated by three Sisters. This place had so many glass jars filled with assorted candy, that it would take me a lifetime to eat. Even the Daily Newspaper was made here. It was like paradise. Then why did this wonderland end ? Something called a Mall came to town, and the Downtown evaporated over time.

I lost my place that I could become hidden within. Around 30 years later, the Malls themselves, became replaced by the online sellers and turned into skeletons. This may be the reason why the down towns have not faded away. They are slowly being updated and offer a brighter tomorrow. They will never be my sanctuary as they were in the past, But I will never forget that at times, they were better than being at home.

Chapter 129

I'm Proud of My Sin - 3/20/19

I meet people everyday, they live for today and think that they will live forever, or at least the next 20 years. They have no fear of a higher power, or any other person. They only live for what they want and get it any way that they can.

They are proud of their accomplishments, all of them, the good and the Bad. They like to brag about all the enjoyment that they got out of their lives, even if it was something wrong that they did. They tell stories about it, over and over, they relish the event and tell all of those around them. They have no worry that someday things will get them in the end. They talk of affairs, times they destroyed others property, and how they got away with things.

They invite trouble to come to them, when it does, they welcome it with open arms. They lie about most everything. They claim to be a professional in a vocation, they talk like one, walk like one, and give advice like one. But they fail to see their error. A real Doctor would not engage others to talk about whats wrong with them in a public place. But unlicensed 'Doctors' do it, because they feel no one will challenge them. They have an answer for everything. When confronted about their claim that they are a real, some fly off the handle and get angry, they yell and cuss a blue streak. Whenever the stakes are too high, they walk away, but yell all the way out the door, that they are right.

Some claim to be a professional in many fields, even as they spew out a thousand lies. They lie about their education, how they became top in their league. They proclaim that they know more that everyone else. When pressured or heavily questioned, they change the subject or make an excuse to end the conversation.

A few of these people, in order to make others think that they are what they say they are, fake events. One would ask to use another's phone. Then fake the call to a local hospital, they would act like pressing buttons and then have a one sided fake call. Then would chatter off their state Doctor's license number, to make others think believe that they are a real Doctor.

Every time that they make a fake call like this, the number they rattle off is different. A state license number has a set number of digits, They never seem to get that right. One time, I caught them using their Social Security number. Their brains never realize just how many dumb errors that they make. No real Doctor would discuss a persons medical condition in public.

Then those that talk of their conquests, they go through every affair that they had for over 40 years. They are proud of their times with married or unmarried partners. I had so many Girls that I could make a volleyball team out of them. They boast that other members of the opposite sex, want them and nothing will get in their way. They repeat this over and over, almost word for word.

This type of person thinks that everyone respects them, because they tell others that they are so great. That everything they do is right for them and they become great at what they do. But, others know that they are great liers and sinners. Over time, more and more people avoid them. They are starting to have less people that they think they control. Over time, they will have none to listen to their lies. So they go to a new location and then they rev up their, same old, same old lies. They have a new audience, but for how long ?

This becomes a never ending pattern of a man that boasts over and over, I will tell any lie to draw attention to Me, as I talk constantly and give nobody a chance to say anything. I always want control. Everyplace I go, I make it my personal stage, and I want no one to stop Me

There are others that hang around this type of person, they are self centered as well. They are users, that enjoy getting things given to them so they can be lazy, stuff their faces with anything that they can get. They have a menu like a King, and the pockets of a pauper. They eat 4 meals a day and snacks between their snack breaks. They don't care about their health as others foot the bill. They are always in search of their next meal. They go to one restaurant for snacks, after eating a large meal at another.

They then brag about every food on their menu, and proclaim how they consumed everything, including dessert. They can say, I had a good meal, I stuffed myself so much that I could not put my hands into my pockets. They love to be users and see nothing wrong. Their weight is morbidly obese, but they don't care. The food comes first, even if I am a glutton and break the rules. I too, am proud of it and will boast to the world.

P.S. is there enough that I can have seconds, or was that thirds. Can I get a doggy bag to take home. I might get hungry on the way home for a late dinner.

Some do not get the idea that others see what they are doing. They really don't care, they do what makes them happy and then brag how great they are. They never quit saying in their own way, I'm Proud of My Sin.

Chapter 130

Past Two Months - 3/21/19

It has been just a little over 2 months that my life was changed forever. It was like a thief in the night, that silently visited, and set the stage that ended Her life. We became an I, then I must go forward and do the things that We had done.

There was many hurdles, The first one was this. One of our kids denied that their Mother had died. I can still remember that this child, did not attend the Funeral. Nothing that anyone else had done prevented anyone to not be there. In My case, my own mother, slammed the door by telling me that I had to leave or be arrested. So when their Mother passed away, nothing stood in their way. It was open arms to all.

Some have said, why were things not done to prolong Her life. Several years earlier, Rayne and I went to an Attorney and had legal documents made. This gave Her and I the final say as what to do when facing the end of life. Rayne had made her choice and did so. She did not want to live by machines for year after year. So this was her choice. Don't look for blaming anyone. However, I feel that there is one or two that still thinks that she should still be in Intensive Care.

Now comes the other main issue. The financial balance that must be done. Before she passed, there was her income. 80% of Hers went to the place where she was taken care of. There was 20% to cover co-pays and things that she needed and items she wanted. I made this system work for about 5 years. Now I am capped as to how much income that I get. This means that things that I normally would have, are not possible anymore. I have to cut back. There is nothing that I can do. This means the in the future, I will have to move from the place that I have been living for the past 36 years. I have spend over half of my life in one place. I see it coming to the end.

Nobody is the same, and changes that need to be done, are not the same for everyone. Some get higher payments in retirement. Others have less cost to live, because they prepared better for their golden years. I planned for later years as well, but I would not get the higher income as others. Part of it is gross earnings over the years, and the other part is that I could not build up a 'Nest Egg' for the Golden Years. I see where others did better than myself, But I did better than others. There is only one final question, did I do enough ?, Time will tell, as to how long my ship will stay afloat.

Others around me seem to waste the things that are needed to make living better. They don't seem to care, as it is not their money being used to live on. At times, they seem to sabotage the ship and don't care. It places me between a rock and a hard place. Before I had two crew members to run the ship, I only have one to do it. I am on my own. I will have to revisit this in about another four months.

With the loss of a spouse, it is never the same for anyone. Some things that I face, may be like others, but not all. I now have to make daily decisions that will allow my ship to continue to sail. In other words, I must sort out things that I face and choose the right ones to keep me walking forward on my narrow path. There is nobody else to walk the path with me. I have to do it alone. My shadow can do nothing, as it tags along with me. I was not ready to have by life partner begin to evaporate before me, day by day. Every since the 1st day of the year, parts of her personality and connection to the world begin to disconnect.

If I could turn back time, would I do it. I say no, going through this once is hard enough. I would not want to go through this same thing again. Maybe this is why the thief came in the night, as my Wife also walked along the many rough roads, that were in her life. She passed peacefully, it was best for her. Going though this a second time may be too much for her and for Me. I could not prevent or change things, I had to accept whatever the outcome would be.

I have had many problems, because of Mother Nature's handing out a tough winter. It will take months to make repairs. If my boat begins to sink, I have to find a way to save it, or abandon ship and go elsewhere. I am in the position of Captain. I have to do the best that I can, with what I have. I have to keep moving forward, as I am not ready to write the Final Chapter.

Chapter 131

Living by Machine - 3/22/2019

About a week into the new year, Rayne had a bad night sleeping at the Riverside Hospital. We would not know how bad until the next morning. The Nurse came into her room with her medications. She went to get a glass of water so Rayne could take her medicines. But something was wrong, Rayne had labored breathing and her lip looked puffed up a bit. This looked strange to the Nurse. It also looked like there was a cut on the lip.

A call was placed to get another Nurse in her room. They put on gloves and inspected Rayne's lip, mouth area, and then opened her mouth. They saw a puffed up tongue and some cuts on the inside of the cheeks. The then looked at her medicine list and then checked her medical records. They finally realized that she had a seizure, and this caused her to bite her tongue and the cheeks. Rayne's breathing was labored, and they tried to see if she could swallow. But she could not do that correctly, because of the swelling and damage. It was time to call in the Doctor.

The Doctor then looks over the situation and says that the swelling may increase a bit, and she has had a time with low oxygen in her system. This caused addition damage to her brain activity. With the stroke that she had a week earlier, and now a seizure, she is in trouble, and if we leave this alone she could pass away with a few hours or days. As being Rayne's Husband, I was filled in with the Doctor's evaluation and what they were planning to do. He clearly stated that if something wasn't done, she would not live very long.

So the Doctor told the Nurses to get a breathing tube ready, and supplies ready and prepped to insert a feeding tube through her abdomen and into the stomach. This would allow the staff to feed her and enter medications into her body. The crew started to hustle to get things ready, then get the Doctor back into the room. He had to leave to check on another ICU patient. One support staff member was on the computer checking what medications that she could use. Then the staff explained what they were planning to do and why.

I asked the important question. "When you do these things, what will life be like for Rayne and how long will these items be needed. Will she recover from the damage from the seizure ? ". They said that once she gets these installed, she will need them for as long as she lives. We see no recovery since she was short of oxygen for more than 2 hours. She will need to be fed and would need a breathing assist machine. Then they asked me a question.

They wanted to know if I had any opinion about what they are doing, Since I now was given the Power of Attorney. Two Doctors did agree it was time to sign the transfer of the P.O.A. I told them to ask Rayne. They said that she may never talk again. I asked them, did they check her file for a Living Will. They commented back, "Does she have one ?". I said, "Yes, why didn't someone check to see ?". They thought that Rayne did not have one because she was on Medicare. I stated that I remember that We had one made for each of us, about three years ago. This was done when problems arose while she was in a Nursing Home.

I told them what Her Doctor's name was, where the document was, and what Attorney wrote up the documents. They should read what Rayne wanted for herself, before my decision about this is needed. A Nurse went onto the computer and searched for it. It was found and then read by the Nurse. She tells the Doctor that because of this document, we can't place the breathing or feeding tube. The Doctor then reads the document and agrees. The document says that she did not want to live a life that depended on machines to keep her alive, in a vegetable state.

So no further procedures could be done. They then proceeded to pack things up, took off a few monitors that were hooked up, and prepared to move her to the hospice area. Nature would be allowed to take it's course. I was told that she could pass away within hours. I told them it would be a few days, because Her relatives would becoming in a few days to visit her. It was now time to move her to a Hospice room.

So about a half hour later, she was moved in new room with less than half the items still hooked up. I contacted relatives and found out that they were coming on Saturday, three days from now. After Rayne was sleeping, I left the Hospital. I came back on the second day, and she still was alive, but breathing was a little labored. Later that day, I returned home, The relatives would show up tomorrow.

On Saturday, I had the information when our relatives would be at the Hospital. I had to meet them in the lobby, as they had no idea where ICU was or the Hospice area. I brought them up the elevator and to Her room. I sat next to the bed and the 4 others were next to the foot of Rayne's bed. We spent the next few hours talking about the past, present, and what Rayne went through. It was around 4pm. Our Daughter and her Fiance was there, Rayne's Sister and her Daughter. There was 6 of us in the room.

The relatives where chatting, but I heard a change in what my wife's breathing was like. It was about 4:10 in the after noon. I quit chatting with the others and listened closely to Rayne. At 4:16, I could not hear her breath. I watched to see if I saw any movement. I saw none, I pressed the call button. After that, I told my Daughter's Fiance to hold my Daughter's hand, and told Her to put her arm around Him. I then informed her that her Mother had passed away. She burst into tears, and held onto her Fiance. Within a minute, the Nurse came into the room. I pointed to my ears, then My heart, and then pointed at my Wife. I spoke no words. The Nurse the used her stethoscope and listened to Rayne's heart. She then pushed her pager for the other Nurse.

The Other Nurse repeats the test and agrees, They said that she had passed away, then my Daughter reacts to this news. The Nurse then says that they will mark the time of death at 4:20 pm. It now ends the daily pain that Rayne had and now, she will not be a living vegetable on display. She remembers what her Sister looked like after a car accident decades in the past. Rayne did not want to end up looking like her with more than a dozen machines doing everything for her.

After a short time, Her Sister and Niece had to go back home, it was about a two hour drive. My Daughter and Fiance had to work the next day, so they were next to leave. I spent time with Rayne, I then left to go home, realizing that I am now a Widower, and no longer married. Life was going to be full of changes each day.

Rayne lived 3 days, living off of her own body's energy, after the staff said that she could pass away within hours. She fought to stay alive to hear her Sister, Daughter, and the others, one last time. This was a Saturday, I realized that Monday was going to be busy for me. I needed to find a funeral home and proceed with the other needed items. I wrote her Obituary and a Poem for her funeral. I informed the other relatives. It was a busy week, Her funeral was on the next Saturday, one week after she passed away. Her Obituary was in the local paper two days in a row.

Every thing was done, I did every task that needed to be done. It was not easy dealing with this, But I did everything for Her.

I kept walking forward on my path, and completed my task. Saturday arrived and the Funeral was held. I had everything in place, she would be at the same place as our Son, who passed away almost 28 years before. They would be together, forever. I keep coming up with this question, Why did I have the only child that died, and then have the only Wife that passed away, among all of my Brothers ?.

It has now been over two months ago. I have everything done that needed to be done. I am back walking down my path, walking into the future, and to the place where We will all be together again.

Chapter 132

Noise of Silence - 3/23/2019

. Living in a world of partial deafness, I see a world that others do not. I also hear a different world when hearing aids are needed and used. I hear noise pollution that years ago was overlooked because sounds around me were normal and I did not focus on unwanted background noise.

. But, Life isn't what it was. Having hearing aids is another learning curve. This is something that if you don't have a hearing loss, you do not know what the problem is. I face problems of the deafness every day, and only other's that share this problem can relate to the issues.

. I remember at times when my hearing loss was so great that I could not hear the engine on my vehicle when I started it, or was driving. I had to find other ways to know when it was operating. Many will never know what that is like.

. The simplest sounds disappeared, the key clicks of a computer, automatic doors opening and closing, the simple sounds of a Cat. I saw the mouth move, but no sound was there, I was in my own version of being on a stranded island. I could feel the breezes, and see the sights, but heard almost nothing.

. When people were talking, I could not hear all of them talk. Others, I could only hear parts of their conversation. I felt disconnected from the world. I was on the path walking alone, alone and being sealed in a chamber that muffled any sound that was partially there. I felt that I was Gilligan, and on the island. Not with 6 other passengers, But I was alone. there was no radio and nobody to talk too, not even the Native's drums on the nearby island could be heard. I was all alone.

. The only place that I can replicate this feeling is when I look back into history. I visit cemeteries and search for past relatives. Its like walking through a time portal. All I see are the Names and dates etched in the granite trail. I can't hear the birds or the wind. It seems like I am walking through a 5 acre tomb, maybe this is why I remember the dates and names. I can recall over 150 locations of these marble and granite lined paths. I remember the faces that are bonded to them. I remember the photo etchings that are on the back of a few of these. I see every kind of things that were the most important to the person whose name is cut into the stone.

. I see farms down in a valley, Cars, Semi trucks, symbols of their belief in a higher power. I see their pets, their hobbies, their jobs, and something from their careers. These stones can't talk and tell their story. Even if they did, I can not hear it. Being in a place like this sets me free from the demands of the world. It does not make a sound, this place talks in silence with the photos, Etched pictures, the scripture verses, and personal poems. I can even sense the presents of the touch of an Angel.

. At these places. I feel that I belong here, to share time with my Maker. I feel as I am the teacher and all of the headstones are the desks of all my students. I learn from them, a valuable history of the past. As I walk by, Those that are buried here, have a friend. I have not abandoned them, like some of their relatives have. I feel that I have been touched by all those that I pass by, as some of those silent stones can make me shed a tear for them. Many innocent children are here, I have one that is there as well. My child, and all of the other children connect to me, in my heart and soul. I can hear them, even if, they cant even make a sound.

. When I am among the generations of those that have gone on before me, I hear them loudly in my soul. They make a joyful Noise of Silence.

Chapter 133

Loss of Parent - 3/24/2019

The loss of a parent isn't easy for all who have went through this. Since my family was like a shattered dish, as there was no possible way to fix it, I felt differently when my Father died. It was so twisted of a family, it ended up by my mother telling me I was not allowed to attend his funeral. My circumstance was rare, as both of my parents were in the marriage for things that each one wanted. There was no common goal for all, and the children were bargaining tools.

The 4 of us were used by one against the other. So when the first parent died, one brother had already died. One was in prison, another one had already became my mother's favorite, and I was cast out in the cold and the door slammed behind Me. Like the shattered dish, there was no way to return it back into what it was. Our family was an empty shell, that came out of the house of hell.

3 out of 4, saw families that managed to stay together for decades. The 4th one went to prison and this caused great rifts within that family and it ended in divorce. The next brothers passed away before their wives. I was the one that was expelled by my mother on more than one occasion. So the loss of a parent, was not a total loss to some of the 4 children. Some may have thought it was more of a blessing. Some of us ended up not honoring our parents.

When it came to Me, I walked the roughest road, I was the one out of 4 that saw a child pass away. When Rayne passed away earlier in this year, She became the first wife of the 4 of us to die. I became the first widower. All the others, the wife became a widow as they are still living. I only saw this in my Paternal Grandfather, it took two generations to see this being repeated, that the wife passes away first. It looks like my life will be a repeat of his, as long as I live.

Nobody saw it coming that my Wife would have a stoke. The risk was there, as she had a small stroke about 9 years before. After she had the first one, she never worked again. Those around her never knew that she had one because they saw no changes in her or her lifestyle. They thought that her age ended her job, as well as the recession of 2008. Rayne had larger issues as she refused to quit smoking, until she had her heart surgery. After she quit, she was getting a little better, until the first mini-stroke.

Then aging and her heart issue, were added to by her failing hip and leg joints. This caused her to end up at a nursing home. This caused more problems, so she went into assisted living. She was there exactly 3 years, then the next morning, she had the second stroke. She ended up in ICU, about a week later, the final straw that broke the camels back appeared. She could no longer talk, eat by mouth, or breath correctly. Her end of life was coming soon. The Staff said it could happen in hours, I said she would live long enough so her Sister, Our Daughter, and others could visit one last time.

Rayne passed away at 4:16, on Saturday afternoon, Jan 12th. There was 5 visitors there, But our Son did not show up for anything. After he was told that his Mother had Passed away, He screamed, No she did not. He was in denial. Sometimes people do this as they don't want to accept changes in their lives. But it did happen, I can't change things, I wish that she had lived one more day. When Rayne died, It was on our Daughter's Birthday. This was tough on my Daughter, because our family history repeated itself. When our second Son died, He died on his Grandmother's Birthday.

When It came to My two remaining children. One felt that she had lost a major part of her life. As for or Son, he denied it even happened. I never thought that this was possible, But when a Parent passes away, there in no way you know what will happen until it actually happens. I see troubled waters heading my way. I see the glass dish in a risky position. Will it fall and shatter, and My remaining family members scatter, or does My family end up like my Grandfather's after my

Grandmother died. His became a reunited family. Can this happen for me, time will tell

My children now have to face holidays without their Mother, This should be a wake up call to the masses.

Honor your family, be united and share part of your life with family members. Make them part of your life, Or someday, your chance to do this, will not be there. Nobody knows the reason or time, when one of your parents could pass away. Better to build a bridge than a wall. The pain of a loss will be less over time, But it will never be forgotten. Your parents were part of your past and the source of your life. They will always be part of your life as you go forward through time.

Chapter 134

Body of Evidence - 3/25/19

It has been about ten weeks since my life would be changed forever. Losing a spouse is never easy for anyone. I am seeing that at this time, I am worn down for dealing with the aftermath of Rayne's death. I see many changes that have happened in just a few months since her stroke. I have see things that I should have never seen at all.

Daily living for Me, is trying to get back to normal, what ever that is. My daily pattern of living changed on the same day that my Wife passed away. Death ended the partnership and the marriage of 37 years. I have to move forward now as a single individual.

Other people try to tell me what it is to go through something like this, they are right on some things, but other times, can be very wrong. No two families are the same, when it comes to an event like this. Yes, parts of it are the same, but not everything could be the same, or would be the same.

Having a bad winter does not help. With about 53 inches of snow during the month of February, was not fun at all. Dealing with snow piles that were over 6 feet tall, has not happened like this before, in my lifetime. Not having reliable help wore me down. This year is a challenge that I have to meet.

Dealing with everything that needs to be done, is like a military mission. I can't stop until everything has been completed, or it's in the final stages. Running the affairs for two lives, eventually begins to wear you down. The decisions came at me like a speeding locomotive. I hit many bumps in the road, even today. Today would have been the 65th birthday of Rayne's only brother. But, He passed away about 4 years ago.

I spent the last few years looking into the past. I did locate her past relatives, this offered many links to her Fathers origin. Another relative of hers and I, uncovered the missing history of Rayne's past. The facts of her family's past had been hidden away for over 60 years. It is now available for all members to now know, and understand their roots. This should have been done ten or twenty years earlier.

Yesterday it felt like I had finally ran into a brick wall, and writers block had arrived. I need to keep writing just a few more chapters. When I finish this one, I want to make at least 9 more. I see the completion of my second book coming soon. After I get the remaining chapters made, then I can begin to do the other things, that I need to complete. Many of these were put on hold, since Rayne had a stoke on New Year's Day.

Getting the many tasks done will take weeks. they have to be completed before I confront the issues coming my way. I cannot drift off my path. I am not the only person that can do it. I do not have a backup that can step up to the plate for me. So I forge ahead and get things done, step by step. This is also how I also move forward along my path.

My future is uncertain, the biggest threat to my style of living is the costs. Since my family has lost a member, it lost part of the income as well. I now have to see what can be done to reduce the costs, or I will need to find another living location and this changes my financial liability.

I see this issue will be the last hoop to jump through. I have to back up my life style, as it was 40 years ago. I will return to my single lifestyle and make the best out of it as I can. As of now, I am the Captain of my ship. I need to look at what needs to be done to survive on the long run. I can't lose sight of my goal, of having a family reunion in the future.

As for now, I have to stay a leader and deal with all of the changes that are coming my way. I may need to slow down that pace, but I will get things done. I will consider seeking help from others, as to get the best information that I will need.

I will need to gather all of the facts, My financial liabilities and assets, and what I can do and what I can't. I will need to sit down with others and go over the facts. Find out what help I need and how much. I need to assemble a Body of Evidence about my options. Then make the best choices. It will not be easy as I continue on my path.

Chapter 135

Dream Vacation - 3/26/19

I can't have the vacation that I wanted. I don't have my life partner to take the trip with. And now I am facing a restricted budget, and this greatly reduce my chance of traveling more than a few hours from home. My Wife and I wanted to take a few trips, but our time ran out, just like it did for Her time on Earth.

We wanted to go out west and see the sights that her Father's adaptive parents had gone on. They went to many national parks, across many states. They went to canyons, mountains, desert country, petrified forests and the big redwood trees. I remember seeing a photo, where a car was driven through the trunk of a living Redwood tree. They took along a small camper to spend more time on the road. They even went to Yellowstone national Park and saw Old Faithful. They went to stay under the starts of the big sky country of Montana

If I want to go on a trip to Montana, it has to be south of Pine Valley. Not the state where the buffalo roam and the deer have a playground. All we wanted was to see how the relatives of the past had their vacations. It all ended in January, as Rayne made a trip on her own, to lie down in green pastures and beside the still waters.

So now, all of my vacations must come out of my dreams. there is no other way. I had to reset my goals to a slower lifestyle and this gives me a chance to have more time to remember the times that we had together.

In my mind I can go back 35 years to the breezes off of the saltwater ocean. I am not alone as I walk along Venice Beach. I smell the variety of foods for sale along the walkway. I see the Hoffy Hot Dog signs and Muscle beach, as my Wife sees the many handmade crafts. I hear the roller blades and roller skates, as they scuff along the walkway. The sun makes it a warm day and our first ever vacation away from home. I recall seeing the Cab that had the checkerboard design. I see the Ferrari and the Rolls Royce, as well as the 1960 Corvair. It looks like it was right out of the series of Route 66. I don't have anything here that interferes with my stroll along the beach.

I recall being at the Wild Animal Park, this is where the talking bird stole the show. We were also at the San Diego Zoo. There was Shamu the Orca whale, and the indoor laser light show. There was a double decker bus that gave us a ride around the place to see all of the other animals.

We spent time with members of Rayne's family, and many days with my oldest Brother's family. One day we left the country and explored Mexico. Another day we went to places with Rayne's Sister and Mother, we went around where some rodent called Mickey lived. This was truly an enjoyable time.

Then years later, there was times We traveled to nearby states. Even if these places were closer to home, they gave us an enjoyable time traveling around see all of the sights. We went high up on cliffs looking for miles over the land. We crossed over the mighty Mississippi several times. Other times we drove along the Great lakes.

The places we went to, were far away from the world that I had to endure. Other places were close by, as in the lands of Paul Bunyan, These places helped me to find inner peace, even if the house of hell was torn down seven years before. The pain and the problems of living there, would remain for a lifetime. Trips of any kind would offer me a chance to see a better world.

At the present time in my life, I don't see another real vacation in my lifetime. Because I can't have another, any that I do have will need to come out of my memories.

My Dream vacation of today, is stored deep within my mind. Each one of these Dream Vacations will always be along with me, every day of my life, to enjoy over and over. This is also the only version of a Vacation trip that I will ever have again, and I only need reservations for one.

Chapter 136

Video Complaints - 3/27/19

I run by this over and over, Too many that view my videos feel that the must comment with their guesses, as what may have effected the making of my Video at the Chicago North Western train depot. They think the reason is that I have Cerebral Palsy or Parkinson's Disease. These 2 afflictions are not in the list of my half dozen physical issues, that I face on a daily basis.

Many things are at issue as why the beginning of some videos are a bit off, or to others, the video does not seem normal to them. Here are some reasons as why the videos don't look like what they expect, 1. Ground is unstable, 2. I am holding on to 20 pounds of electronics to make the video. The VHS deck is around 10 pounds, the camera and connecting cable is another 8, and the backup battery is another two pounds. (Unlike today, My all in one Digital camera & Battery weighs 12 ounces).

The next reason that is to be considered. I was there to record the look of the remains of the Chicago North Western Depot, The train passing by was an extra bonus, but the vibration from the train passing by, could effect the video as well. In trying to get the train in the video, I can't correctly frame it with a Manual Focus camera. This is due to the fact that I have no depth perception at all. and I can't frame it and focus at the same time, it is a 2 step process.

The next reason, I am the forerunner in Home Videos, I can't read a how to book, there was none, I had to write my own. I made Dash Cam videos years before these cameras actually existed. It's call learning on the Job experience. Many told me this could not be done, I proved them wrong. As time passes, My videos get better, even with the disabilities that I have.

The fifth reason, my Videos were Never intended to be in public Hands, so I was not trying to make them perfect. I made them as life was presented before me. I have made over 15,000 videos, these were intended for me in case of any of my conditions getting worse. As an example, not being able to drive. This is why I made the driving videos, I could see the places that I actually visited. After having children, these videos were intended for them to see what my past, what it was and the many things that I did. As the children were growing up, I aired some of my videos on the local Public Access TV channel. I even got my Son to have a program of his own. this has been done since 1993, over 25 years ago. The internet offered a new window for others to remember the past. I have thousands of One of a Kind Videos, in the Time frame of the 1980's & 90's, Nobody has any others like this.

So instead of trying to find fault with the my videos, you should think about this.. without my video, you would have none at all. Any handicapped individual, would not find any humor in others looking for the reason or fault, as why the video isn't studio quality. You should take these videos as what they are, a Free Gift that looks at the past. You can see my videos with both of your eyes, as you peek at my recordings of the past. A past that will never be repeated again.

I wrote a book, and in it, I explain why the things for Me are the way they are. I explain why I can't make my videos, to look like you expect. It teaches hard lessons from a live style that others did not have to endure. Any Handicapped person that quits trying to do their best, isn't going far in this world. I have overcome obstacles that would have stopped many. Making Videos was a challenge, I was behind the 8-ball, But I did it anyway that I could.

My first book was released 2/22/17, Living With The Evidence. People should enjoy my videos and not waste time nitpicking them apart. I can't go back and do them over. Complainers should show me their videos. They don't have any, so they should enjoy what I freely have given them. Without my videos, even if they are not perfect, there would be nothing else. Over time, I do make better videos. I had to learn by doing, and I made these videos expecting nothing in return, except for these to be enjoyed by others.

Chapter 137

Floor Flood - 3/28/19

I try to get by on the income that I have, I now have to concentrate on the basics. I am now living the widower world. Two incomes are now one. My cost remain the same. I am trying to do a balancing act, and stay afloat in the world of today. But having to cover the costs of having another live at the house may be that anchor that sinks the ship. I try to keep a tight ship and track every penny. But having another in the house that adds no income, and causes the total liabilities to rise, is what may end up sinking the ship for all.

I have a way to save myself from the ship, if it sinks. I can go to another place and lower my costs, as I can get a place that the rent cost depends on personal income. This could be what I need in the future. But I still need to keep what I have afloat and go forward for the near future, as my current lease expires at the end of the year. So I have to do what I can now, and keep me at the place where I am. But the other resident in the house keeps sabotaging my chance for staying afloat.

I keep telling him what I expect, and he keeps going like I have all the money in the world. This logic is a sure plan for failure. He has done many things around the house that is costing me money, and it looks like he never learns after he makes a mistake once or twice. He continues like he did nothing wrong. Every blunder of his is costing me, I am getting into a time in my life where my income is only enough to cover the costs for one. It is stretched a bit having another passenger aboard my ship. But having the passenger that does not care about others property, is a sure sign of an approaching Iceberg.

The day starts as usual, I get up in the morning and start my daily routine. I come into the kitchen and my feet get wet. I look down and see the floor has water covering the area by the sink. I had this disaster before. This is when the passenger tried to flush some uneaten food down the sink. In a very short time the drain pipe was plugged and backed up the water in the sink. This led to an overflow and made the floor fill with water. He never admitted what he had done, but he was the only on in the house. After a few hours, I found the clog and saw what it was. I told him that this place isn't like homes of other people that he knew. I mad it very clear, We do not have a garbage disposal, stop letting food enter the drain.

This event has happened a few time in the last year or so. He keeps letting food enter the drain and down the pipes. After telling him over and over, We don't have a garbage disposal, I thought I gave him this sermon enough times, But I was wrong. Even doing nothing around the house as a team member, I hoped that he would take care of the house like a team member and do what he could to make this a better place to live for the both of us. I ended up being wrong again, He just does not give a damn for anyone else's property, except his own. This is what happened again today. He clogged the drain again. Never said a thing as he did not care that the longer this event lasted, the higher the cost would be for me.

The floor again had over a quarter of an inch of water on it. I look at the sink, and it's holding water without a drain stopper. This time I can't fix it like I did the last time. He really must have screwed it up even more that he did in the past. I had to spend money of repair items that were not in my budget. Well, he still does not care as what he does, as he does not have enough money to pay for the damages that he has caused in the last two years. It all adds up to having a less comfortable lifestyle. He is wasting my resources in his carelessness and then he whines that he wants more things for himself. He shot himself in the foot with this idea, the more damage he causes, he spends my money faster. This causes a shortage of funds for the both of us.

When will he ever learn to take care of others property better, I wish I knew. His is like a wandering iceberg, and if he hitting the ship over and over, the leak might not be repaired and the ship will sink to the bottom. I have a life raft that fits me, but he has none. So why does he keep risking the safety of the ship when he has no way to save himself. The Captain of the Titanic wanted to set a record crossing the Atlantic and went full steam ahead, this ship sank. Other ships in the area, stopped for the night to keep save. My passenger is different, He just does not care about others, even at the risk of harming himself. He is like Captain Edward J Smith, yelling Full Speed Ahead.

Chapter 138

Poised to Kill - 3/29/19

I am confronted by many things that do not make common sense. Too many places, Doctor's offices, and other places that you have to set appointments to get services, come to mind. Also manufactures assume that they are making a safe product that anyone can use, But they are so wrong. They could be endangering the lives of those that use their product.

I just went to check on my next appointment at a local clinic. I was there the day before, but I was not given a appointment schedule card or given a copy of my future appointments on a printed page. This happens once and awhile, some places are busy and it slips through the cracks. So I go back the next day and ask for a copy of my upcoming events. The receptionist does what I requested, She hands Me a printed page with my future appointments. I look at it and I can't read it, The font is so small that it would not even be large enough for a sidewalk in Flea Town. Too many assume that you can read the page, because they can. People need to understand that no two people can do all of the same things. I did not think that I needed to bring my reading glasses with me. This reminds me of labels that are not readable by all.

I first think of food products that have several names for identifying sugar. They use corn syrup and dextrose as a fancy name for it. I have trouble when the package states Spices. Spices, just what are they, maybe I might have a reaction to one of them. Some people die when they have a reaction. When I eat a Six dollar meal from a local grocery store, I can't stand the flavor added to the corn. I look at the ingredients, can't find any item that added the flavor. This is a totally bad idea. No food should be listed as spices added. Why can't I know what ones are used. For someone who reacts more than I do, There could be a killer in the corn.

Manufactures of products are the other source of this problem. Just what is this danger, poisonous gasses and chemical burns come to my mind, as well as skin burns and severe illness and possibly death. The risks come from not clearly informing all of the public, about the dangers of their product that can be read by everyone. This again, has to do with the font and style of the print on their package. This package of cleaner has 12 lines per inch on the bottle. The letters are 0.04 of an inch. 25 letters stacked would be 1 inch.

This package also has white letters over pink. Very poor contrast, this package also uses pink over brown. This product if misused could cause death. Laws should have this as black letters over white. This package has the skull and crossbones, but I can't clearly read the warning, and what to do if someone ingests the product. This package also has warning in Spanish, but that takes more letters to give the same information that is in English. This product needs to be placed into a box for it to be sold. The box would allow larger print, and a sheet inside of the box that would have larger print. The print on the bottle needs to be 0.08 of an inch. This is the size that I can read without error. The largest letters used, is less than a half of an inch tall. The height of the Skull and crossbones is less than a third of an inch.

I see that the rules are slacking in selling dangerous products. They need to properly post the warnings so the nobody gets harmed by their product. They need a package that is clearly readable. I see a possible lawsuit because they are making a product that is Poised to Kill.

Chapter 139

Million Tears - 3/30/19

. I shed a million, tear after tear
. Wish today that I still had you here
. Now am living a single life without you
. I remember all of the days, when there were two
. I recall our time along the ocean, back in eighty five
. While we were there, the many walks we had made us feel alive
. We had many chances to steal a kiss
. We would never have another time like this
. A stroll along Hollywood walk of Fame
. Every star that we saw, we knew the Name
. We were married five years, before We had our Son
. Our second Son died early, we only have the one
. Later we had our Daughter, she was the third child to come our way
. Fate would deal us a bad hand, You passed away on Her birthday
. You never saw a Grandchild, or held any of them, left you crying
. Our Son and future Son in Law, would have the same name, of Ryan
. I walk all alone through the Cemetery looking for You
. There is no marker or evidence for the space of two
. I hope to get a headstone for two
. I will get one for Me and for You
. We were married a long time, We were together thirty seven
. My reservations have been made, I will be with you in Heaven

Chapter 140

Lost Holidays - 3/31/19

As the year progresses, I see more dark clouds ahead. I see storms and possible disasters. I am like Christopher Columbus. I got married and set out into the world, by having the First Mate with me on my lead ship. Later 3 small ships joined in to make our adventure into the unknown world. We are on our way to enjoy the holiday time with our family friends and discover new friends in our journey, in our cluster of 4 ships.

Once the First Mate got aboard my ship, we waited 5 hours for the others. We set sail on our new life and what was beyond the horizon. We assemble our group of 3 new Crew Members and took our 3 small ships along with us. The JR, Ryeson, and the Nee Nee. We set our sails and off we go. We thought that it would be clear sailing ahead for the next 37 days on our adventure

On our search for our happy holiday times, a storm arrived quickly and within 3 hours, Ryeson was in deep trouble and it sank below the surface and never would be seen again. This was a great personal loss, but it did not stop our quest to have happy times. We sailed on and came to a group of islands. We stopped at the largest valley island, filled with a pine forest. This was a place called Rhieann. The crew member that was on the Nee Nee, disembarked and set up a place to colonize this island. I then had the First Mate take over the Nee Nee and sail along with me, now we had 3 ships and and 3 crew aboard.

We set out sail again for the search of our own land of happy
Holidays. We faced a fierce wind and hurricane with torrents of rain,
and thunder. While we were approaching a strange new world on our
37th week of travel, we tried to get out of harms way by getting into a
small oxbow lake. A lightning strike at the stoke of midnight, hit the
Nee Nee. the First Mate could not keep it afloat and was lost. The Nee
Nee, with the First Mate aboard, sinks below the surface in the Lake,
with a view of etched pillars and symbols. We would have to come back
to this place later.

Now with the loss of 2 ships and 2 of the crew members, one was
my First Mate, we were in a new world. But it was a restless place. I
wanted to know what happened to the First Mate and the original crew
member of the Nee Nee. So I set out on this journey alone. The crew
of the JR was left at home. So I, the Admiral of the Ocean Sea, set out
to go back to the Lake with a view of pillars. I finally arrived there and
spent many days searching where my First Mate was. I could not exactly
find the location as where She was. So I have to wait until the stormy
season is over, and bring a navigator to mark the position of where the
ship went down below the surface.

As for now, I sailed back to where JR was and to see what, if any
future life I can have there. If this can't be done. I will have to see both
of us on a new trails, so the two of us will be parted and each sent on
a different path.

I look into the future and see where I may never find our Happy
Holiday. It could be lost forever. I only have one hope. My next trip
will be back to the Island of Rhieann, where among the pines, I find
the crew member of the Nee Nee. She tells me of Her wonderful trip
to the sights along the coast of the western ocean. She was there with
a native of the land. I am told that She and the Native, who is related
to Royalty, are planning to get married. This is the only light on the
horizon that I see at the end of day.

Nee Nee proclaims that she has more than one Royalty among her
ranks, and was helping out carin' for the other crew members. So I,
with the Nee Nee Captain and Her Native, will now set out to find a
happy holiday for all. It may take years, but we will not stop working
together to have happier times. So in the future, I will give the Nee
Nee Captain away to be with her Native. This way, there will be a new

direction for our family to grow. Then we will sail away into the sunset. We will hope, that we will not fall off the edge of the Earth. But, We will find a rainbow at the end of our stormy adventure, and time to find our Happy Holidays again.

Chapter 141

Family Times - 4/1/19

Spring is here and its time that the Family gets together for a Birthday Party for the twins. My Daughter's twins are 5 and it will be a big change for her family. This year they will be getting the twins, Rachael and Rob ready for school. So this family get together will be wing-ding special. There was a few brats and cots for the ones with the lazy bones.

We all gathered at Horseshoe Island and enjoyed a warm day on the shore of Oxbow Lake. Had many games that a Grandpa like me, could play with them. Grandma was a bit slow in her old age, but She helped out with the picnic and had all the food ready for the little Kids and big ones too. Some snacks looked like chiggers and crabs. Goofy Grape was the beverage of choice for the kids.

My Son-in-Law's family arrives and joins in setting up the events, Now the twins had all grandparents, and their Paternal Aunt and uncle joined us with their 4 year old. The youngsters are starting to burn off their energy, its like they were a candle burning at both ends. The adults were talking of events happening within the family. I brought up this fact, the twins Great Grandpa was born 100 years ago. He was born in 1919. This is what a family event should be, and everyone is involved with others and the children are having a memorable birthday time.

Time to call the rugrats over to the Picnic table for some grub. A Marble Birthday cake awaits them. The twins can't make up their minds as what cake they wanted, Chocolate or White cake, so now they have both. My Son-in-law wants to try his luck at fishing later, but it's Hot dog time with a few burgers thrown in. With kids around, there was a few corn chips thrown around to see if they could fly.

After everyone got their belly filled, the kids ran off like a rocket to the playground. It was time to relax a bit for the adults, the over 50 crew. We are all enjoying the sunlight and the stories of the past. There was fun times in the sun. A few times, a kid or two, would sneak back for a handful of chips. Then the kids were trying to stuff the squirrels with salted peanuts, and see their puffy faces. One asked, how long can a Squirrel run before you change it's battery ?

The Twins had a great day with their Grampas and Grannies, with a few extra relatives thrown in. This was the time of their lives to remember and enjoy, before they go off to school in about 5 months. They came up with an idea that each of them could go to a different school.

It is time to pack up the goodies and everyone to get back home, as it begins to get overcast. A light April shower is forecast for tonight. This was a memorable day for the twins and everyone else. They ate most of the cake and had a big grin, showing off their milk moustaches.

Rayne was packing up what we brought and then we were on the way home. She went into the house with a few snacks for later, I put all the lawn chairs in the garage and headed to the house. It was a long day for 2 pair of grandparents. It seemed like Grandma added a full year to her age, in one afternoon.

Before I got into the house, I grabbed my cellphone to call up family crew members to say, April Fools !

Chapter 142

Voice of the People - 4/2/19

Many things in life should not be so difficult for people with physical limitations. I am deeply disappointed that there is no easy way for people with limited abilities to complete a task with ease.

My Wife passed away over 10 weeks ago, and I could not locate any map of the Pine Valley Lakeview Cemetery Lot Numbers. All I knew was Section D, and the Lot number. Just where it was, who knows ?. Communication by phone is not my best choice. I tried to find the Sexton many times.

There is a Section Map of Lakeview online, Why can't I find a map with the Lot numbers. You sell grave locations by numbers, so why isn't there a map to download any section.

I took a video of every headstone in section D, I spent hours mapping the names with the lots. I closed in on the area I wanted to find. I researched over 150 names.

I Finally found where my Wife is, on April 2nd. This should never have happened. There should be a chart or map on line of every Pine Valley Cemetery, that has the Sections and the Lots.

Chapter 143

Beginning of the End - 6/5/2019

Today's errands takes to another supermarket that I have not been to in a few years. This one has other surprises for me. This place was easier to navigate because it is a smaller size than Pineman's. After getting a few things that I could use, I was ready to checkout. I was distracted because of a worker that was there, was known to me. I left without attracting her attention.

Getting outside, the rain had began and I made it to my vehicle and left the parking lot to drive home. I went to check the mail box and then drove up the hill to get home.

As I turned the corner off the main road, I saw something that I did not expect. 2 local police cars were at the end of the street. Now what has my Son done now, is what comes to my mind. This isn't what is expected after the previous event a few weeks ago. But it has happened.

I left my vehicle and approached the Officers and they informed me that he contacted 911, again. They said there was voices on the call and then the call ended. This is a repeat event, and it should not have been. They inform me that they went to the door and again he did not answer the door. My Son's luck ran out, I entered the house and opened his bedroom door and informed him that the Police want to talk to him, and if he does not come outside to see them, I will allow the officers into the house.

He gets ready and goes outside alone to talk with the officers. I do not know what they talked about, but because of the past events, I can put the pieces together. I informed the police that he has a tablet that can operate on WiFi, and this is where the second voice came from when he placed the 911 call. They said that they must track down every 911 call due to policy of leaving no stone unturned as why the call was made.

My talk with the Officers gave them more information. Now they will be turning up the heat to get him placed somewhere where his problem can be worked on.

I know now that his time is limited, there is another source of pressure to get him out and moved to another place, that can work to resolve his issues. He does not know it yet, but the Steam Locomotive is building up speed and will be riding him out on a rail. The train will be facing no red lights. His time living his life as he does now is rapidly coming to the end.

What else is there that I can lose now. I saw my life walking along the path alone, and it has became a reality, sooner that I thought. With 2 in the cemetery and another adrift, I am on that path walking alone.

I look back and have a vision of me being in the hospital nursery for months after months, I was alone among strangers that cared for me in 6 hour shifts. I had no family there, I was alone and could not even walk on my path as I could not walk at all. This is a vision that I do not want to see happen again. No wonder Rayne did not want to be living an extended life hooked up to machines. She would have been like a baby, that could never walk again.

I recall walking a path through a roadside attraction called the Biblical gardens, I walked the trail looking at a collection of biblical events. Eve tempting Adam, Abraham ready to sacrifice Isaac, Daniel in the lion's den, and more, the last thing I saw was a final resting place for a young woman. then the path opened up to a sunny green pasture. I need to find this place like this again, but it is nowhere to be found.

My life has truly followed my prophecy of my original poem written in 1969. It has a one word title of Death.

Although I am a Friendless Friend. I must fight to the end, the end of my life. Although I am half blind, and have trouble with the mind. I must fight for what I have today Life, or tomorrow I may have Death.

So I am walking along the path again, going forward, even if I am doing it alone. The light at the end of the tunnel seems so far away, but I can still see it. It feels that I have demons lurking behind, hiding in the shadows. They have not stopped me yet and I don't plan on letting them do it now. I walk along along the narrow path, as I have been doing it for decades and I can't quit now.

I can't explain as to why me, I just do not know. I can't let things derail me. I must go forward, even if I limp along at times. I has been 40 years since I lived alone. I have been through some bad times before, so I have experience in this area. But I expected that I would have someone to grow old together, but this isn't in the cards for me. I am adrift again to walk on my path alone through time.

I will keep on my path and more forward, even if my shoes wear away beneath my feet. I can never lose sight of my path as I move along. In the past my sight faded away from me, I was steadfast in what I had to do. When my vision returned, I picked up the pace, I even kept this event hidden from others for decades. I know my odds and they did not look very good. I never let it get in the way and lose my way on my path.

I have not been stopped yet, and I will keep the pace to keep moving forward. The Doctor's said in the past that I would not be expected to live 6 hours, but I have extended that to over 60 years. I see no end in sight. I will keep walking and hope there will be new things for me, but there is no guarantee. So it's one foot in front of the other.. I venture forward on my path and I see nothing stopping me. I did this alone in the past and I can do it again.

The sounds begin to fade and the light is filled in with shadows, as I travel forward on my path. I am moving forward at a slower pace, as I wonder just where the beginning of the end is.

Chapter 144

Deja Vu - 6/24/19

I am going down my past and I am seeing the same things that I did over 28 years ago. only thing is that I am seeing it in reverse, and this time, I am seeing it alone.

Back then, a House fire started the events that forever set the stage. This fire event happened in the morning. Searching for a new house became the next thing in life. We had insurance money to replace the house with the same brand of home. The one in the fire was a 2 bedroom and We replaced it with a 3 bedroom. A growing family was on the horizon, we had one Son and another child on the way. Not knowing if it was going to be a boy or girl, we still needed the space. It was a cold time after the fire, We slept in the fire charred house for one night.

Then in February, My Grandmother, the oldest in the family passes away, in 1991. She was at the same funeral home that her husband was at over 30 years before.

Around 5 weeks later another death in the family, our newborn Son is born and dies the same day, He was the youngest in the family tree. He was at the same Funeral Home as his Great Grandmother. The Infant dies on his Grandmother's Birthday.

For over 6 months the expenses exceeded our income. This short period of time should never have been repeated, as it has many uncommon happenings.

As time marches on to 2019, The world gets flipped over. The oldest in my family dies, This reverses the last time when the youngest in our family dies. It's no longer ours, as my Wife was the one that passed away. She was at the same funeral home as our youngest son was 28 years before. I had the same problem back then as I did now, getting money to cover the burial. Our 2nd Son and now my Wife are at the same Cemetery. I have now had to walk the second trip along this path alone.

For a 2nd time, 6 months becomes the time frame of events. In January, my Wife passed away. Now about 6 months later, I have lost another house. It is considered totaled as a large tree fell and caved in a portion of the roof. The exterior wall has buckled and damage to the porch has happened. The repair cost will be too great, so for the 2nd time in my life, the house will be condemned. This time money issues will stand out again, as I do not know if I will get any insurance from this event. So buying a third house will may only be a pipe dream.

For another time financial losses with extend through months of time. For a 2nd time, I am spending the 1st night in the damaged home, but this time I am doing it alone. No Wife, or Son is with me this time.

The power is restricted and the natural gas has been turned off. How many of these tragic events do I have to encounter. I have seen it once & now I am seeing it again.

The first time, the fire made the 10 pm news, wonder what news this time will make. I am now walking alone down the path where I have traveled before as a team. My path is getting very rocky again.

Many questions remain. Will I get insurance or did others cause me to get nothing this time around, time will tell. I look down the hallway, and I see pitch black, same as before. But, this time around the smell of burnt wood is missing, it was replaced the the echo of loneliness.

Going through a loss of a family member and a house within a short time is a terrible thing to deal with, but seeing it twice in less than half of my lifetime are odds I can't compute. How about this fact, both homes were lost at the same address. When do I find my green pastures and the still waters.

I have been seeing too much of fire, wind, water, and brimstone. This can't stop my walk down the path, even if I now will have to travel it alone. I don't even know for how long, or where it will take me next. I really do not want to see a three-peat. How much of this does a person have to endure, I guess that I am being put to that test.

For the 2nd time, The headstones mark the years of the double events. The dates are now etched in stone.

If this happened twice, why can't lightning strike the same place twice, The odds are the lightning's favor.

CPSIA information can be obtained
at www.ICGtesting.com
Printed in the USA
BVHW070126140620
581354BV00001B/29

9 781796 042627